The Treasures of
English Freemasonry
1717 – 2017

The Treasures of English Freemasonry
1717 – 2017

Edited by
Richard Gan

in association with
the Library and Museum of Freemasonry

Consultant: Diane Clements

Dedication

To my wife Niki
for her patience, encouragement and support

also

to my mother, Czesia
who will now be able to show her friends
something about the organisation her son has been
involved with for the last forty years

Acknowledgements

I would like to record my thanks to:

Dr Ann Pilcher – Copy Editor
Robert Wilcockson – Production and Design

All the staff at the Library and Museum of London,
especially Peter Aitkenhead

Colleagues from the featured Museums and Libraries including:

Bristol: Gary Williams, John Martin; *Derbyshire:* Colin Clayton; *Essex:* Pierre Waddoups;
Hertfordshire: Brian Tierney MBE; *Leicestershire:* Donald Peacock;
Northumberland: Ian Brown; *Nottinghamshire:* Geoffrey Bond OBE, DL, FSA;
West Lancashire: Vic Charlesworth, Caroline Crook; *Worcestershire:* John Tapson;
and *Jewels of the Craft:* Robert J.G. Smith; Scots Lodge No. 2319: Ian Rainford.

for their help and assistance in the writing of this book

First published 2017

ISBN 978 0 85318 531 4

All rights reserved. No part of this book may be reproduced or transmitted in any form or by any means, electronic or mechanical, including photocopying, recording, scanning or by any information storage and retrieval system, on the internet or elsewhere, without permission from the Publisher in writing.

© Richard Gan 2017

Published by Lewis Masonic, an imprint of Ian Allan Publishing Ltd, Addlestone, Surrey KT15 2SF.

Printed in Malta.

Visit the Lewis Masonic website at www.lewismasonic.co.uk

Copyright

Illegal copying and selling of publications deprives authors, publishers and booksellers of income, without which there would be no investment in new publications. Unauthorised versions of publications are also likely to be inferior in quality and contain incorrect information. You can help by reporting copyright infringements and acts of piracy to the Publisher or the UK Copyright Service.

Contents

Introduction 6
About the Editor 7
An Unexpected Treasure 8

Chapters

1 **An Overview** 10
  Richard Gan

2 **The Early Years of Freemasonry** 44
  Professor Aubrey Newman

3 **The Antients and the Moderns** 64
  Dr David Harrison

4 **The Formation of the United Grand Lodge of England** 90
  John Belton

5 **A Cornucopia of Freemasonry** 120
  Diane Clements

6 **My Cup Runneth Over** 138
  Richard Gan

7 **The Craft of Symbolism** 178
  Hugh O'Neill

8 **Freemasons' Hall, London** 196
  Dr James Campbell

9 **English Freemasonry Overseas** 218
  Dr James Daniel

10 **Freemasonry and Charity** 244
  Dr John Reuther

11 **Royal Freemasons and the Rulers of the Craft** 268
  Dr Paul Calderwood

Appendices

Location and Contact Details of Featured Museums and Libraries 296
Catalogue and Index of Images 297
The Contributors 303
Image Acknowledgements 304

Introduction

Richard Gan

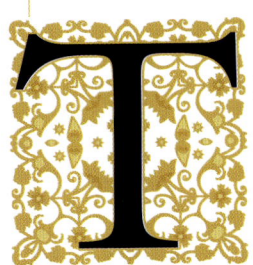
The year 2017 sees the celebration of the Tercentenary of the formation of the first Grand Lodge and with it the formal organisation of Freemasonry in England and indeed the world. Since 1717 many millions of men have become Freemasons and in England alone over 9,500 lodges have been constituted. Whilst some of these lodges have come and gone, others have survived as long as Grand Lodge itself. All however have left a footprint – in some instances so shallow as to be almost imperceptible and which has long since disappeared, whilst others have left an indelible and long-lasting impression.

The record that remains is multifaceted and reflects the social history of the last 300 years; which in the case of Freemasonry means an organisation which can boast a membership ranging from Kings and royalty at one end of the spectrum to the poor and destitute at the other; and from the artisan to the highly skilled artist – all of whom have had a part to play and all of whom have left their respective mark.

It is no surprise that over a period of 300 years a substantial number of items with Masonic decoration and connections have been made and collected. Many of the finest examples can now be found in the Library and Museum of Freemasonry in London and other Masonic Museums up and down the country. These objects include examples of regalia, jewels, manuscripts, books, magazines, newspapers, photographs, prints, engravings, postage stamps, documents such as Patents of Appointment, certificates, Warrants and Charters, portraits, glassware, porcelain, pottery, ceramics, furniture, silverware, presentation pieces and ephemera.

Whilst to some the word 'treasure' has the connotation of high monetary value, the treasures or objects contained in the book might not be all of great financial worth, but many are priceless and most are irreplaceable.

Over 200 Masonic objects that reflect all aspects of Freemasonry over the last 300 years have been carefully selected, professionally photographed, and categorised into one of ten different themes. The themes form the chapters in the book, each of which has an introduction, based on the images, written by an acknowledged Masonic scholar: 'The Early Years of Freemasonry' – Professor Aubrey Newman; 'The Antients and the Moderns' – Dr David Harrison; 'The Formation of the United Grand Lodge of England' – John Belton; 'A Cornucopia of Freemasonry' – Diane Clements, 'My Cup Runneth Over' – Richard Gan; 'The Craft of Symbolism' – Hugh O'Neill; 'Freemasons' Hall, London' – Dr James Campbell; 'Freemasonry Overseas' – Dr James Daniel; 'Freemasonry and Charity' – Dr John Reuther; 'Royal Freemasons and the Rulers of the Craft' – Dr Paul Calderwood.

The Editor has endeavoured to provide an overview that connects the ten themes and puts them into a social and historical context. In addition he has written detailed descriptions, based on information provided by colleagues at the Library and Museum of Freemasonry, and wherever possible comprehensive explanatory notes amplifying the background and history for each of the objects.

The overall style is intended to appeal to the general reader, whether or not a Freemason. The approach adopted enables the book to be enjoyed either by reading it sequentially from cover to cover or by dipping in and out, concentrating just on the photographs. The images can be enjoyed on an individual basis, as their accompanying notes provide more than enough information to make them both meaningful and interesting.

It is hoped that this book will serve not only as a celebration of 300 years of Freemasonry in England, as illustrated through more than 200 objects, but also as a definitive catalogue of the finest treasures relating to English Freemasonry.

About the Editor

Richard Gan is a senior Freemason and a Grand Officer in all the major Orders of Freemasonry. He retired in June 2010 as Deputy Grand Secretary of the Grand Lodge of Mark Master Masons.

Born in 1950, he was educated at the Becket School, Nottingham, and is a graduate of London University, where he took an Honours Degree in Geology and subsequently studied part-time for a Masters Degree in Education. He is also a graduate of the Open University, where he took a Bachelor of Arts Degree in Management Studies. Whilst at the Institute of Education he combined winning a double distinction in the Postgraduate Certificate of Education with serving as President of the Students' Union.

He has enjoyed a number of successful careers during his working life – as a teacher and head of faculty; a local government chief officer in educational administration; bursar and clerk to the governing body at a grant-maintained school; Assistant Grand Secretary and subsequently Deputy Grand Secretary of the Grand Lodge of Mark Master Masons based in St James's; and finally Editor of *The Square*, an independent magazine for Freemasons. He is a full member of Quatuor Coronati Lodge No. 2076, the premier Lodge of Masonic research. Having fully retired in 2014, he now has more time to develop his writing and research into Victorian Freemasonry and the Orders beyond the Craft.

He lives near Lincoln with his wife Niki, who is a former preparatory school Headmistress.

An Unexpected Treasure

Information such as the type of font used in the printing of a book is usually contained on a page right at the beginning of most books and more often than not completely ignored by the majority of readers.

In this particular instance however, the font used to print this book is thought to be of some significance, not least because it can itself be considered one of *The Treasures of English Freemasonry*: Granjon.

George William Jones (1860–1942) was a master printer, described in *The Times* on the occasion of his 70th birthday as 'Printer Laureate', one of the most celebrated letterpress printers of his generation.

Born in Upton-upon-Severn, he entered the printing profession in 1873 as an apprentice and on completing his indentures progressed from being a jobbing printer, gaining experience in Sheffield and Leicester, until he became a works manager in Edinburgh. In 1889 Jones moved to London to start up his own business, which eventually became the *Sign of the Dolphin Press*. In doing so he came into contact with Bro James Thomson, a printing manager who was at the time Secretary of Scots Lodge No. 2319 and with whom he became great friends.

George Jones was initiated into Scots Lodge No. 2319 in January 1892 and he remained a member until his death on 14 May 1942. He was an enthusiastic and prominent Freemason, joining no less than six other lodges and three Royal Arch Chapters. Having been installed as Master of the Scots Lodge in 1904, he received very rapid promotion, being appointed as Junior Grand Deacon in the United Grand Lodge of England in 1906 and in the following year as the Provincial Senior Grand Warden in Hertfordshire.

As a printer he was heavily influenced by the work of William Morris – that is evident from the Summons that he first printed for Scots Lodge in 1906 and which is still in use today (➤).

In 1921 Jones was appointed Printing Adviser to Linotype & Machinery Ltd, where he was responsible for designing and developing a number of classic typefaces for line composition including Estienne, Baskerville and – what is considered to be his finest achievement – Granjon, which dates from about 1928. Jones based his font on that originally designed by Garamond in 1592 but, because there were a number of different variants of Garamond coming onto the market at that time, he decided to call it Granjon to avoid any possible confusion. The Granjon font family is a classic font that has stood the test of time. An exemplar is shown on the facing page. It was a remarkably easy decision to make when choosing a font to be used in the design for this book – a truly unexpected Treasure.

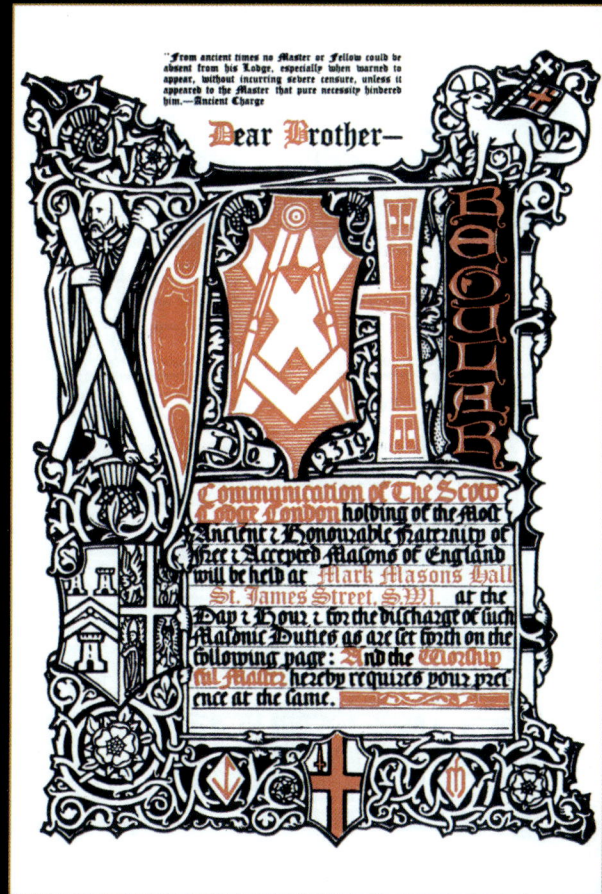

An Overview of Three Hundred Years of English Freemasonry

Richard Gan

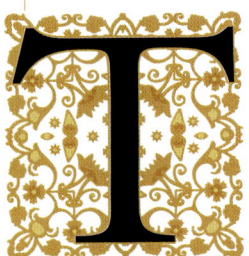he history of any institution or organisation, especially one that is over 300 years old, will have its high and low points with some aspects more interesting than others, and in this regard English Freemasonry is no different. *The Treasures of English Freemasonry* charts the progress of English Freemasonry, as opposed to Freemasonry in England, from its formal inception in 1717 to the celebration of its Tercentenary in 2017. It does so through the medium of more than 200 objects and in doing so provides the opportunity for a very different perspective to that normally associated with the more traditional type of history.

The beginnings of English Freemasonry and its formative years take place primarily during the period from 1717, with the formation of the Premier or Moderns Grand Lodge, up to the establishment of the United Grand Lodge of England (UGLE) in 1813. In the period following the Union right up to the present time, whilst Freemasonry has developed and kept pace with changes in society in general, including a greater emphasis on 'openness' over the last fifty years, it would be true to say that there has been considerable stability after 1813 compared with the first 100 years.

The quotation attributed to Sir Francis Drake is very apposite as far as Freemasonry is concerned: 'There must be a beginning of any great matter, but the continuing unto the end until it be thoroughly finished yields the true glory.'

In terms of design, a chronological approach has been adopted for the period 1717-1813 with chapters covering: the Early Years, the Antients and the Moderns, and the Formation of the UGLE. A thematic approach is more appropriate for the years from 1813 to the present, with chapters on the constant threads that run throughout Masonry during the time in question: Masonic Charity, the long-standing connection with the Royal Family, Masonry overseas, and Freemasons' Hall in London. The one key factor which distinguishes the operative stonemason from the Freemason is the use of symbolism and, as such, warrants a dedicated chapter. There are many day-to-day aspects of Freemasonry which come alive through the objects that have been left behind. These, if put in separate chapters, would not have the same impact as when brought together in the chapter entitled 'A Cornucopia of Freemasonry', which demonstrates the sheer variety of different items that have been generated by Freemasons. The majority of the objects will be found in the Library and Museum of Freemasonry in London, whilst others are from the many Masonic Museums up and down the country.

Freemasonry is the oldest and largest initiatory, non-religious, fraternal organisation in this country and indeed the world. The key principles that have been in place since the seventeenth century include: a requirement to believe in God, a male-only membership, charitable giving and receiving, and the members to be of good morals. It is hardly surprising therefore that the sheer variety and quality of objects contained in this book reflect those principles and give a unique insight into an organisation that has undoubtedly left its mark and made a considerable contribution to society over the last 300 years.

In the chapter on 'The Early Years of Freemasonry', Professor Aubrey Newman explores the history of Freemasonry in the period before and immediately after the formation of the Premier Grand Lodge in 1717. Whilst the earliest recorded incident of the Initiation of a Freemason in England was that of Elias Ashmole in 1646, the earliest documentation relating to the duties of Freemasons goes back to 1583. The membership in those early days was drawn primarily from the upper reaches of society. Other lodges, within the London area, soon joined the four founding lodges and by the 1730s there had been a great increase in lodges outside London, and indeed some outside the British Isles. It was in these early years that English Freemasonry evolved an elaborate structure of Masonic jewels, collars, and aprons, making differentiations between the various Officers of Grand Lodge, the Officers of individual lodges, and the rank and file of the ordinary membership.

A desire by those who were mainly artisans and craftsmen to become members of the Fraternity, and who were unable to do so, caused a major rift within the world of Freemasonry. Freemasons, many of whom had been initiated in Ireland but were now working in London, decided in 1751 to form their own Grand Lodge, which in due time became known as the Antients, for reasons that are explained in the chapter by Dr David Harrison on 'The Antients and Moderns'. The competition between the two Grand Lodges encouraged the development of Freemasonry with these two organisations operating on a national scale, both reaching out to the Colonies and each spreading their own particular influence.

The disagreements between the two Grand Lodges continued until 1813, when, as described by John Belton in the chapter 'The Formation of the United Grand Lodge of England' (UGLE), and following many years of negotiation, the two Grand Lodges finally came together due to the influence and determination of two royal Princes – the Duke of Sussex and the Duke of Kent. One of the most significant outcomes of the Union was that it brought stability to the world of Freemasonry at a time of turbulence. Freemasons today are still feeling the benefits arising from the events of 1813.

Many objects can be used to help illustrate one or more themes whilst others defy specific classification, in particular items of Masonic ephemera. These have been grouped together in the chapter entitled 'A Cornucopia of Freemasonry', in which Diane Clements provides a fascinating account of the history of the Library and Museum of Freemasonry based in Freemasons' Hall in London. This is now very much the jewel in the Masonic crown and one of the foremost Museums in the country. The Library and Museum has also served as a tremendous role model for the formation of similar establishments throughout the country. Whilst none can compete with London in terms of size and resources, they nevertheless house important Masonic treasures of local interest that are often unique. A number of local Museums have provided such items, which have been included in the chapter 'My Cup Runneth Over', amply illustrating the wealth of Masonic treasures that are to be found up and down the country and which emphasise the importance of the local perspective and its impact on the history of Freemasonry.

Freemasonry is described in the ritual as 'a system of morality, veiled in allegory and illustrated by symbols'. A number of Freemasons find the whole concept of symbolism – or what is sometimes termed esoteric Freemasonry, with its many levels of understanding – one of the more difficult subjects to understand. Hugh O'Neill presents a very clear explanation and at the same time provides a deep insight into the philosophy of Freemasonry in the chapter on 'The Craft of Symbolism'.

There cannot be a more iconic building for Freemasons throughout the world than Freemasons' Hall in London. The building was officially opened in 1933 and is an outstanding example of the art deco period which more than merits its Grade II* listed building status. It is a far cry from 1717, when the Grand Lodge of England, with just four lodges, met for the first time in a room in the Goose and Gridiron Tavern in St Paul's Churchyard. The idea for a building for Grand Lodge was not mooted until 1768 and the first Freemasons' Hall opened in 1776 in Great Queen Street in Covent Garden. The style and quality of a headquarters building reflects the standing and status of an organisation. In the chapter 'Freemasons' Hall, London', Dr James Campbell traces the absorbing history of the various Halls that have stood on or near the present site in Covent Garden from that time until the present.

Once Freemasonry had become formalised in the British Isles with the establishment of Grand Lodges in England (1717), Ireland (1725) and Scotland (1736), it quickly spread overseas – initially in the early eighteenth century by means of British emigrants in the colonies but also by traders, soldiers and sailors on the one hand and foreign visitors to British lodges on the other. It is from these lodges, formed overseas, that a great number of Grand Lodges throughout the world became established. Dr James Daniel explores 'English Freemasonry Overseas': how the Fraternity developed in different parts of the world and the legacy that it has left behind, including less well-known aspects such as Freemasonry at war, when Masons managed to continue to meet in the most adverse of circumstances.

Charity over the last 300 years has been and continues to be a central tenet of Freemasonry. In many ways Freemasons originally replicated the principles of the early trade guilds in terms of self-help. At the time when there was no state welfare net, lodges were able to provide for those who were unable to work or fell on hard times, to give financial assistance and where necessary medical care, as well as providing for dependents of Freemasons and, in the most unfortunate of cases, to make it possible for them to receive a dignified funeral. Times have changed, and whilst today Masonic Charities still do support Freemasons and their dependents in circumstances where the State is unable to do so, the focus for a number of years has been and continues to be the provision of sizeable financial grants to other charitable organisations within the wider community – which, by definition, means they are non-Masonic – and in 2014-15 the Grand Charity made grants amounting to £3.2 million to non-Masonic charities. In the chapter 'Freemasonry and Charity', Dr John Reuther charts the foundation and development of the various Masonic Charities and how they have changed and adapted to mirror changes in society in general over the last 300 years.

One of the most striking and enduring features of Freemasonry has been the powerful appeal and enjoyment that it has extended to so many of the nation's rulers, including members of the Royal Family. The first member of the Royal Family to become a Freemason was Frederick Lewis, Prince of Wales, who was initiated in 1737, only twenty years after the formation of Grand Lodge in 1717; and after an almost unbroken connection with royalty since that time, HRH the Duke of Kent will celebrate fifty years as Grand Master in 2017. Dr Paul Calderwood, in the chapter 'Royal Freemasons and the Rulers of the Craft', examines this long-running association that has generated an abundance of treasured items illustrating the history of the Fraternity, and the strong appeal that the organisation has had for many of the nation's most distinguished figures.

The story of 300 years of Freemasonry through more than 200 objects brings Masonry to life in a very tangible way. A prime example is that of the 'The Wren Maul' **[A1]**, believed to have been used by King Charles II at the laying of the Foundation Stone of St Paul's Cathedral in 1675, and which Sir Christopher Wren presented to the Lodge of Antiquity – one of the four founding lodges of Grand Lodge – in 1717. The range of different objects available is both astonishing and considerable and some form of categorisation is necessary to make it more meaningful and easier to assimilate and appreciate. It is of course possible to categorise the items by age or, as has been done in this book, by putting them into broad themes. It is also useful to look at them by type – to see how they have developed and changed over time, which is the format adopted in the Index of Images.

Regalia

From those earliest times Freemasons have worn regalia at their meetings. Masonic aprons were modelled on those worn by operative stonemasons, made of white lambskin and frequently decorated with hand-painted Masonic symbols. The designs used were very much a matter for the individual and not to any standard design, not least because until 1717 there was no one ruling or governing body. Even then, many lodges ploughed their own furrows as far as regalia was concerned. It was not until after the Union of the two Grand Lodges in 1813 that designs for regalia, including aprons, collars and jewels **[A2]**, were standardised and which in turn coincided with the ability to manufacture commercially all types of regalia on a large scale.

Jewels

Jewels, or medals as they might be referred to in the wider world, have given ample opportunity for exquisite design and craftsmanship **[A3]**. It is no coincidence that eminent and successful artists such as William Hogarth **[A4]** and Alphonse Mucha, the Czech patriot **[A5]**, have designed some beautiful and delicate pieces, whilst examples of the intricate work by jewellers, such as Thomas Harper in particular, may be considered as works of art. The tradition has been continued up to recent times, with individual lodges being able to exercise some freedom in the design of lodge jewels for Founders, members, and Past Masters, which reflect the character of the lodge and provide some of the earliest-known examples of what might be described as a corporate image.

The art of the Masonic jeweller is not always appreciated, and there is the celebrated incident of a female descendant of the Earl of Moira altering the Masonic jewel, presented to him for his services to Masonry, into a piece of fashion jewellery. Given that the cost of the original was some £1,500 – nearly £88,000 in today's money *[henceforward itm]* – one cannot really blame her; and the jewel, depicted in this book, was ultimately restored using paste gemstones.

Manuscripts, Books, Magazines, Newspapers, Music, Poetry and Literature

Books, magazines and newspapers about Freemasonry have been available since the early eighteenth century. The first Masonic book to be published was the *Book of Constitutions* of 1723. Antagonism towards Freemasonry has existed right from the outset, and many of the early publications were anti-Masonic, purporting to reveal the secrets and ritual of Masonry. These publications must have been quite accurate in their interpretation as they frequently sold out, needing to be reprinted to satisfy the wants of their largest audience – Freemasons themselves. As there was no official printed ritual at the time, it was the only means by which Freemasons could obtain a copy. The first Masonic magazine published in 1738 was followed by a variety of Masonic journals and two weekly newspapers – *The Freemason* [A6] and *The Freemason's Chronicle,* which ran from 1869 to 1951 and 1875 to 1957 respectively. The quality of the literary content of books and magazines has always been consistently high, not least in the early years, with poetry, literary pieces and music featuring large: a reflection on the intellectual quality and expectations of the membership at the time. The works of authors such as Rudyard Kipling have been influenced by their membership of the Craft [A7]. Sibelius composed music specifically for use in Masonic ceremonies, whilst at the other end of the scale Freemasonry even featured on stage in the music hall of the late nineteenth century [A8].

Photographs, Prints, Engravings and Documents

Photography did not make a commercial impact until the end of the nineteenth century: prior to that metal engraving was effectively the only means by which multiple copies could be achieved. It is, for example, interesting to compare the widely-distributed engraving by Francesco Bartolozzi – of the painting of Ruspini leading the procession of girl pupils of the Royal Cumberland School into Freemasons' Hall in 1802 – with the original painting by Thomas Stothard [See K7 and K8]. The art of the engraver features not only in the broadsheets published in the eighteenth and nineteenth centuries but also in certificates, Warrants, Charters, lodge Summonses and Loyal Addresses [A9].

Portraits

Portraiture has always been a popular medium and the great and the good in the world of Freemasonry have throughout the period in question been the subject of portraits. Some appearing in Masonic regalia, others in everyday clothes, but all reflecting the social style of their particular age [A10]. Sculpture is another medium often employed, more often than not in the form of a more manageable bust rather than full size or a larger-than-life example – the case of the sculpture of the Duke of Sussex being a notable exception [A11].

Glassware, Porcelain, Pottery and Ceramics

Dining at the conclusion of Masonic meetings has always been a characteristic of English Freemasonry; indeed, in the eighteenth century meetings were held around a dining table, usually in a suitable tavern. It is no surprise therefore that lodge members, and tavern owners specifically, commissioned tableware and glassware, including specially-designed firing glasses. In time more sophisticated and expensive porcelain and decorative ceramic pieces with a Masonic theme were produced and collected, amply illustrated by the examples of Meissen and Sèvres.

Meeting Places

Lodges originally met in taverns, indeed the first meeting of Grand Lodge took place in one – The Goose and Gridiron [A12] – but after the formation of the UGLE in 1813 Masonic Halls were built, specifically designed to cater for the needs of Masons, one of the first being in Bath in 1819 [A13]. Masonic Halls and rooms were also built overseas; the one in Kaira in India [A14] was in operation in 1822 and provides an interesting contrast with Freemasons' Hall in London.

Furniture

Masonic furniture, used in lodge rooms, would often include ornately carved and suitably engraved items, often rich in Masonic symbolism, made specifically for individual lodges. Chairs in particular can often survive despite extensive use, with that of the Master decorated with the Square and those of the Wardens with the Level and Plumb rule respectively. At the top end of the market is the throne commissioned for the Prince of Wales – later George IV – as Grand Master. Other more mundane examples include such things as lodge Tracing Boards.

Silverware and Presentation Pieces

Presentations and testimonials, including salvers, caskets, medals and candelabra in precious metal – paid for by voluntary subscription from the individual members and presented to Brethren who had rendered great service, usually at local or Provincial level – are testimony not only to the generosity of the members but are also indicative of the appreciation of the considerable contribution made by senior members of the Craft [A15].

Austerity

One of the more visible and visual aspects of Charity is that of the charity jewel, issued annually for the Festival by the Masonic Charities and worn with pride by members who have made a sufficient financial contribution to qualify as a Festival Steward. The Festival jewels are made using metal or metal gilt, save in the war years when the jewels were made of printed card. Similarly, in times of austerity Freemasons have ever been resourceful, even making regalia from cardboard and calico.

Ephemera

Masonic ephemera is defined as something that was meant to exist for only one day – or for a one-off specific event – and examples include such things as lodge Summonses, tickets, newspapers, broadsheets, invitations, and letters. Fortunately for us many Freemasons are also 'magpies', and hence examples that should have been thrown away after use can still be found in Museums today, helping to provide such a vivid picture of Freemasonry through the last 300 years.

Miscellany

Some items almost defy classification or categorisation: these include such objects as an Egyptian maul [A16], an engraved powder horn [A17], a cowrie shell snuffbox [A18], William Preston's death mask [A19], and a lodge meeting depicted in a bottle [A20]. Items that have been produced specifically for the Masonic market include jewellery [A21] and such novelties as Masonic toast holders and jelly moulds [A22] [A23]. Surprising as this might be, the presumption has to be that these items were manufactured because there was a market for them! Yet all add something to our overall knowledge and have their place in *The Treasures of English Freemasonry*.

A1: Wren Maul, 1675.

It is believed that King Charles II used the 'The Wren Maul' at the laying of the Foundation Stone of St Paul's Cathedral in 1675. It was presented to the Lodge of Antiquity by Sir Christopher Wren, who was described as 'Worshipful Master of this Lodge and Architect of that Edifice'. The silver plate was added in 1827 by order of the Duke of Sussex, Grand Master and Master of the Lodge. The Maul has been carried in at the head of the procession at the special meetings for the 250th and 275th anniversary celebrations of the founding of Grand Lodge in 1967 and 1992, and – all things being equal – will do so again at the Tercentenary celebration to be held in 2017.

A2: Collar Jewel for the Past President of the Board of General Purposes, 1894.

The jewel belonged to Thomas Fenn, who was President of the Board of General Purposes from 1884 to 1893. A Joining Member of Prince of Wales's Lodge No. 259 in 1860, he served as Grand Steward in 1863 and was the representative Grand Steward at the laying of the Foundation Stone for the second Freemasons' Hall.

The Board, which acts as the Executive Committee of the UGLE, was formed in 1813 at the Union of the Antients and Moderns. Its functions are prescribed in the *Book of Constitutions*. The Board is presently composed of the President, the Deputy President, the Grand Secretary, Grand Treasurer, and the President of the Committee of General Purposes of Grand Chapter, together with no more than seven additional members.

A3: Sackville Medal, 1733.

The Sackville Medal takes the form of a medallion, minted in the same way as a coin. It was produced to commemorate an event rather than to be worn as the membership jewel of a Masonic lodge, and is one of the earliest known 'English' Masonic Medals.

Charles Sackville (1711-69) was Earl of Middlesex from 1720 and, on the death of his father in 1765, 2nd Duke of Dorset. The medal was struck whilst Sackville was in Florence on the Grand Tour, to commemorate a lodge meeting in the city.

A4: Grand Steward's Hogarth Jewel, c.1789.

The jewel is believed to have been designed by the artist William Hogarth. Hogarth (1697–1764) was a Grand Steward and member of Grand Stewards' Lodge. Since 1835 the jewel has been worn by the Master and Past Masters of the Lodge.

The Annual Investiture is the meeting at which the Grand Officers of the year are appointed and invested. It is followed by the Grand Festival, or celebratory dinner. The arrangements for the Grand Festival have, since the earliest days of Grand Lodge, been organised by the Grand Stewards. Nineteen 'Red Apron' Lodges have the privilege of nominating the Grand Stewards of the year, for appointment by the Grand Master. They rank as Grand Officers during the year for which they are appointed; Past Grand Stewards, as such, are not Grand Officers. Grand Stewards present and past are entitled to wear a crimson apron – hence the derivation of 'Red Apron' lodges. The nineteen Grand Stewards form that year's Board of Grand Stewards, which is responsible for arranging the Grand Festival in such a way that no costs fall on Grand Lodge, even to the extent that they have to make up any financial shortfall, without help from their lodges. In 1735 the Stewards of Grand Lodge were allowed to form (without a Warrant) a special Stewards' Lodge. In 1792 it was placed at the head of the roll of lodges without a number: a position and distinction that it retains to the present day. The membership of Grand Stewards' Lodge is restricted to those who have held the office of Grand Steward.

A5: Jewel designed by Alphonse Mucha for Dilo Lodge, Czechoslovakia, *c*.1920.

The jewel, in the art nouveau style, is in gold-plated metal with enamelled decoration and was designed by the Czech artist and patriot Alphonse Mucha (1860-1939), whose poster and advertisement designs were typical of the art nouveau style of the late 1800s. The jewel features many familiar Masonic symbols such as gavels, triangles and the letter G, all executed in a unique Slavonic style.

Freemasonry has had strong associations with the struggle for national independence in a number of different countries including the USA, Chile, the Philippines, Poland, and Finland. Alphonse Mucha played a leading role in the formation and creation of the identity of the newly-formed independent state of Czechoslovakia in 1918, including providing the design for the country's new bank notes and postage stamps. He took a leading role in the re-introduction of Freemasonry into Czechoslovakia which, under the Austro-Hungarian Empire, had been banned since 1794. The first President of Czechoslovakia, Thomas Masaryk, was a Freemason. In the 1920s Mucha designed the jewels for the newly-formed National Grand Lodge of Czechoslovakia and for at least five Czechoslovakian lodges, including the Jan Amos Komenský Lodge in Prague, of which he was a Founder in 1918 and which was named after the seventeenth century Czech patriot.

A6: *The Freemason* newspaper: title page of the first issue, 1869.

The Freemason was a weekly newspaper, published in London from 1869 until 1951. It published a wide range of articles, including in-depth studies on various aspects of Masonry and detailed accounts of the debates in Grand Lodge. Whilst it did not shirk from publishing articles of a controversial nature, in the main it provided a record of the various Masonic meetings that had taken place during the previous week – all of which clearly appealed to a very wide Masonic audience and which accounted for its continuing success. In addition, the cost of *The Freemason* at 2d. represented good value.

Masonic periodicals have been published for a little over 200 years, with the first English Masonic example – the *Freemasons Magazine* – appearing in 1793. The magazine folded in 1798 and there followed thirty-six fallow years when no Masonic periodicals were published. The period from 1834 to 1917 can be described as the golden era of Masonic newspapers and periodicals. The price of a daily newspaper fell from 7d. to 1d. and ultimately to ½d. A combination of factors enabled this to happen: the removal of the newspaper tax in 1855 and paper duty in 1861; the advances in technology and production; and the development of the railway, which made possible an effective distribution system.

THE FREEMASON

"Truth is the Body of God, and Light is His Shadow."—PLATO

REGISTERED FOR TRANSMISSION ABROAD.

No. 1.]   SATURDAY, MARCH 13, 1869.   [PRICE 2D.

TABLE OF CONTENTS.

	PAGE.
OUR ADDRESS	1
THE MASONIC PRESS ABROAD	1
REPORTS OF MASONIC MEETINGS:—	
THE CRAFT—	
Metropolitan	2
Provincial	2
THE ROYAL ARCH—	
Metropolitan	3
Provincial	6
ORDERS OF CHIVALRY—	
Knights' Templars,	
Provincial	6
Red Cross of Rome and Constantine,	
Metropolitan	6
Foreign	6
MEMORANDA	4
PARLIAMENT OF FREEMASONRY	4
ZETLAND COMMEMORATION FUND	4
THE ROYAL MASONIC INSTITUTION FOR BOYS ...	4
THE EDITOR'S PORTFOLIO	4
MASONIC JURISPRUDENCE	5
MULTUM IN PARVO	5
MASONIC ANTIQUITIES	5
POETRY	5
SIR KNIGHT W. R. LITTLE'S ADDRESS ...	6
ADVERTISEMENTS	7 and 8

OUR ADDRESS.

IN assuming the *rôle* and responsibility of editorial functions, we do so with a hearty fraternal greeting to all our readers. Upon their indulgence we rely to excuse imperfections, and to their sympathies we confidently appeal for support in this attempt to establish a journal which we hope will become a worthy organ of the great Masonic Fraternity.

It is beyond dispute that the progress of Freemasonry, not only in England but in every part of the globe, has been for some time past almost incalculable. Candidates for admission throng the hallowed porch-ways of our Temple, while men of every clime and creed, are found zealously promoting the welfare of the Craft by the study of its mysteries and the dissemination of its principles. A society at once so admirable and so extensive, and which embraces within its ample fold so many members of talent and influence, ought to be, we conceive, as fully represented in the Press of Great Britain as it is in that of Germany, France, or the United States of America. It will therefore be our mission to act as the exponent of our brethren's enlightened views, as well as the historian of their proceedings; and in the discharge of this duty we shall sedulously avoid giving publicity to any document, from whatever source, which might in the slightest degree infringe the laws of the Order by disclosing the arcana of Freemasonry. We invite the cordial co-operation of *every Mason*, as our columns will be opened to reports of meetings in *every established degree* and *every existing rite*.

Among other subjects to be considered or discussed in THE FREEMASON, will be found "Masonic Jurisprudence." Under this heading we purpose giving expositions of the *laws* of the Masonic institution in its several branches, according to the most generally received interpretations, and not merely as our own editorial opinions.

The utility of "Masonic Notes and Queries" is unquestionable; many stray facts may be jotted down, and many little incidents brought to light through the medium of this unpretending mode of inquiring, or of communicating information.

The "Antiquities, Records, and Bibliography" of the Order will occupy the position due to the importance of those monuments of the past, and we rejoice to hail our esteemed Brother HUGHAN as the first craftsman in this department of labour.

In our "Portfolio" we shall give excerpts from choice publications; and this being a work in which all our friends can lend a helping hand, we earnestly solicit them to forward suitable extracts from books in their possession. *Non omnia possumus omnes* was the saying of an ancient sage, but it is fair to add that we may *all* achieve *something*.

A prominent feature in THE FREEMASON will be leading articles upon subjects of interest to the Order, or upon remarkable events in its history and progress. The "Craft Universal" will, of course, first claim our attention, and we promise to devote our utmost endeavours to promote the success of those noble charities which are near and dear to the heart of every true Mason. Arrangements will also be made to obtain foreign Masonic intelligence, and we shall be glad to receive from our brother editors in America and on the Continent copies of their magazines or journals in exchange for THE FREEMASON.

This, friendly readers, is our programme.

Regarding Freemasonry as a pure system of ethics which contains every element that can constitute real greatness and goodness in life, we shall honestly and fearlessly advocate its interests in the most comprehensive sense of the word. We shall direct attention to its principles and its practices, investigate its records, and demonstrate its utility. In short, it will be our constant aim to sustain the reputation and enhance the renown of an Institution which has been so long

To fame immortally allied,
And crowned with glory.

Our readers will observe that our frontispiece is an engraving of Freemasons' Hall, Great Queen-street, the Grand Temple of English Freemasonry, and we trust this will be accepted as an evidence that, whilst working under the ægis of lawfully-constituted authority, and paying due deference to the ordinances of ruling powers, we shall ever remember that we are "free" Masons, and vindicate our position as such by maintaining a just independence as the organ of a great and "free" fraternity.

THE MASONIC PRESS ABROAD.

One of the best magazines published in America is the "Masonic Monthly," of Boston. We extract from it the following apposite remarks upon Masonic Literature :—

The existence of a Masonic Science, and a Philosophy of Masonry, suggests and renders possible, a Masonic Literature. Science and philosophy are essential to the existence of any literature. They are its food and its life. The existence of the one presupposes that of the other.

Of late years the literature of Freemasonry has assumed large proportions. It has been developed to such an extent as to give considerable prominence and importance to the question—What is its mission and its duty. It is a weighty matter how the conductors of the Masonic Press solve this problem. We much fear that some of them have not given the subject very much of their thought, while some, we imagine, regard the earnings as of more consequence than the influence of their organs.

We consider that the mission of the Masonic Press is to occupy the field of Masonic science, history, and philosophy, and to disseminate the principles of true Masonic life, with the end in view of winning back the Craft into the old ways of our ancient brethren, who sought to penetrate into and obtain a mastery over every department of Masonry. The lodges have neglected the pursuit of science and philosophy, and confined themselves simply and exclusively to Masonry as an art. Masonic literature is, or should be, a reaction to this tendency, and as a reaction may we hope for it all success.

A7: 'The Mother Lodge', 1896.

Rudyard Kipling (1865-1936) was initiated on 5 April 1886 in Lahore, India in the Lodge of Hope and Perseverance No. 782. He was appointed the Secretary of the Lodge the same evening – and as such wrote up the details of his own Initiation in the Lodge Minutes.

The Lodge into which a Freemason is initiated is known as his Mother Lodge, even though he may well become a Joining Member of other lodges in the future. The importance of the Mother Lodge to a Freemason and the relationship of Freemasonry with ethnicity, religion and occupation are best summed up in his poem – 'The Mother Lodge'.

'The Mother Lodge'

There was Rundle, Station Master,
An' Beazeley of the Rail,
An' 'Ackman, Commissariat,
An' Donkin' o' the Jail;
An' Blake, Conductor-Sergeant,
Our Master twice was 'e,
With 'im that kept the Europe-shop,
Old Framjee Eduljee.

Outside – "Sergeant! Sir! Salute! Salaam!"
Inside – "Brother", an' it doesn't do no 'arm.
We met upon the Level an' we parted on the Square,
An' I was Junior Deacon in my Mother-Lodge out there!

We'd Bola Nath, Accountant,
An' Saul the Aden Jew,
An' Din Mohammed, draughtsman
Of the Survey Office too;
There was Babu Chuckerbutty,
An' Amir Singh the Sikh,
An' Castro from the fittin'-sheds,
The Roman Catholick!

We 'adn't good regalia,
An' our Lodge was old an' bare,
But we knew the Ancient Landmarks,
An' we kep' 'em to a hair;
An' lookin' on it backwards
It often strikes me thus,
There ain't such things as infidels,
Excep', per'aps, it's us.

For monthly, after Labour,
We'd all sit down and smoke
(We dursn't give no banquets,
Lest a Brother's caste were broke),

An' man on man got talkin'
Religion an' the rest,
An' every man comparin'
Of the God 'e knew the best.

So man on man got talkin',
An' not a Brother stirred
Till mornin' waked the parrots
An' that dam' brain-fever-bird.
We'd say 'twas 'ighly curious,
An' we'd all ride 'ome to bed,
With Mo'ammed, God, an' Shiva
Changin' pickets in our 'ead.

Full oft on Guv'ment service
This rovin' foot 'ath pressed,
An' bore fraternal greetin's
To the Lodges east an' west,
Accordin' as commanded,
From Kohat to Singapore,
But I wish that I might see them
In my Mother-Lodge once more!

I wish that I might see them,
My Brethren black an' brown,
With the trichies smellin' pleasant
An' the hog-darn passin' down;
An' the old khansamah snorin'
On the bottle-khana floor,
Like a Master in good standing
With my Mother-Lodge once more.

Outside – "Sergeant! Sir! Salute! Salaam!"
Inside – "Brother", an' it doesn't do no 'arm.
We met upon the Level an' we parted on the Square,
An' I was Junior Deacon in my Mother-Lodge out there!

A8: 'Act on the Square Boys' – a Music Hall song, c.1875.

'Act on the Square boys', written by Alfred Lee, is one of the songs most associated with 'The Great Vance', the stage name of Alfred Peek Stevens (1839-88), one of the great stars of Victorian music hall in the 1860s and 1870s.

Pictorial music covers became common from the middle of the nineteenth century following the invention of colour lithography, which enabled multi-coloured printed work to be produced in quantity and cheaply. At the same time a change in the regulations governing theatrical performance led to the development of the music hall. The first purpose built Music Hall was opened in 1852 and by 1875 there were 375 Music Halls in London alone. Songs formed the largest part of the entertainment at Music Halls and singers were amongst the best-paid performers. 'Act on the Square boys' has four verses. The chorus and final verse are as follows:

(Chorus)

Act on the square boys
Act on the square
Upright and fair boys
Act on the square
(repeated once)

I never liked a round game, nay
Round tables cannot bear
And in a Circus I can't stay
So I live in a square.
Now brothers all and Masons too
Of good let's do our share
And when a chance presents itself
We must act on the square.

VANCE'S ACT ON THE SQUARE BOYS.

faithfully yours
Alfred G. Vance

Act on the square boys, Act on the square,
Upright and fair boys, Act on the square.

WRITTEN BY **ANTHONY**, COMPOSED BY **ALFRED LEE.**

SUNG WITH GREAT SUCCESS BY

THE GREAT VANCE.

A9: By-laws of Royal Denbigh Lodge No. 505: Frontispiece, 1787.

The By-laws or rule book of the Royal Denbigh Lodge No. 505 include an illuminated front page depicting a lodge room layout. It has a chequered carpet, pedestal, Volume of the Sacred Law, Square and Compasses, Level and Plumb line, three candlesticks, and Doric and Corinthian columns; with an All-Seeing Eye symbol above these objects.

It was illustrated in 1787 by one of the first Initiates of the Lodge, John Owen, who was a young lawyer at the time. The script is known as Chancery Hand, a calligraphic style used in legal documents. The Royal Denbigh Lodge No. 505 was warranted on 5 August 1787 and constituted the following day in Chester. Meeting in Denbigh, the Lodge was renumbered 414 in 1792 and erased on 6 February 1811.

A10: Silhouette of a Freemason, c.1820.

A Masonic example of the late eighteenth and early nineteenth century fashion for creating portraits, generally in profile, from black card. This shows a Freemason of the time in his regalia as a Senior Grand Warden.

A11: Statue of Augustus Frederick, Duke of Sussex, 1847. ➤

The statue of the Duke of Sussex was commissioned from the leading sculptor Edward Hodges Baily (1788-1867), who was also responsible for the sculpture of Nelson that sits atop Nelson's Column in London. The statue of the Duke originally stood in the Grand Temple designed by Sandby, in the alcove behind the throne, as seen in the painting by Sigismund Rosenthal [H7]. Having survived the fire of 1883, it is now situated in the corridor leading to the old Boardroom of the Board of General Purposes.

A12: Goose and Gridiron, 1892. ⱽ

Watercolour by B. Angel Roberts.

The Goose and Gridiron Tavern, in Paternoster Square in London (adjacent to St Paul's Cathedral), has iconic status amongst Freemasons as having been the location of the meeting place of the oldest surviving lodge in the English Constitution, the Lodge of Antiquity, now No. 2, from 1716 to 1729. It is also believed to be the place where the Premier or Moderns Grand Lodge of England met for the first time on 24 June 1717, when Anthony Sayer was installed as the first Grand Master. The tavern was demolished in about 1894. Fortunately, B. Angel Roberts, an artist who specialised in making a pictorial record of taverns in London prior to their destruction during the latter part of the nineteenth century, was able to paint this watercolour, which is one of the finest representations of the Tavern.

A13: Jewel commemorating the dedication of the Freemasons' Hall in Bath, 1819.

A silver medal with, on the obverse, a relief bust of Augustus Frederick, Duke of Sussex (1773-1843); and on the reverse a relief depiction of Freemasons' Hall in Bath. The text reads: *FREE MASON'S* [sic] *HALL A.L. 5817 / DEDICATED / SEPR. 23 1819.*

Until comparatively recently most lodges met in inns and taverns, rather than Masonic centres – some still do. The Hall in Bath was one of the first dedicated Masonic Halls outside London. It was designed by William Wilkins but unfortunately became too expensive to run and closed in 1823.

A14: Lodge Room at Kaira, India, 1821.

George Sallisbury, a military surveyor and member of the Lodge of the 17th Regiment of Light Dragoons, enclosed the drawing with the Annual Returns to Grand Lodge in 1822.

Lodges have always met and continue to meet in a variety of different premises. The Lodge Room at Kaira provides a very vivid contrast to the Headquarters building of English Freemasonry in London.

Kaira, also called Kheda, is a town in east-central Gujarat state, west-central India, situated in the lowlands between the Sabarmati and Mahi rivers. The 17th Regiment of Light Dragoons Lodge No. 285 (Antients) was granted its Warrant in September 1794 whilst in Netley, Hampshire. The Lodge met at numerous locations during its working life, including Kaira, before returning to England in 1823; it was erased in 1828.

A15: Epergne in silver and glass, 1887.

Epergne in silver and glass presented to Richard Charles Else, Deputy Provincial Grand Master for Somerset 1883-1902, by the Freemasons of Somerset on his marriage in July 1887.

The Taunton Courier, and Western Advertiser on 4 January 1905 reported: '… the death of Mr. R. C. Else, JP of the County of Somerset and an ex-Mayor of Bridgwater, at the advanced age of 81 years; he had for upwards of a quarter of a century occupied the position of Deputy Provincial Grand Master. The deceased gentleman, who was an engineer by profession, and was associated with Mr. Brunel in the construction of the Bristol and Exeter Railway, and also the Saltash bridge, was Mayor of Bridgwater in the Jubilee Year (1897), and had the honour of being presented [to] Queen Victoria. In Bridgwater [he] had also filled the positions of president of the Conservative Association and chairman of the School Board. In 1887 [he] married the widow of Mr. Richard Smith, solicitor, of Bridgwater, P.P.G. Secretary of Somersetshire Freemasons.'

A16: Ancient Egyptian Mason's Maul, *c.*1,400 BC.

The maul, carved from one piece of wood, was found in a tomb in Memphis, Egypt in 1914. Whilst there have been some ill-thought-out attempts to try and link modern Freemasonry back to the time of the ancient Egyptians, it is probably best to take this item entirely at face value and simply acknowledge the fact that since time immemorial masons have used a maul.

A17: Powder Horn, 1820.

A powder horn decorated with military and Masonic symbols.

A18: Snuffbox made from a silver-mounted cowrie shell, 1810.

The surface of the lid is decorated with engraved Masonic emblems and the monogram 'G.F'. It was made by the silversmith Joseph Taylor (1767-1827), who was based in Birmingham.

Joseph Taylor is recorded in marks in the register of the Birmingham Assay Office from 1773 to 1801. His work initially seems to have involved making small-work such as watch cases, caddy spoons and vinaigrettes. In 1813 he became a Guardian of the Assay Office; he also had a showroom in Bouverie Street, London and left £18,000 in his will.

A19: William Preston – Death Mask, 1818. ➢

A plaster cast made from the face of William Preston, who's portrait [C5] appears with additional personal information relating to him on pages 72 & 73.

A20: Lodge Meeting in a Bottle, made by a French Prisoner of War during the Napoleonic Wars, c.1795. ➢

The model depicts a military lodge meeting around a table on which are laid out the Working Tools. The Master stands at the head of the table on a small box and is framed by the arch. The figures and scenery have been carved in wood and painted. The hair is styled in the military fashion with a long ponytail and made of real hair, whilst the aprons are fashioned from scraps of real leather.

In the latter half of the eighteenth and the early part of the nineteenth centuries, when England and France were periodically at war, considerable numbers of captured French prisoners of war were brought to England. In the period 1803-15 over 100,000 prisoners were interred. To keep occupied and to make money, the prisoners often fashioned items from whatever materials were to hand, including figures and models from paper, bone, wood and straw. Many prisoners were Freemasons and not surprisingly made items with a Masonic content.

A21: Pocket watch and case mounted with Grand Steward's Hogarth Jewel, *c.*1770.

Silver and gilt pocket watch and case made by James Neild. The outer case is set with brilliants and mounted with a representation of the Grand Stewards' Lodge Hogarth Jewel. Both James Neild and William Hogarth (1697–1764) were Grand Stewards and members of Grand Stewards' Lodge.

A22: Masonic Toast Rack, *c*.1872. ➢

Toast rack of electroplated silver with dividers of a Set square and Compasses design.

A23: Masonic Jelly Mould, *c*.1921. ▽

Jelly mould in copper, in the shape of an eight-pointed column with a Set square and Compasses on top, made by Benham and Froud (1855-1924), who were particularly well known for their copper jelly moulds.

There has always been a market for a variety of domestic items decorated with Masonic symbols.

The Early Years of Freemasonry

Professor Aubrey Newman

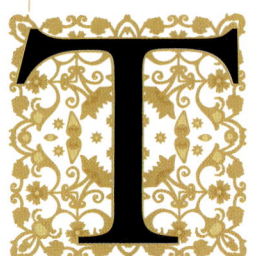There is a great deal of uncertainty amongst the students of English Freemasonry about many aspects of Freemasonry and particularly about the nature of Masonic lodges prior to the eighteenth century. Doubts about the existence of meetings of Freemasons prior to the beginning of the eighteenth century were expressed for many years, but the discovery of a pamphlet dated 1698 addressed *'To all godly people in the Citie of London'* **[B1]**, condemning the holding of secret meetings and the swearing of oaths, seems to have resolved such issues. It would seem therefore that there were Masons' lodges at that date and that an essential part of their procedures was the reading of documents describing the duties of the members, the *Old Charges* to which every Mason had to swear acceptance on admission. For this reason, every lodge had a copy of its Charges, occasionally written into the beginning of the Minute Book, but usually existing as a separate manuscript roll of parchment.

They usually have a three-part construction, starting with a prayer, a description of the Seven Liberal Arts (Logic, Grammar, Rhetoric, Arithmetic, Geometry, Music and Astronomy), and then followed by a history of the craft. The last part consists of the Charges or regulations of the lodge, and the craft of Masonry in general, which the members are bound to maintain. There are a number of copies of these *Old Charges* still in existence. Most of the *Old Charges* are thought to be copies of earlier documents, either exact copies or interpretations. *The Haddon Manuscript*, dated 1723, **[B2]** has precisely the same wording as the *Shadwell Clerke Manuscript*, which in turn was a near copy of another *Old Charge*, the *Antiquity Manuscript*, both of which are dated 1686.

It was the coming together of four of these early lodges into what was originally termed the Grand Lodge of London and Westminster which led to the replacement of individual versions of the *Old Charges* by a uniform printed version. As this first Grand Lodge gathered momentum, the Revd James Anderson was commissioned to digest the 'gothic constitutions' into a more palatable form. The result, in 1723, was the first printed *Book of Constitutions* **[B3]**. While manuscript constitutions continued to be used in unaffiliated lodges, these printed versions saw them die out by the end of the century. Anderson's introduction advertised a history of Freemasonry from the beginning of the world. Anderson's Regulations, the second part of the book, followed on a set of Charges devised by an early Grand Master, George Payne, during his second term of office. Charges and Regulations were geared to the needs of a Grand Lodge, necessarily moving away from the simplicity of the originals. Anderson's *Constitutions*, subjected over the following centuries to constant revision and amendment, have formed the basis for organised Freemasonry throughout the world. This first edition was reported in 1735 as having been out of print and subjected to unofficial pirate reprints, therefore suggesting the need for a second and revised *New Book of Constitutions* which appeared in 1739.

The Frontispiece [B4] of the first edition of these Regulations is of particular interest, depicting the formal passing of the Compasses and Regulations by one Grand Master (the Duke of Montagu) to his successor (the Duke of Wharton). Montagu's Wardens are shown in an early form of Masonic regalia, and they are carrying regalia for the incoming, newly-appointed Officers accompanying Wharton.

Details of the early years of this new Grand Lodge are obscure until the appointment of William Cowper as Secretary to Grand Lodge and the beginning of the official recording of the proceedings of Grand Lodge in a series of Minute Books, the first of which is shown [B5]. In time the manuscript Minutes were replaced by more formal printed papers, but essentially their format has been preserved.

The initial founding lodges were soon joined by other lodges within the London area, the so-called area covered by *The Bills of Mortality* (weekly mortality statistics for an area, fixed in 1636, which expanded out from the original City, but which by this time was much smaller than the real limits of London), and there was soon sufficient public interest to warrant the printing of *Lists of Lodges* associated with Grand Lodge, indicating when and where such lodges were meeting. The usual meeting place was a tavern, if only because inns and taverns were usually the only places with rooms large enough to hold such meetings, and in consequence lodges bore the name of the tavern in which the meeting was held. This particular list is dated 1725 [B6]. That there was an increasing public interest in Freemasonry is shown by the appearance of a plate on Freemasonry in a work of engravings by Bernard Picard, *Cérémonies et coutumes religieuses de tous les peuples du monde* [B7], published in 1737. This plate is one of the earliest illustrations of English Freemasons in a lodge, and where the back wall is replaced by a List of Lodges. Also shown is a portrait of Sir Richard Steele (1672-1729), an Irish writer and politician, but not known as a Freemason. A less flattering observation of the consequences of a lodge meeting is depicted in the picture *Night* by William Hogarth in 1738 [B8].

The list of 1737 also illustrates the phenomenal growth in the number of lodges associated with this Grand Lodge; the list dated 1725 (see above) includes some lodges outside London, but by the 1730s there had been a great increase in lodges outside London and indeed some outside the British Isles.

One feature of Freemasonry in London had been the public processions of Freemasons in full regalia, especially from the annual general meeting, at which the Grand Master had been elected, to the particular Hall in which the Feast was being held. But not all publicity was necessarily good publicity and in 1742 an anti-Masonic group had organised a counter-procession which attracted a great deal of public interest, and led to the publication of a large engraving claiming that it was a depiction of *A Geometrical view of the Grand Procession of Scald Miserable Masons* [B9]. It was this demonstration (and this print) that led to the discontinuation of the public procession.

It was in these early years that English Freemasonry evolved an elaborate structure of Masonic jewels, collars, and aprons, making differentiations between the various Officers of Grand Lodge, the Officers of individual lodges, and the rank and file of the ordinary membership. At its meeting in March 1731 Grand Lodge laid down rules for the jewels appropriate for each rank of Officers and for the colours of the ribbons and collars from which they were to be worn. The regulations specified the size and nature of aprons to be worn by each grade. In 1735 and again in 1739 Grand Lodge had to insist that 'The Laws relating to the proper Cloathing of the

Brethren should be directed to be strictly observed'. It had become important for the proper provision of the Annual Banquet that there should be a regular organisation of Stewards. Partly in order to encourage an appropriate number of volunteers for this office, those who were Stewards or who had already served as Stewards were permitted to wear their jewels suspended upon a red ribbon and to have their aprons trimmed in red. One such Grand Steward was Colonel John Pitt MP, Governor of Bermuda, whose portrait [B10] shows not only his collar and apron but also his gauntlets, which at this time were still plain white but later were also adapted to indicate rank. The *Portrait of a Senior Grand Warden* [B11] shows the development of a range of regalia. He is holding the jewel of his rank, suspended by a ribbon round his neck. On his left hand he is wearing a gauntlet, at the same time holding the right-hand gauntlet. His apron is bordered in blue, indicating that he holds Grand Rank, but it is without the tassels and levels that were to appear at a later stage of development. The early apron [B12], which dates from about 1730, shows the apron had already evolved from the protective garment of an operative stonemason to the symbolic badge of a Freemason. This example is made from a complete lambskin to which has been added a number of symbols, chosen from a wide range of Masonic emblems.

Such symbols and jewels were appearing also at a lodge level, and over the years a number of jewellers and instrument makers were commissioned to prepare suitable artefacts for individual lodges. One such prominent instrument maker was Jonathan Sisson, and illustrated here is probably the only surviving example of his art, the jewel of a Past Master of a lodge [B13]. Hanging from a Masonic Set Square is a plaque, on which is inscribed a diagram that usually accompanies the proof of Pythagoras' Theorem.

An increasing concentration upon the minutiae of regalia and regulations does not always reflect upon the activity of the members of the Order. It must be admitted that the last years of this first period of Freemasonry show a decline from what can be discerned as an early excitement. The Grand Master who had been installed in 1747 failed to appear at any meeting of Grand Lodge until 1752; there was in consequence no change in either the Grand Officers or the Grand Stewards. There were indeed in these years only seven meetings of Grand Lodge itself. While it would be over-simplistic to attribute the appearance of a rival Grand Lodge to these weaknesses, there was now certainly room for the appearance of what might well be a more enthusiastic alternative.

That such a step was not destructive of the main body of Freemasonry is amply illustrated by the Wedgwood jasperware vase [B14] produced in 1992 to mark the 275th anniversary of the formation of the Premier Grand Lodge of England.

B1: 'To all godly people, in the Citie of London', 1698.

A very early and rare example of a printed leaflet publicly expressing strong antipathy towards Freemasonry. It is ascribed to M. Winter and printed by R. Sare at Gray's Inn-gate in London in 1698.

It is a matter of some regret that since the earliest days of Freemasonry there have always been certain elements that have expressed hostility and antagonism towards Freemasonry. This particular leaflet that is 'Set forth as a warning to this Christian generation' was published nearly twenty years prior to the formation of the premier Grand Lodge in 1717.

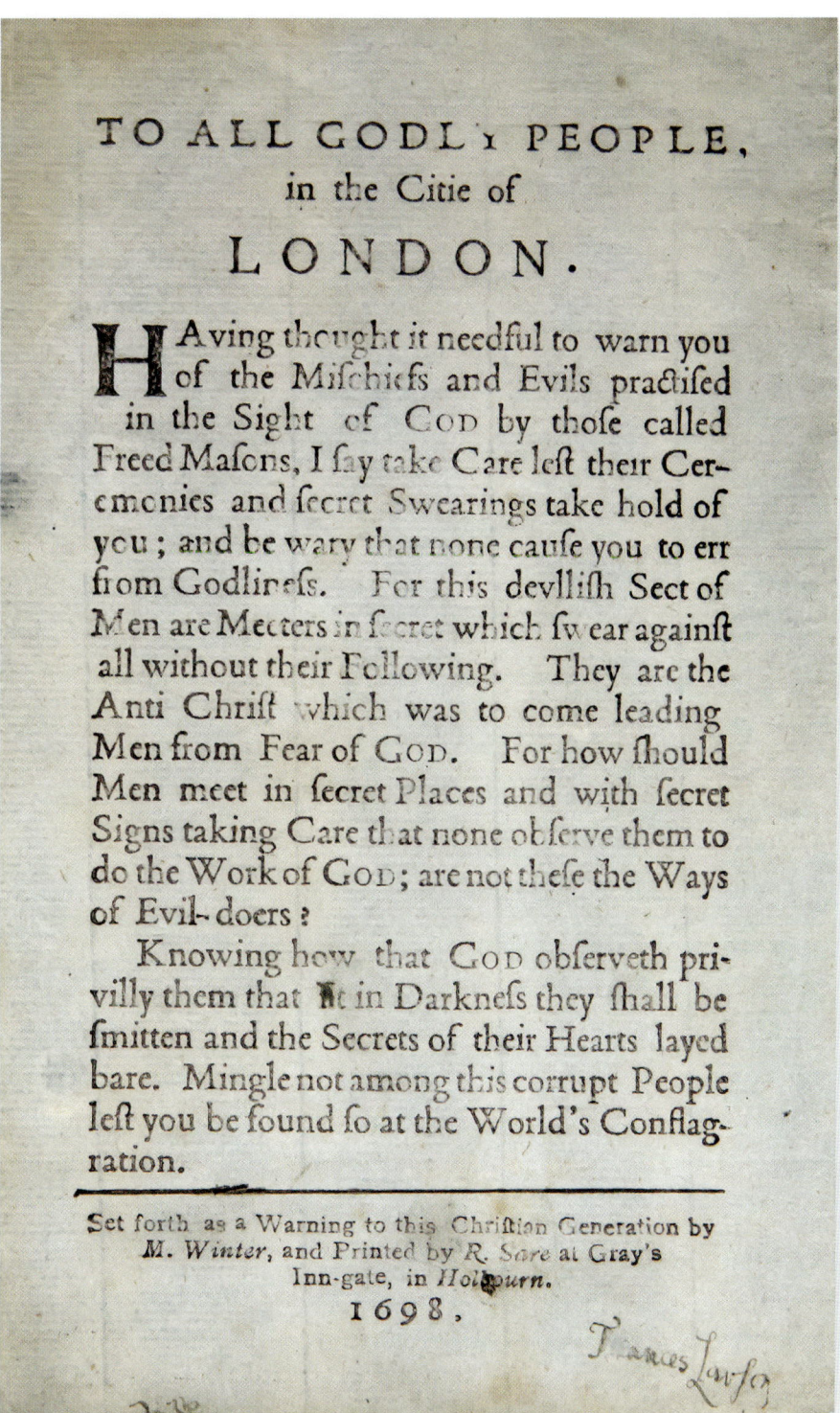

B2: *The Haddon Manuscript, 1723.*

This example of an *Old Charge* features the coat of arms of George I, flanked by the arms of the Masons' Company on the left hand side and the arms of the Rutherford family on the right. The connection between the document and the Rutherford family is unknown but a Hew Rutherford is listed as a member of the Lodge of Antiquity between 1723 and 1725.

The *Old Charges* or *Constitutions* are the popular name given to over 100 old manuscripts, some almost 600 years old; most are English but there are examples also found in Scotland. They provide some of the earliest examples of the history and rituals of Freemasonry, as well as describing the duties required of members. The *Old Charges* were gradually superseded by printed *Constitutions*. Many of the various manuscripts are named: for example the *Halliwell Manuscript*, also known as the *Regius Poem* (the original of which is in the British Museum), is the earliest of the *Old Charges*. It consists of sixty-four vellum pages of Middle English, written in rhyming couplets. In this, it differs from the prose of all the later Charges. The manuscript *Grand Lodge No. 1* was acquired by the UGLE in 1839 for £25. It is the first of the Charges to bear a date, which is just discernible as 25 December 1583.

Most of the *Old Charges* are thought to be copies of earlier documents, either exact copies or interpretations. *The Haddon Manuscript*, dated 1723, has precisely the same wording as the *Shadwell Clerke Manuscript*, which in turn was a near copy of another *Old Charge*, the *Antiquity Manuscript*, both of which are dated 1686. It is named after James Stradling Haddon (1851-1904), a draper from Wellington in Somerset, who was initiated in Lodge of Fidelity and Sincerity No. 1966, Wellington in 1882 and who donated the manuscript to Grand Lodge in 1896.

of the Father of Heaven, with the wisdom of the glorious Son, through the grace and the goodness of the Holy Ghost, that be three persons in one Godhead, be with us at our beginning, And give us grace, so to govern us herein our life, that we may come to his bliss that never shall have ending. AMEN.

and fellows our purpose is to tell you how this worthy Science of MASONRY was begun, and in what manner, and afterwards how it was founded by worthy Kings and Princes, and by many other honourable and worshipfull men. And also to those that be here, we will declare the Charges that belong to every true Mason to keep. For in good faith and if you take good heed thereto, it is well worthy to be kept for a worthy craft and curious Science. there be Seven liberal Sciences, of which Seven, it is One, And the names of the Seven Sciences are these. Grammar, and that teacheth a man to speak truly, and write truly. second is Rhetorick, and that teacheth a man to speak fair in Subtil terms. third is Dialectick, and that teacheth a man for to discern, or know Truth from Falshood. fourth is Arithmetick, and that teacheth a man for to reckon, and count all manner of Numbers. fifth is called Geometry, and that teacheth a man mete and measure, and all other things. Sixth is called Musick, and that teacheth a man the perfect method of Song, and Voice & tongue, with Instruments as Organ, Harp and Trumpet. the Seventh is called Astronomy, and that teacheth a man the course of the Sun Moon and Stars. These be the Seven liberal Sciences, the which Sciences take their foundation, of Geometry, for Geometry teacheth a man mete and measure, and weight of all manner of things on earth. For there is no man that worketh any Science, or Craft, but he worketh by some mete, or measure, or weight, and all this is Geometry, and Merchants and all Craftsmen, and all other of the six Sciences, especially the Ploughmen, and Tillers of the Earth, for all manner of Grain, Seeds, Vines, Plum-trees, Or planters of Fruit; for neither Grammar Arithmetick nor Astronomy nor none of the other Sciences, can a man find mete or measure in, without Geometry therefore me thinketh, that the Science of Geometry is most worthy, from whom the other proceed

that this worthy Science was first began, I shall tell you: Before Noah's flood there was a man that was called Lamech, it is written in the Bible, in the 4th Chap. of Genesis and this Lamech had two Wives, and the one wifes name was Adah, and the other Zillah : by the first he had two Sons, and the one was called Jabal and the other Jubal, And by the other wife Zillah, he got a Son and a daughter, and these four Children founded the beginning of all the Sciences in the world, And the elder Son Jabal founded the science of Geometry, and he departed Flocks of Sheep and Lambs in the field, and first wrought houses of Stone and Timber, as it is noted in the Chapter aforesaid. And his younger Jubal found the science of Musick, as Song Harp and Organ, and the third brother Tubal-Cain, found Smiths craft of Gold Silver Copper Iron and Steel, And the daughter found the craft of Weaving, each of these Children knew that their

B3: *Constitutions of the Free-Masons, 1723.* ▽

James Anderson produced the *Constitutions of the Free-Masons* in 1723 by adapting the legends and rules contained in the *Matthew Cooke Manuscript*, the second oldest of the *Old Charges* or *Gothic Constitutions* of Freemasonry. It is the oldest-known set of Charges relating to the stonemasons' lodges written in prose to come down to modern Freemasonry. The *Constitutions* were first published some five years after the formation of the first or Premier Grand Lodge, also known as the Moderns Grand Lodge, in 1717.

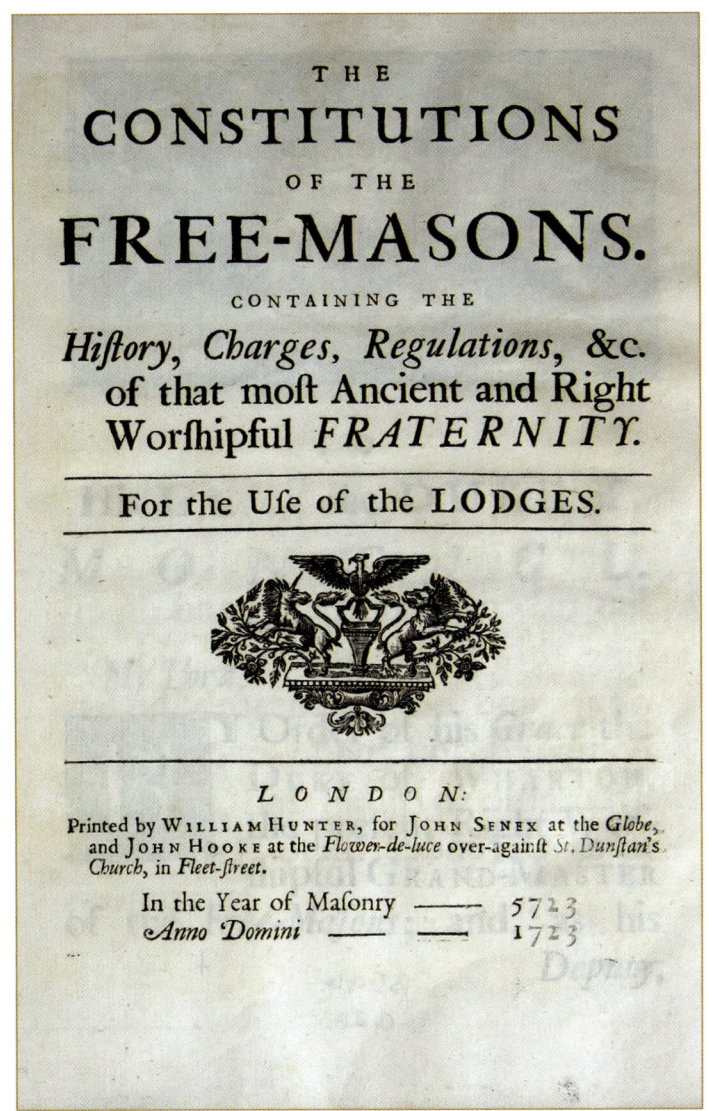

B4: *Book of Constitutions:* Frontispiece, 1723. ▷

The engraving shows the Grand Master, the Duke of Montagu, handing over the *Constitutions* and Compasses to his successor Phillip, Duke of Wharton. Each man is accompanied by his Deputy and Wardens. One of Montagu's Wardens carries aprons and gloves for the new Grand Officers. This is one of the earliest depictions of Masonic regalia. The architectural setting and depiction of the sun god Helios are used to place Freemasonry in the classical tradition.

Engrav'd by Iohn Pine in Aldersgate Street London

B5: Earliest Grand Lodge Minute Book, 1723.

Although the first Grand Lodge was formed in 1717, the earliest extant Minutes date only from 1723 and they coincide with the publication of the first *Book of Constitutions*.

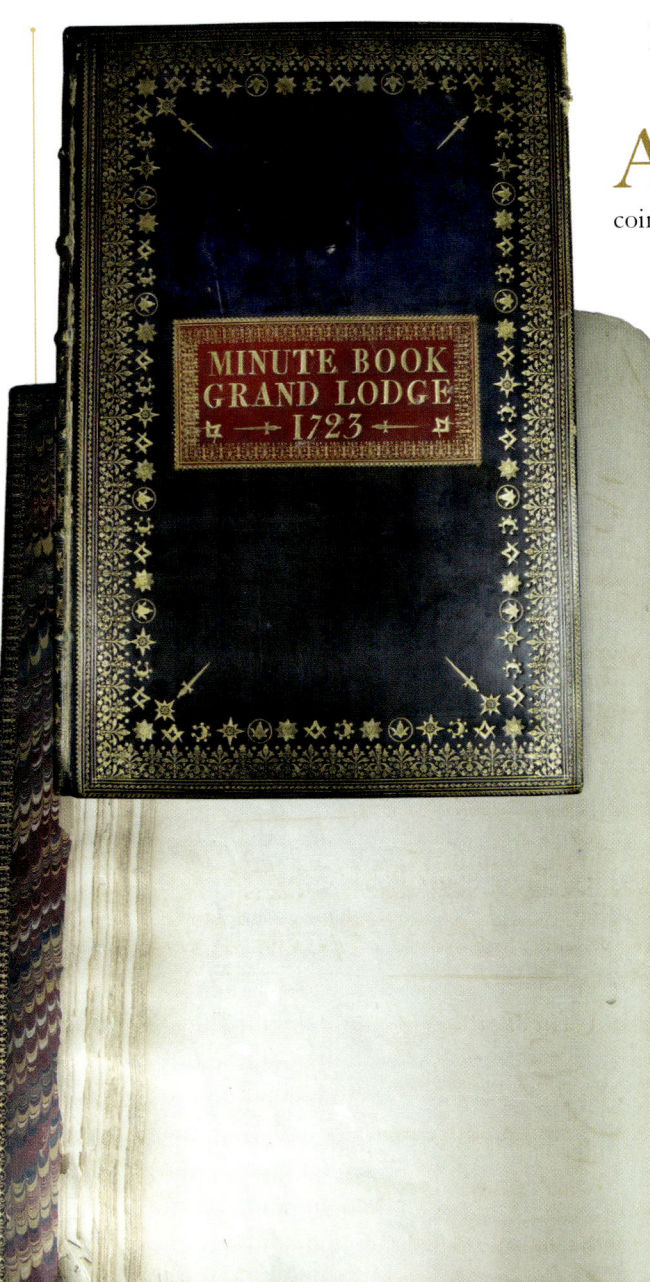

B6: *Engraved List of Lodges, 1725.*

Lists of lodges were produced from the 1720s to record where and when lodges were meeting. Lodges were not named but were identified by the sign of the taverns where they met.

The term *Engraved Lists of Lodges* is applied to the annual lists, detailing lodges working under the Premier or Moderns Grand Lodge of England, that were published from 1722 to 1778. The list for 1725 contains details of some sixty-four lodges of which fifty were based in London. The entries are elaborately engraved with the sign and name of the tavern at which each lodge met, together with the lodge's number and the meeting days. The inclusion of a lodge in an *Engraved List* demonstrated its regularity in the Constitution and, in future issues, its seniority. The first official engravers to Grand Lodge were Bro John Pine and Bro Emmanuel Bowen. After 1778 the *Engraved Lists* were replaced by the *Calendars* of the Grand Lodge of England, the forerunner of the present *Masonic Year Book*. The *Engraved List* of the Antients Grand Lodge was first produced in 1753.

Frater J. Thornhill Eq. inv.   J. Pine Sculp.

EN LA ROSE IE FLEURY

The Most High, Puissant, and Noble Prince Charles Lenos, Duke of Richmond & Lenox, Earl of March and Darnley, Baron of Setterington, Methuin and Torbolton, 1725.

GRAND MASTER.

A List of the REGULAR LODGES as CONSTITUTED 'till MARCH 25th 1725.

	Lodge	Meeting
	St. Pauls Church-yard	every other Monday from ye 29 of April inclusive
	Knaves Acre	every other Wedn. from ye 2t of April inclusive
	Turn stile	First Wednesday in every Month
	Westminster	Third Fryday in every Month
	Ivy lane	every other Thurs. from ye 20 of June inclusive
	Newgate street	First Monday in every Month
	Silver street	Second & Fourth Wednesday in every Month
	in the Strand	First Fryday in every Month

Printed for & Sold by J. Pine Engraver over against little Brittain end in Aldersgate Street

B7: Cérémonies et coutumes religieuses de tous les peuples du monde, 1737.

In the foreground there is depicted the layout of a lodge room with members wearing regalia; while in the background is a chart listing some 130 lodges then known to be in existence in England.

B8: *Night* by William Hogarth, 1738.

Night is the fourth and last of a series entitled *Times of the Day* by William Hogarth (1697–1764). In the foreground, the principal figure (slightly the worse for wear) is the Master with the collar and Square, who is being escorted home by the Tyler of the Lodge. The figure on the right holding a mop is possibly an allusion to the practice of drawing symbols on the lodge room floor and washing them off when the lodge was closed. The Lodge met in nearby Channel Row (near to what is now Northumberland Avenue) at the Rummer and Grapes Tavern, and was one of the four that formed the Premier Grand Lodge in 1717. It has been suggested that the Master is Sir Thomas de Veil, a member of Hogarth's first Lodge; and the Tyler with the sword, key and lamp is Bro Montgomerie, the Grand Tyler.

B9: *Grand Procession of Scald Miserable Masons, 1742.*

A geometrical view by A. Benoist of the *Grand Procession of Scald Miserable Masons*, designed as if they were drawn up against Somerset House on 27 April 1742.

From 1721 onwards it became the custom for members of Grand Lodge to assemble at a tavern and walk in procession to hold their Assembly and Feast at the Hall of one of the City Livery Companies. In 1741 a mock procession was held by anti-Masonic elements, for the sole purpose of bringing Freemasonry into disrepute. The event was repeated in 1742 and commemorated in a long engraving by A. Benoist, originally published some years later, and with the last edition being dated 1771. The term *Scald* meant 'shabby' or 'lousy'. As a consequence, public processions by Grand Lodge were discontinued after 1747 and up to the present day there are restrictions in place regarding unauthorised appearances in public in Masonic clothing.

B10: Colonel John Pitt, *c*.1750. ▿

The painting of John Pitt is attributed to the artist William Hogarth (1697-1764) and shows him seated behind a table, wearing the regalia of a Grand Steward. He was the first Master of Britannic Lodge No. 75 (now No. 33) in 1730. Pitt was also a member of what is now St George and Corner Stone Lodge No. 5, being appointed as a Grand Steward on 2 March 1732. The jewel he is wearing was originally worn by the Master of the Grand Stewards' Lodge, and is thought to have been designed by Hogarth, who was himself a Grand Steward.

Colonel John Pitt (1698-1754) was a politician, soldier and colonial administrator. After Eton he went into the army, where he rose to the rank of Lieutenant Colonel and served as an aide-de-camp to George I. At various times between 1720 and 1734 he served as a Member of Parliament for three different constituencies; and from 1728 to 1737 as Governor of Bermuda.

B11: Senior Warden of an Early Lodge, *c*.1735. ▸

The portrait shows an unknown Freemason wearing a Masonic apron and the collar and jewel of the Senior Warden of a lodge.

Stonemasons traditionally wore long, leather aprons that were tied with a loop at the front, with the ends hanging loose; and this has been replicated in Freemasonry. Over time the aprons became smaller and elaborately decorated. After the Union between the Grand Lodges in 1813 all regalia was standardised, and this resulted in a much smaller apron, traditionally made of white lambskin, with a triangular flap. Previously tied by ribbons, the fringed ends have become stylised as the tassels on a modern apron.

B12: Early Masonic Apron, *c.*1810. ➤

This particular example shows the transition from the traditional, long stonemasons' leather apron, tied with a loop at the front with the ends hanging loose, but is smaller, made from lambskin, and decorated with somewhat clumsy Masonic symbols.

B13: Sisson Jewel, *c.*1727. ▽

A Past Master's collar jewel made around 1727 for the Lodge meeting at the Swan and Rummer in London. The Lodge paid Jonathan Sisson (1690?-1747), a scientific instrument maker, to make lodge 'jewels'.

The silver Set Square has suspended from it the 47th proposition of Euclid, which is infilled with light blue enamel; the design is still used for the jewel of Past Masters. It is thought to be the oldest surviving jewel of this type. Jonathan Sisson was an English scientific instrument maker, with a shop in the Strand, and is renowned for inventing the modern theodolite, which for the first time incorporated a telescopic sight. Sisson was a member of a Lodge that met at the Fountain Tavern in the Strand and was one of those acknowledged in Anderson's *Book of Constitutions* of 1738.

B14: Wedgwood Vase, 1992.

Vase in Wedgwood blue jasperware, commemorating the 275th Anniversary of the formation of the Premier Grand Lodge of England.

The blue jasperware vase with applied, white relief decoration was specially commissioned in 1992 by the United Grand Lodge of England from the Wedgwood Company.

Only three vases were produced: one given as a gift to the Grand Master, HRH the Duke of Kent; one to be placed on display in the Museum; and the third to be kept by the Company.

The Antients and the Moderns

Dr David Harrison

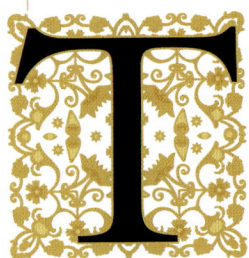

The formation of a second Grand Lodge in 1751 caused a major rift in English Freemasonry that would last until 1813, with two Grand Lodges operating on a national scale, both reaching out to the Colonies and each spreading their own particular influence. The later Grand Lodge, somewhat ironically, became known as the Antients and the original or Premier Grand Lodge of 1717 as the Moderns [C1]. They practised different methods of administration and had differing attitudes to ritual. An example of the former relates to the way in which the Antients enabled new lodges to purchase the Warrant of a lodge that had ceased operation, thereby retaining the number of the former lodge. The Moderns issued each new lodge with a brand new Warrant – this helps explain why there are gaps in lists of lodges and why some lodges have a lower number than older lodges above them in the list. In terms of ritual, the two Grand Lodges both practised the three degree system, but it was the on-going argument, right up to the Union in 1813, concerning the situation of the Royal Arch which marked a difference between them. The Antients considered the Royal Arch an integral part of Craft Freemasonry whilst the Moderns considered it – and indeed worked it – as an additional degree [C2].

Laurence Dermott was the leading light in the 'Grand Lodge of England according to the Old Institutions' – the Antients [C3] – founded in London in 1751 by mainly Irish Brethren, who had settled in London and found it difficult to become members of lodges under the Moderns, which by and large had a membership with a somewhat higher social profile. After Dermott became Grand Secretary, the new Grand Lodge began to attract Masons who, amongst other things, had become dissatisfied with what they considered to be the modernisation of the Craft. The Antients firmly identified themselves with the older Grand Lodge of York and the Edwin legend, which held that a general assembly of Masons was convened at York in 926 AD by Edwin, son of King Athelstan. Some alarm was caused amongst the Moderns when the Antients were formally recognised as an official Grand Lodge by both the Scottish and Irish governing bodies. The discontent being expressed by some members of the Craft with their leaders at the time was exemplified in 1764, in an anonymous publication entitled *The Complete Free mason: or Multa Paucis for Lovers of Secrets*, which attempted to reproach the 'wicked' Lord Byron for the development of the Antients, even though the actual causes of the rebellion dated back to before he became Grand Master.

The Antients soon became extremely influential, their lodges being founded far beyond London, notably in Bristol, which had its own traditional working of the ritual. By 1755, an early

Antients lodge could be found in Warrington, the town where Elias Ashmole had become a Mason more than a century before; and Liverpool also boasted a number of early Antients lodges. From ports such as Bristol and Liverpool the influence of the Antients soon spread overseas to America, other British Colonies and the Continent, mainly due to the Antients granting travelling Warrants for the setting-up of lodges within regiments of the British Army.

It was Dermott who can be credited with the use of the terms Antient and Modern to distinguish the two English Grand Lodges. Dermott was born in Ireland in 1720 and joined a Dublin Lodge in 1740, which came under the jurisdiction of the Irish Grand Lodge. After moving to England, he joined a lodge under the jurisdiction of the Premier Grand Lodge in 1748, but switched his allegiance after helping to establish the Antients in 1751. When *Ahiman Rezon* – the Antients' Book of Constitutions – was first published in 1756 **[C4]**, it was almost entirely the work of Dermott, who was careful not to show any disrespect towards the Moderns' Freemasonry. After a number of years though the rift between the two Grand Lodges deepened, and later editions of Dermott's Constitutions became increasingly hostile and antagonistic towards the Moderns, who, in turn, continually tried to ridicule both Dermott and the Antients.

The Earl of Blessington, who had been the Grand Master of the Irish Grand Lodge in 1738, became the Grand Master of the Antients – Dermott no doubt seeking aristocratic patronage to legitimise the new Grand Lodge. It was certainly advantageous that the first edition of *Ahiman Rezon* was actually dedicated to Blessington, which must have also helped to cement the relationship between the Antients and the Irish Grand Lodge.

Other Grand Masters of noble birth followed, the most prominent being the third Duke of Atholl, who was installed in 1771, and who in turn expedited the relationship between the Antients and the Grand Lodge of Scotland; Atholl becoming the Grand Master of the Grand Lodge of Scotland in 1772. His son, the fourth Duke of Atholl, was installed as Grand Master in 1775 following the death of the third Duke the previous year. The fourth Duke took office again in 1792, following the death of the Earl of Antrim, and then served as Grand Master until December 1813, when he stood down in favour of Prince Edward, the Duke of Kent, and thus paved the way for the Union between the Antients and the Moderns.

Whilst at local level there are examples of members interacting and visiting each other's lodges, there were undoubtedly differences between the two Grand Lodges, particularly amongst the leaders of both. There is also ample evidence of sustained competition and animosity between the two rival Grand Lodges. Masons from either side, who decided to change their loyalty from one to the other, had to swear allegiance and be *'remade'* or *'healed'* to accord with the ritual of the receiving body. It seems that the *'remaking ceremony'* was even required for members of the Grand Lodge of Scotland wishing to join an English lodge, as occurred in 1774 when two Scottish Masons joined an Antients' lodge. Needless to say there was a fee involved: in September 1785 the sum of one guinea had to be paid for a Modern Mason to be *'re-made'*, to become an Antient Mason.

The movement of members between the Moderns and Antients continued until the unification in 1813. Thomas Harper, a silversmith and maker of Masonic jewels, was appointed Deputy Grand Master and became a leading figure in the negotiations that united the two Grand Lodges. Harper was a member of both the Moderns and the Antients, but was expelled and then reinstated by the Moderns seven years later. William Preston **[C5]**, author of *Illustrations of Freemasonry*, had been a member of a lodge under the Antients; switched allegiance to the Moderns; then threw in his lot with the Grand Lodge of All England at York, in order to assist in the foundation of a new Grand Lodge – the Grand Lodge of All England south of the River Trent – but eventually returned to the Moderns.

Whilst there were differences between the workings of the two Grand Lodges, there were also very many similarities. It is, for example, difficult to discern any marked differences between the symbolism expressed on the aprons worn by members of the two rival Grand Lodges [C6] [C7] [C8] [C9]. Whilst there may have been considerable variations in the design of various jewels, these could not be ascribed to differences in approach by the respective Grand Lodges [C10] [C11]. Lodge meetings, both Antient and Modern, were held around a dining table, usually in a suitable tavern. It is no surprise therefore that lodge members, and tavern owners specifically, commissioned tableware and glassware, including specially-designed firing glasses [C12] [C13] [C14] [C15] [C16] [C17].

As time went by, local decisions were being made on the matter of *'remaking'*. For example, in the Warrington-based Modern Lodge of Lights, it was agreed in 1803 that if a Brother from an Antient lodge was to be re-admitted, he should be charged the sum of £1. 11s. 6d., whereas a Brother re-admitted from another Modern lodge should only pay £1. 1s.

Some local lodges seemed to hedge their bets, such as the Royal Gloucester Lodge No. 130 in Southampton, which actually held two Warrants – one from the Moderns and one from the Antients. On a number of occasions the members of the Lodge transferred their allegiance from one side to the other, never quite being able to decide with which Grand Lodge to stick. Antient lodges, such as No. 86, transacted lodge business in a decidedly Modern manner; whilst in Modern lodges, such as the Lodge of Relief No. 42 in Bury, the terminology used was that of the Antients, as in 1792 when the lodge raised 'Master Masons Ancient'. Other lodges, such as the Union Lodge, founded in York in 1777, were able to bring together both Antient and Modern Masons in perfect harmony, well before the official Union of 1813 [C18].

Instances can be found of rivalry at a local level between the Antients and the Moderns. In Chester, for example, five months after an Antient lodge had been constituted at the Star Inn in 1766, it found itself usurped by a Modern lodge. An Antient lodge founded at the Bear's Paw in Frodsham near Chester in 1770 had lapsed by 1794. In the second half of the eighteenth century lodges owing allegiance to the Antients were founded in towns on the fringes of Cheshire – in places like Macclesfield, which had three, and Stockport, which had five – all operating well away from the Modern stronghold of Chester [C19].

The Antients Grand Lodge was very adaptable in the way it dealt with lodge Warrants, much in the same manner as that adopted by the Grand Lodge of Ireland. To all intents and purposes Warrants were considered as transferable. This policy was extremely useful as it meant that new lodges did not have to be consecrated or constituted with all the attendant expense, but could easily be established in other areas simply by transferring an existing Warrant from elsewhere. An example is that of the Lodge of St John, founded in 1765 in Mottram, Longendale in Cheshire. The Lodge seemed to have floundered and the Warrant was transferred to Saddleworth in Yorkshire in 1775, with the Lodge meeting there until 1784. The Warrant then seemed to have been kept in the possession of one of its old members, who took it with him when he moved to Stockport and, after getting it endorsed in London, started the Lodge afresh in 1806.

This transfer and re-use of lodge Warrants was very popular. In Liverpool the Antient Lodge No. 25 appeared in 1755, disappeared in the 1760s, only to resurface as an entirely new Lodge in Liverpool in 1786. Warrants could also be quickly transferred to other parts of the country, such as the Warrant of Lodge No. 189 – an Antient Lodge founded in Macclesfield in

1774 – which, after the Lodge was disbanded in 1801, was reissued to the All Saints Lodge in Northumberland the following year. Warrants were hand-engrossed and often embellished with Masonic symbols, as shown in the one issued to the Lodge meeting at the King's Arms Punch Bowl, Shad Thames, London [C20].

Warrants bearing an older number were much sought after by members of the Antients. It seems then, as now, that the older the number of the lodge, the more prestige it appeared to carry within the Masonic Fraternity. At the Union, lodges on both sides had the same number and to resolve the situation lots were cast, and won by the Antients. As a consequence, Grand Master's Lodge of the Antients became No. 1 on the roll of the UGLE, whilst the older Moderns Lodge of Antiquity became No. 2 – something that still rankles today. Lodge numbers were then allocated alternately in order of seniority, which helps to explain why most of the early former Antients lodges have odd numbers and those of the Moderns even ones. It was only natural that when lodges were renumbered after the Union, and indeed on two subsequent occasions in later years, many lodges, both Antient and Modern, became upset.

Many of the early Antient lodges were short-lived and there are no complete surviving records, but the Minutes of one Lodge in particular, the Lodge of Benevolence founded in Stockport in 1759, survived. The Lodge, which seemed to operate in a similar fashion to a contemporary Modern lodge, got entwined in a financial dispute and surrendered its Antient Warrant, defecting to the Moderns in 1789. The original Warrant of the Lodge of Benevolence was transferred to an Antient Lodge in Birmingham in 1811.

In Warrington, an Antient Lodge was founded in 1755 that met at The Cock in Bridge Street but, again, the Lodge was short-lived, lapsing just over a year later and leaving no records. In 1765, the Modern Lodge of Lights was founded and was to dominate Freemasonry in Warrington. The situation was reversed in Liverpool, where during the closing years of the eighteenth century there were seven Antient lodges while the Moderns could only muster four.

The formation of independent rival Grand Lodges became almost fashionable during the late eighteenth century. The reasons were manifold, and included such things as personal ambition, disputes, or even the desire to work a particular version of the ritual. In 1762, the Antient Grand Lodge dismissed a certain David Fisher, who was the Grand Warden elect, after it came to light that he had attempted to form his own Grand Lodge, and had offered to register fellow Brethren for 6d. each. Ten years earlier, Thomas Phealon and Dr John Macky, two Brethren under the Antient Grand Lodge, had also conspired – in a somewhat bizarre and maverick fashion – to initiate men into Freemasonry for the price of a leg of mutton. Macky had also initiated Brethren into the Royal Arch, without having any knowledge whatsoever of Royal Arch Masonry, making up the ceremony and instructing that, through his teachings of a mysterious Masonic Art, an Initiate could become invisible. As a result of these ashamedly blasphemous activities, Dermott expelled Phealon and Macky and ordered that the two men should never be admitted to an Antient lodge ever again. Another maverick who tried to create a rebel Masonic lodge was Sir Francis Columbine Daniel. He was a doctor, and was first made a Freemason in Lodge No. 3 under the Antients, but he later joined the Royal Naval Lodge that came under the Moderns Grand Lodge. Daniel was Master of the Royal Naval Lodge from the time he joined in 1791 until 1808, and, as a result of issuing Certificates on his own authority as Master of the Royal Naval Lodge of Independence, he was dismissed by the Antients in 1801. By 1810, the Moderns also moved against Daniel because of his desire to claim independence for the Royal Naval Lodge. He had initiated almost 1,000 men of naval extraction and, due to the large and rapid expansion of the Lodge, Daniel seemed to have thought that it was large enough to become independent from the Moderns. Daniel had complained to the Moderns in 1801 about unorthodox Masons who had been 'encouraging irregular meetings and infringing on the privilege of the Ancient Grand Lodge Of All England assembling under the authority of H.R.H. the Prince of Wales'.

The Moderns were also strict when dealing with lodges on issues of conformity, especially with certain lodges that wanted to express their individuality. An example was that of the Country Stewards' Lodge, which in 1795 petitioned Grand Lodge to wear aprons trimmed with green to mirror the privilege of Grand Stewards wearing red aprons. The Country Stewards' Lodge was composed of Masons who served in the office of Steward at the Country Feast of the Grand Lodge. The members of the Lodge had already been given permission to wear a green collar and a distinctive jewel. The request was originally granted and then rescinded, causing considerable acrimony, to the extent that the last Country Feast took place in 1796 and the Lodge closed in 1802 [C21].

Laurence Dermott, who had twice served as Deputy Grand Master, was fiercely loyal to the cause of the Antients and greatly opposed to any form of unification with the Moderns Grand Lodge. It was not until after he finally retired from the post in 1787 and after his death in 1791 that the process of reconciliation between the two Grand Lodges slowly began. As early as 1794, when departing Lower Canada (Quebec) for Nova Scotia, the Duke of Kent, when replying to a farewell address jointly signed by the Antients and Moderns Deputy Provincial Grand Masters of Lower Canada – in which they expressed the hope that his 'conciliating influence' could bring together the Antients and the Moderns so that 'Freemasonry in his Majesty's dominions will soon be united' – responded: 'You may trust that my utmost efforts shall be exerted, that the much-wished-for Union of the whole Fraternity of Masons may be effected.'

C1: *Book of Constitutions*: Frontispiece showing the interior of Freemasons' Hall, 1784.

The *Book of Constitutions* of the Moderns Grand Lodge was originally published in 1723 by James Anderson. A number of editions followed: the frontispiece of the one published in 1784 contains an engraving by the artist Cipriani (1727-85), showing the interior of Freemasons' Hall, designed by the architect Thomas Sandby.

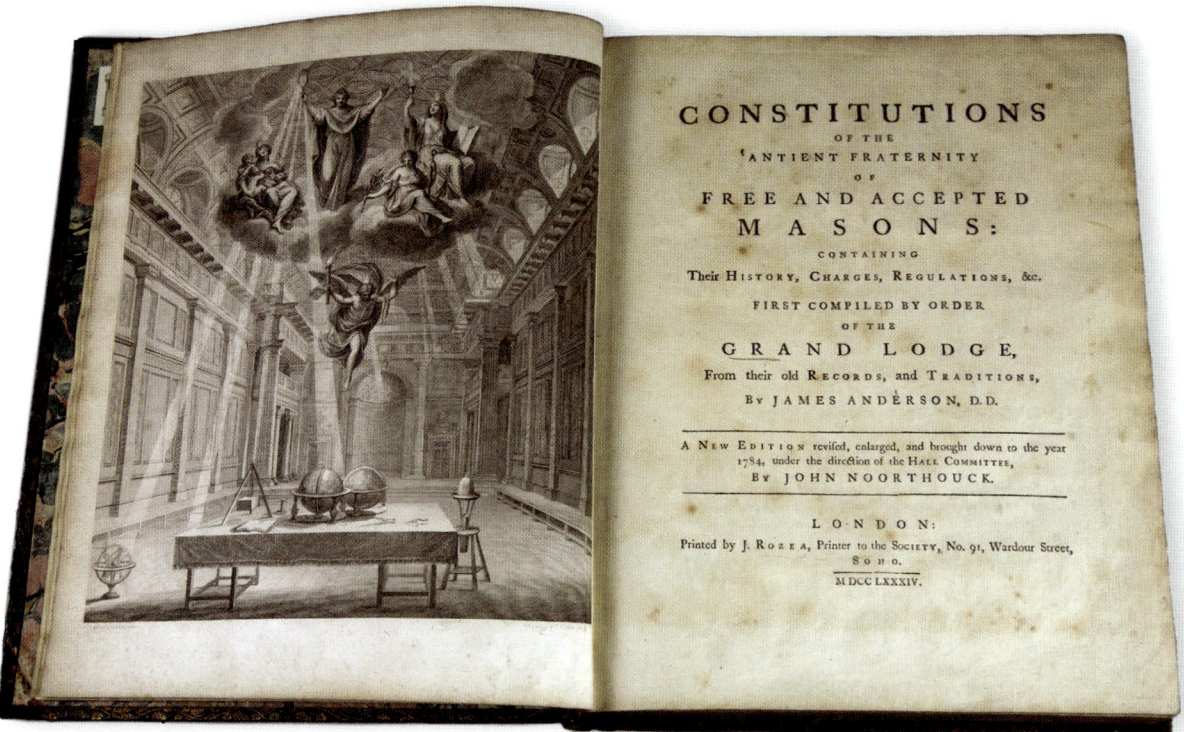

C2: Swan and Rummer Lodge Minute Book, *c.*1725.

Minute Book of a Masters' Lodge meeting at the Swan and Rummer Tavern, Finch Lane, London (1726-34): the oldest extent Minute Book of any private lodge.

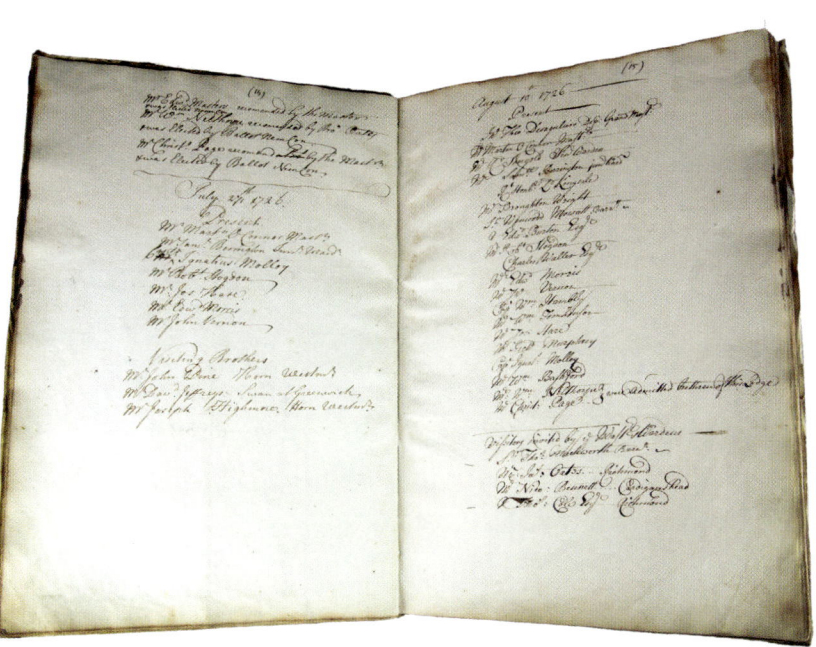

C3: Enamel jewel with Antients Grand Lodge Coat of Arms, *c*.1755.

Oval jewel in enamel, decorated with Masonic emblems and the arms of the Antients Grand Lodge.

C4: *Ahiman Rezon* with the bookplate of Laurence Dermott, 1756.

The first Constitutions or rulebook of the Antients Grand Lodge, published in 1756 and written by Laurence Dermott, the Grand Secretary, to whom this copy once belonged.

The premier Grand Lodge, the Moderns, was formed in 1717; and the 'Grand Lodge of England according to the Old Institutions' – better known as the Antients – in 1751. The Constitutions or rulebook of the latter was written by their Grand Secretary Laurence Dermott (1720-91) and first published in 1756 with the rather strange Hebrew title of *Ahiman Rezon*. Over the years there has been much inconclusive debate as to the meaning of the title – including 'A Help to a Brother' (the original sub-title) and 'Faithful Brother Secretary'. Laurence Dermott was a highly influential member of the Antients, serving as Grand Secretary from 1752 to 1771 and then as Deputy Grand Master from 1771-77 and 1783–87. The first edition relies heavily on Spratt's *Constitutions for the Use of Lodges in Ireland*, published in 1751. Three more editions were published in the lifetime of Dermott and a further four before the Union of the two Grand Lodges to form the United Grand Lodge of England (UGLE) in 1813. Later editions featured far more original work. The second edition published in 1764 devotes 118 of the 224 pages to poetry and songs.

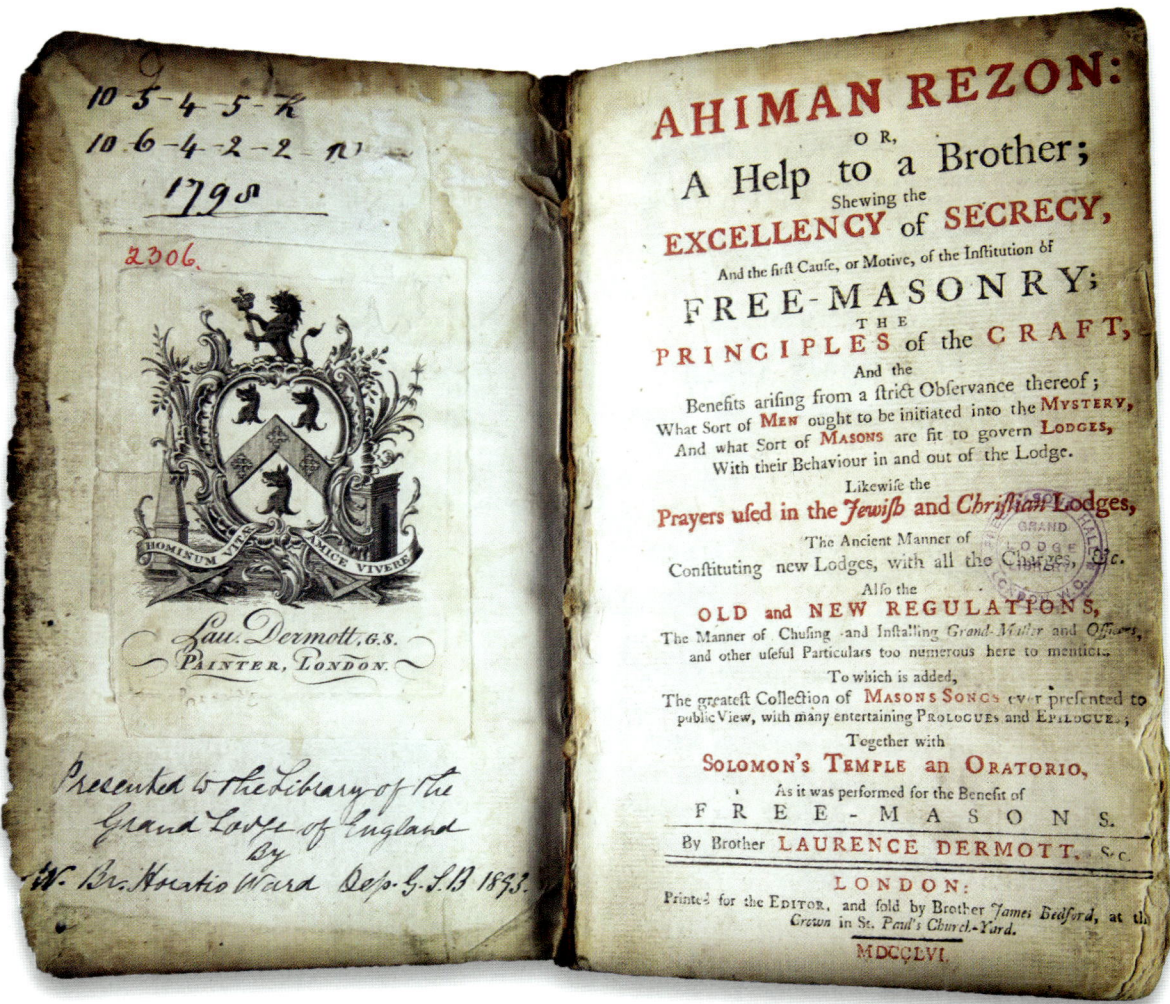

C5: William Preston – Portrait, 1800.

The portrait of William Preston (1742–1818) in contemporary dress, by John Russell RA, was presented to Lodge of Antiquity No. 2 in 1878 by Bro Woodford, a Past Master of the Lodge.

Best remembered for his influential *Illustrations of Freemasonry* and as the instigator of the Prestonian Lecture, William Preston was born in Edinburgh in 1742, attended Edinburgh University but left before completing his degree. He moved to London in 1760 and worked as a compositor and later a proof-reader for William Strahan, the King's Printer. Strahan died in 1785 and left an annuity of £30 for life to Preston, who subsequently became a partner in the firm with Strahan's son Andrew; and in 1794 a member of the Stationers' Company.

He was initiated in London in 1763 into a lodge composed largely of Scots that met at the White Hart in the Strand. The members would have preferred to have been warranted by the Grand Lodge of Scotland but had instead accepted a Warrant from the Antients Grand Lodge. The following year the members applied for a Warrant from the Moderns Grand Lodge, becoming the Caledonian Lodge No. 325 and subsequently No. 134, meeting at the Half Moon Tavern, Cheapside. Preston became a Joining Member of Lodge of Antiquity No. 1, subsequently No. 2, in June 1774. Involved in a number of disputes, Preston was expelled from the Moderns Grand Lodge in 1779 but ultimately reinstated in 1789.

His greatest contribution to Freemasonry was the publication in 1772 of his *Illustrations of Freemasonry*, which gave an in-depth analysis of the ritual and symbolism of the three degrees of Craft Masonry and which ran to some twelve editions in his lifetime. The American Thomas Webb was so inspired by the work that he largely based his own book *The Freemason's Monitor* on it in 1797. Most lodges in the USA use a ritual based on the Preston-Webb lecture system.

Preston's name is also immortalised in the annual Prestonian Lecture. In his will he left a sum of £300 to the Grand Lodge, to continue to disseminate his system of instruction. The Lectures were given in their original form from 1820 to 1864; the Lecture was revived in 1924 and continues to this day, with each year a Masonic scholar being invited to deliver the Lecture on a Masonic subject of his own choosing.

C6: Moderns Apron, *c.*1790.

A Moderns Grand Lodge leather apron, hand-painted with the arms of the Moderns Grand Lodge together with various Masonic emblems.

Prior to the formation of the UGLE – brought about by the union of the Moderns Grand Lodge and the Antients Grand Lodge – there were no specific regulations regarding the design of the regalia worn by Freemasons.

Masonic aprons are directly descended from those worn by the operative mason. Indeed, on the present-day apron there is a reminder of that, in the form of the two tassels that represent the fringed ends of the ribbons with which the original operative apron was fastened around the waist.

In the latter days of the Moderns Grand Lodge, the Grand Master, his Deputy and the Grand Wardens were allowed to line their white leather aprons with blue silk. The Masters and Wardens of certain lodges could use white silk, and the Grand Stewards of the year red silk.

Candidates on being initiated into Freemasonry wear a white lambskin apron – an emblem of innocence. In certain Jurisdictions, such as those in the United States of America, all Brethren up to and including the Grand Master wear a white apron.

C7: Moderns Apron, *c*.1760.

White leather apron of the Moderns Grand Lodge, with hand-painted Masonic symbols.

C8: Antients Apron, *c*.1806.

An Antients Grand Lodge leather apron, hand-painted with various Masonic emblems, including the All-Seeing Eye.

The Apron was worn by Augustine Harrison, who was initiated into the Antients' Marquis of Granby Lodge No. 24, Canterbury on 31 May 1806. The Lodge was named after the Marquis of Granby tavern where it met. In 1819 it merged with Industrious Lodge No. 416 to become the United Industrious Lodge, re-numbered as No. 31 in 1894, and continues to meet in Canterbury.

C9: Antients Apron, *c*.1790.

White leather apron hand-painted with Masonic symbols, including a full colour All-Seeing Eye on the flap.

The apron belonged to Martin Westmorland, who was initiated on 4 March 1789 into the Antients Lodge No. 3b, now St George's and Corner Stone No. 5.

C10: Pierced Jewel inscribed to John Gale, *c*.1770.

The silver jewel is not hallmarked but has been dated to around 1770; it is engraved with the name John Gale and Lodge No. 184.

The inscription on the Set Square in the centre of the jewel reads *Nous Vivons Sur Le Quarre* – 'We Live On The Square'. The words around the border read *Sola Concordia Fratrum* – 'Harmony Only Among Brothers'.

A pierced jewel is made by cutting out the metal, normally silver, to make the design. Prior to the formation of the UGLE in 1813 there were no regulations regarding the design of Masonic jewels and hence the craftsman was able to incorporate any number of Masonic symbols.

C11: Past Master's Gallows Pattern Collar Jewel, 1815.

Past Master's collar jewel in the form of a gallows of clear, coloured stones, with a pierced, silver-coloured metal 47th Proposition of Euclid attached. It was presented to John Sutcliffe of the Lodge of Probity No. 84 (now No. 61).

The Lodge of Probity was founded in 1738 and met at the Black Bull, Copper Street, Halifax, Yorkshire. Re-named the St John the Baptist Lodge in 1767, it was again re-named in 1795. The Lodge of Probity No. 61 still meets in Halifax.

C12: Glass Rummer, 1700.

Wine glass, engraved with Masonic emblems and 'Lodge No. 199'.

A rummer was a popular beer-drinking vessel. This example was commissioned by the Antients Lodge No. 199. Constituted in 1804, the Lodge met at the Travellers' Rest, Daw Green, Dewsbury, Yorkshire and was erased in 1885.

C13: Bristol Blue Decanter, 1770. ➢

The decanter, decorated with the arms of the Moderns Grand Lodge and other Masonic symbols, was made for the Lodge of Perfect Union No. 241, which met at the White Hart, Chippenham, Wiltshire between 1763 and 1773.

In the early years of Freemasonry lodges met in taverns and inns, with meetings taking place around a table with frequent breaks for refreshment. In later years the meeting took place in a lodge room and was followed by a separate Festive Board. Lodges often commissioned glassware and tableware for use at refreshment or at the Festive Board. The quality often reflected the financial standing of the members.

During the late 1700s Richard Champion, a merchant and potter, developed and patented a formula for porcelain. He worked with William Cookworthy, a chemist, who obtained a monopoly on importing good-quality cobalt oxide from the Royal Saxon Works in Saxony. The combination of fine cobalt oxide and the recently invented lead crystal gave a deep blue glaze decoration on the porcelain producing the innovative Bristol Blue Glass.

C14: Beilby Firing Glass, *c.*1760. ➢

A firing glass, decorated in enamels with the coat of arms of the Moderns Grand Lodge by William Beilby, who worked for a local glass enameller in Newcastle from 1749 to 1797, alongside his sister Mary. He was one of the first in the world to perfect the art of enamelling onto glass.

Masonic Fire is believed to have been copied from the practice followed at military dinners, and is said to replicate the firing of guns in salute. It derives from the time when Masonic lodges were held around a table in a tavern. After the toast had been given, the glass was drained of its contents and banged on the table, in appreciation of what had been heard and to show that the glass was empty and ready to be re-filled. In time, no doubt because of sustained breakages, special firing glasses began to be made – too small to drink out of but with a heavy bulbous bottom which meant that they could be safely banged on the table without fear of breaking – whilst the wine continued to be served in traditional drinking glasses. It would not have been unusual for lodges to commission and own their own set of plain or, as in this case, more expensively decorated firing glasses. These days not all lodges have firing glasses and hence the custom is continued by the rhythmic clapping of hands.

C15: Teapot in Liverpool Creamware, *c.*1780.

Printed with the coat of arms of the Moderns Grand Lodge and various Masonic symbols.

One side of the teapot has a black transfer print of Masonic emblems on a chequered pavement, framed by compasses and a section of an arc, with the text above *DEUM TIME ET / REGEM HONORA*, all enclosed by elaborate scrollwork and flowers with more Masonic emblems. On the other side is a transfer print of the Moderns Grand Lodge coat of arms surrounded by Masonic emblems and two flanking Freemasons, with the text above 'A HEART THAT CONCEALS / AND THE TONGUE / THAT NEVER REVEALS'.

C16: Teapot in Wedgwood creamware, *c.*1794.

Printed with the coat of arms of the Antients Grand Lodge and various Masonic symbols.

One side of the teapot has a black transfer print of the coat of arms of the Antients Grand Lodge. Below the arms are Working Tools and the text 'No. 225 / LONDON, Holiness to the Lord' and Hebrew characters. The Lodge of Temperance No. 225 was constituted on 4 May 1784, re-numbered as No. 169, but was erased in 2004. The other side of the teapot has a scene of Freemasons and buildings with clouds above framing a figure, surrounded by cherubs holding Masonic emblems and the text *VERITAS PRAEVALEBIT* – 'Truth Will Prevail'. The scene is taken from an illustration in Fifield Dassigny's *Serious and Impartial Enquiry* (Dublin, 1744). The impressed mark WEDGWOOD & CO indicates that this article was most likely made by Ralph Wedgwood (nephew of the more famous Josiah Wedgwood), who worked at Burslem, Staffordshire up to 1796. At this time the firm used the WEDGWOOD & CO mark. Ralph Wedgwood left the partnership in 1801, hence the period of use for this mark is *c.*1796-1801.

C17: Jug in Sunderland Lustreware, *c.*1810.

Transfer printed with hand-coloured Masonic emblems, a verse and a view of the Iron Bridge over the River Wear.

The bridge depicted is the first Wearmouth Bridge, opened in 1796. The initial idea of a bridge over the Wear was that of Durham MP and Freemason Rowland Burdon (1757-1838). The opening included a Masonic dedication and procession.

C18: Early Antients Grand Lodge Certificate, 1767.
Issued to Edward Abott and signed by Laurence Dermott.

Laurence Dermott (1720-91) was a truly remarkable and inspirational Freemason. He was the mainstay of the Grand Lodge of the Antients. Initiated in 1740 into Lodge No. 26 in Dublin, he was installed as its Master in 1746. In the same year he was exalted into the Royal Arch and this event provides one of the earliest recorded references to that Order. Working as a journeyman painter he came to England in about 1748 and originally joined a lodge under the Moderns Grand Lodge. He later transferred his allegiance to No. 9, now the Kent Lodge No. 15, and to No. 10, now Royal Athelstan Lodge No. 19, both of the Antients Grand Lodge. Dermott was appointed as the Grand Secretary of the Antients in 1752 and served in that capacity until his appointment as Deputy Grand Master to the third Duke of Atholl from 1771 to 1777, and again from 1783 to 1787. As Grand Secretary he produced a model set of by-laws for lodges and in 1756 compiled the Book of Constitutions for the Antients entitled *Ahiman Rezon*. Dermott considered the Royal Arch to be 'the root, heart and marrow of Masonry', and greatly influenced its development as an integral part of the Antients' system of Freemasonry.

C19: Early Patent of Appointment of a Provincial Grand Master, 1769.

The Patent, dated 13 November 1769, appoints John Allen as the Provincial Grand Master for Lancashire.

John Allen was the fourth Provincial Grand Master for Lancashire (the first having been appointed in 1734) and served for thirty-seven years from 1769 to 1806. The calligraphy and illustrations are the work of Michael Devon, who undertook a considerable amount of work for the Moderns Grand Lodge. The Antients did not have a Provincial system and their lodges reported directly to the Grand Lodge in London.

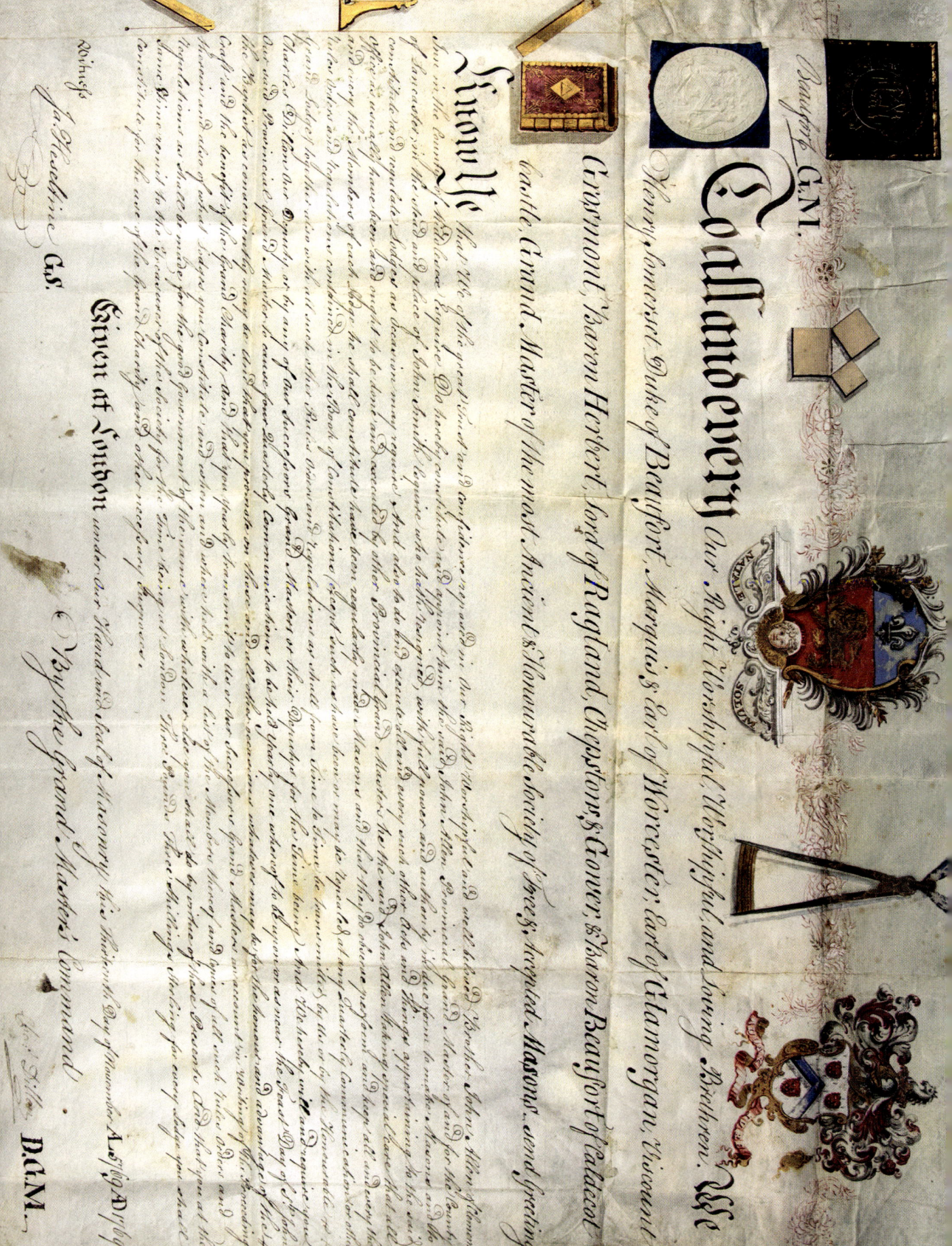

C20: Warrant for Lodge No. 203, meeting at King's Arms Punch Bowl, Shad Thames, London, 1766.

The Lodge was established in 1766, but as was common at the time, never acquired a name. It met at the King's Arms Punch Bowl, Shad Thames, London until it was erased in 1806. The calligraphy and illustrations are the work of Michael Devon.

C21: Country Steward's Jewel, 1789.

Jewel of the Country Stewards' Lodge presented to Thomas Schabner in 1793. The silver medal is cast in bas-relief with a winged Fortuna with her horn of plenty (cornucopia). On the reverse is the text 'GRANTED BY GRAND LODGE / IN / QUARTY. COMMUNN. / 25TH NOVR. 1789 / TO THE MEMBERS / OF THE / COUNTRY STEWARDS / LODGE'.

The Annual Investiture is the meeting at which the Grand Officers of the year are appointed and invested. It is followed by the Grand Festival, or celebratory dinner. In addition to the Grand Festival held in central London, it became customary from about 1737 for Grand Lodge to hold an additional summer Country Feast in what were then rural retreats such as Islington, Hampstead, Vauxhall and Putney. As with the Grand Festival, Stewards were appointed to organise the dinners. In 1789 a Country Stewards' Lodge was formed and its members were granted permission to wear a special jewel, to be worn suspended from a green ribbon. In 1795, the Country Stewards sought permission to wear an apron trimmed with green, to mirror the privilege of Grand Stewards wearing red aprons. The request was originally granted but then rescinded, causing considerable acrimony, to the extent that the last Country Feast took place in 1796. The Lodge closed in 1802, with the Warrant being transferred to what is now the Royal Lodge of Faith and Friendship No. 270 in Gloucestershire.

The Establishment of the United Grand Lodge of England

John Belton

The period at the end of the eighteenth century was a particularly turbulent one in Europe as a whole. The failure of the harvest in the years 1783 to 1785 contributed greatly to the financial collapse in France. The ensuing French Revolution of 1789 and the disruption that followed did not draw to a close until 1802, to be followed by the Napoleonic Wars which only ended with the Battle of Waterloo in 1815.

Not surprisingly, the radical events in Europe in general and France in particular created a sense of apprehension amongst the English Establishment, which to some extent was countered by members of the Royal Family playing a greater part in social affairs. Thus we find the Prince of Wales, later George IV, taking an active role in Freemasonry as Grand Master of the Moderns in England from 1792 to 1812, when he became Prince Regent, and also Grand Master Mason in Scotland from 1806-20. Throughout he was accompanied step by step but a rank below by the Earl of Moira (previously Lord Rawdon), who was Acting Grand Master of the Moderns from 1790 to 1812 and the same rank in Scotland between 1806 and 1808. The very first issue of *Freemasons' Magazine* in 1793 sets the tenor of this change with two cherubic engravings – the first a dedication to the Prince of Wales, and the other one dedicated to Lord Rawdon, showing an interesting combination of Working Tools [D1].

While life in the outside world was full of unaccustomed events then so the world of Freemasonry was equally in a state of revolution. While Grand Lodges took possession and control of the three degrees of the Craft, a number of other degrees beyond the Craft were being worked in England including the Royal Arch, Knights Templar, Mark, and Rose Croix (Ancient and Accepted Rite); some in separate units but many of them within, and as part of, the confines of Antient lodges. Today William Preston is perhaps best remembered for his famous *Illustrations of Freemasonry*, but he was also a searcher after more degrees and greater 'light'. The Lodge of Antiquity, of which he was a member, ceded from the Moderns Grand Lodge to join for some ten years the Grand Lodge South of the River Trent, which worked, or at least promoted, the Rite of Seven Degrees. Preston was no doubt influenced by the work of Peter Lambert de Lintot, whose frontispiece to the Charter of the Lodge of Perfect Union is a marvellous symbolic drawing which includes a double-headed eagle that is a precursor of the Ancient and Accepted Rite. The absence of any organisation of this multiplicity of degrees was a major problem, which did not start to be resolved until after the death of the Duke of Sussex in 1843 [D2].

A major stumbling block between the Antients and the Moderns continued to be the Royal Arch Degree [D3]. The Grand Lodge of Ireland and that of Scotland handled the issue of the Royal Arch and indeed the other degrees of Freemasonry in a very different and pragmatic way. However, the attitude of the leaders of the Moderns in the 1760s had been that the Royal Arch was 'an innovation … to seduce the Brethren'; whilst for Laurence Dermott of the Antients the Royal Arch was determinedly 'the root, heart and marrow of Masonry'. The Antients were never going to give ground on this point, and indeed the importance which was placed on the ritual in general can be deduced from the fact that in 1792 they formed a committee which selected 'Nine Worthies' – nine eminent Grand Lodge Officers – who travelled round the country to ensure that ceremonies were correctly carried out. Each of the Worthies was furnished with a jewel on a gold chain, which on the obverse showed symbols of the Craft and on the reverse those of the Antients' version of the Royal Arch [D4].

The first moves towards seeking a union of the Antients and Moderns Grand Lodges began in 1802, but came to nought. Endeavours were resumed in 1809, when the main actors in the piece were the Prince of Wales and the Earl of Moira – Grand Master and Acting Grand Master, respectively of the Moderns; together with the fourth Duke of Atholl and Thomas Harper – respectively Grand Master and Deputy Grand Master of the Antients. The Lodge of Promulgation was formed to act as a vehicle to progress matters, but discussions faltered throughout 1810 and eventually collapsed in March 1811. The Prince of Wales may well have been distracted by the illness of his father, but the major stumbling block was the democratic stance taken by the Antients, who referred every matter of import to their Grand Committee – which must have driven the Moderns to distraction.

Although no substantial progress was made between 1811 and 1812, other events helped bring about change and action and force matters to a conclusion. The Prince of Wales became Prince Regent in 1812 and the duties of office meant that he resigned as Grand Master of the Moderns Grand Lodge of England – but interestingly not as Grand Master Mason in Scotland. Early in 1813 the Earl of Moira was appointed as Governor General of India. In recognition of the role played by him in attempting to bring together the two Grand Lodges, and the service he had given to Freemasonry over a period of some twenty-three years, he was presented with an exquisite jewel, originally valued at some £1,500 (some £87,500 itm) [D5].

As always the Royal Family was able to fall back on its own resources and in this instance the vacancy of Grand Master was filled by the sixth son of King George III, Frederick Augustus, Duke of Sussex. The contrast in the image and style exhibited in the full-length portraits of the Prince of Wales and the Duke of Sussex speaks volumes [D6].

The Duke of Sussex became Deputy Grand Master on 12 February 1812, Grand Master on 12 May 1813 and appointed Lord Dundas as his Deputy on 7 December 1813. In practical terms a union was now a distinct possibility. When the Kent's only child became Queen Victoria in 1837, Dundas was created Earl of Zetland, perhaps as a result of the financial generosity he had previously shown towards the Duke and Duchess of Kent. Sadly he only lived to enjoy the honour for a relatively short period of time, dying in 1839. Lord Dundas played no active role in the Union, but his son, the second Earl of Zetland [D7], became Grand Master following the death of the Duke of Sussex in 1843 until his own death in 1873.

The membership of the Moderns was largely drawn from the upper reaches of society whilst that of the Antients tended towards that of the artisan. Notwithstanding the nature of its membership, the Antients recognised the importance of having a member of the aristocracy at its head. It is therefore not surprising that the fourth Duke of Atholl [D8], who became Grand Master of the Antients in 1794, retained James Agar as Deputy Grand Master and also appointed Thomas Harper as Deputy in 1801. The events of 1813 gathered pace and the Duke of Atholl retired on 8 November 1813, his place being taken by the Duke of Kent [D9].

Both Moderns and Antients each appointed 'nine worthy and expert Master Masons' to complete the work of the two Lodges of Reconciliation created on 1 December 1813. They met, taking turns to occupy the various offices; and in a breathless dash towards the Union, met on 10, 14, 16, 17, 20, 21, 22 December and even on the day of the Union itself, St John's Day, 27 December 1813. It was just as well that these Worthies were largely those who had played a similar role in the previous Lodge of Promulgation, which had lasted from 1809 to early 1811.

Many differences can be identified between the two Grand Lodges which needed to be resolved for unification to take place. The social divide between the memberships of the two Grand Lodges has already been alluded to; but the fundamental problem was that relating to the Royal Arch, with the Antients insisting that it formed an essential element of the Craft degrees whilst the Moderns considered it to be the Fourth Degree in Freemasonry. Whilst the Royal Arch degree was carried out within the confines of an Antients Craft lodge, it was carried out in separate units – Chapters – under the Moderns. In terms of administration, the Moderns had an extensive Provincial structure whilst the Antients lodges dealt directly with their Grand Lodge. Other differences were primarily to do with matters relating to the ritual. The Antients had an esoteric ceremony of Installation for the Master of a lodge, whilst in the Moderns the Mastership was effected in a very perfunctory manner. Cyril Batham in his Prestonian Lecture of 1981 identified some fourteen differences in working between the two Grand Lodges, including: the preparation of Candidates; abbreviating ceremonies; omitting the Lectures, Charges and prayers; transposing the means of recognition in the First and Second Degree; the layout of the lodge room; the use of Deacons; and the nomenclature used within the ritual. As far as the last point regarding the ritual is concerned, negotiations on the finer details were not concluded until 1816 and even then it was still not possible for the two sides to agree on certain elements. Most of the ritual previously used by the Antients was ultimately adopted, including the ceremony of Installation and the acceptance of the Royal Arch, albeit in separate Chapters. However there still exist today at least two instances where agreement was not possible. Hence in the Third Degree two variations of the Master Word are given to Candidates, one deriving from the Antients and the other from the Moderns; and in the Opening ceremony reference is made to 'the Tyler or Outer Guard'. It is little wonder that negotiations regarding unification took so long when battle lines were such that it was not possible to agree as to whether it should be Tyler or Outer Guard, and this helps to explain why the road to unification was far from easy.

The legalities of the Union were actually completed on 1 December 1813 when the various signatories, including the two princely brothers, signed the two respective copies of the Articles of Union, and then exchanged them with the other party. Of the two copies, only the one belonging to the Antients, which was handed to the Moderns, survived. In practice, the meeting held on the 27 December was only one of acclamation, with another set of carefully-scribed Articles nominally being signed [D10].

The Count Jacob Pontuson de la Gardie, a senior Swedish Brother, was present and records being taken to lodge at 11 o'clock and then 'at 6.30 o'clock we departed to dinner which lasted until 1.30 o'clock in the morning'. He adds that 'I went home at nearly 2 o'clock being I must confess rather tired of the 14 hours I had spent'. There is one sole visual record of that day – an engraving that was published in the *Freemasons Quarterly Review* of July 1838 and reproduced on the base of the Sussex Plate – a silver candelabrum presented to the Duke of Sussex to mark his twenty-five years as Grand Master. It is all we have that visually bears witness to the creation of the United Grand Lodge of England (UGLE) on that momentous day **[D11] [D12]**.

At the meeting itself it was Count de la Gardie who retired with the two Royal Princes to hear the deliberations on ritual produced by the Lodge of Reconciliation in the previous month. He pronounced himself happy with one variant simply because it was closest to his ritual at home in Sweden.

One of the most significant benefits of the Union was that it brought stability into the world of Freemasonry at a time of turbulence. It must have been a real disappointment therefore that there were no representatives from the Grand Lodges of Ireland and Scotland present on 27 December to signify their accord. The notice was short and the distances, with travel by stagecoach of course and in winter, unattractive. Ireland offered to attend after St Georges Day (early May) and so a meeting of the representatives of the three Grand Lodges was convened for St John's Day, 27 June 1814. It was thought until recently that the only copy of the International Compact between these three Grand Lodges was in the Minutes of the Grand Lodge of Ireland, but another copy has been found in the archives of Freemasons' Hall in London **[D13]**. It was the draft copy of the pre-prepared text that was actually taken into the meeting by the Grand Secretary of the Moderns, William White, and annotated by him as discussions progressed. It shows that, in spite of the treaty being carefully worked upon in advance, the negotiations that took place on the day were very real and as a consequence changes were made. The first clause is extremely important because it defined the relationship between the Craft and Royal Arch as agreed between the Home Grand Lodges and which is still in place today.

Putting aside the politics of the Union, some elements have been treasured by ordinary members of the Craft up to the present time. The first of these is Thomas Harper's Chapter jewel. This design by Thomas Harper, Freemason and master jeweller, was first produced shortly after the Union and when one visits lodges today one can see them being proudly worn. Most of those one sees are replicas, produced by the Thomas Harper Lodge No. 9612. They have re-registered Harper's TH hallmark, which they use on their jewels. Any design that has stood the test of time for over 200 years has to be a treasure. Both original and current jewels are fittingly pictured together as testament to that **[D14] [D15]**.

Many of the Grand Masters have simply become names in a long list. The Duke of Sussex is remembered of course, but usually with reservations; however the fourth Duke of Atholl is remembered with affection for his leadership of the Antients for twenty-seven years, and the name is still used as an alternative to 'Antient' – as in the term 'Atholl Lodge' – by members of the Association of Atholl Lodges and by Brethren in general.

There are some more formal traces of the Union worthy of interest. The bag of the Grand Registrar was used at every meeting of Grand Lodge to carry the original Articles of Union into the meeting: they could be thought of as akin to the Warrant of a lodge. Eventually it was realised that this was damaging the actual Articles, so the practice was abandoned. These were in some ways times of excess, and the children of George III were sometimes accused of profligacy. The jewel and apron of the Duke of Sussex as Grand Master epitomises the times of the Prince Regent **[D16] [D17] [D18]**.

It is almost as though that by the end of 1813 Freemasonry simply ran out of steam, and it was not until 1815 that a *Book of Constitutions* was produced **[D19]**. Likewise it would appear that it was forgotten to obtain a Grant of Arms from the College of Heralds, a situation that took over a century to rectify. Eventually in 1919, after almost one hundred years of unauthorised use, the matter was put right – at last – the final act relating to the Union **[D20]**.

D1: *Freemasons' Magazine*: Frontispiece from the first issue, 1793.

The first English Masonic periodical, the *Freemasons' Magazine, or General and Complete Library*, appeared in June 1793 and was published monthly until December 1798.

As the first issue makes clear:

> This Magazine is not only intended as a monthly Register of literary Information, but will also contain Essays, tending to the promotion of good Morals; strictures on the dreadful effects of Vice; together with a variety of such original and pleasing miscellaneous Subjects, as we may think useful or entertaining: these will form one part of our Magazine; the other, we conceive, will be of the most evident utility, and for which this Magazine is principally undertaken, – no less than that of an honourable medium, through which fraternal communications and correspondence may be conveyed one to another ... Finally, we request, as a particular favour, of the Masters, Officers and Brethren of the various Lodges, that they will be pleased, at times, to communicate to us the account of any thing remarkable, which they may think will tend to throw a further light on the Science, or to instruct its Members ...
>
> June 1793

Perhaps surprisingly the first magazine for Freemasons was not exclusively Masonic in content and included as many articles of a non-Masonic nature as it did on Freemasonry. The content was divided, with Masonic articles at the front of the magazine and non-Masonic articles at the back.

THE Free-Mason's Magazine, OR Generall and Complete LIBRARY. VOL: I.

Commissumque teges et vino tortus et ira. Hor:

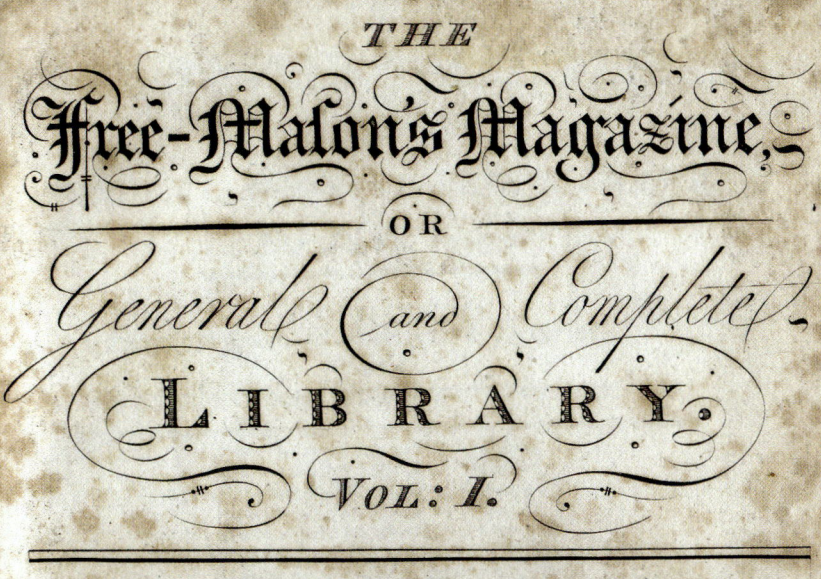

LONDON.
Printed for the Proprietor, & Sold by Scatcherd & Whitaker, Ave Maria Lane, & all Booksellers in Town & Country.
1793.

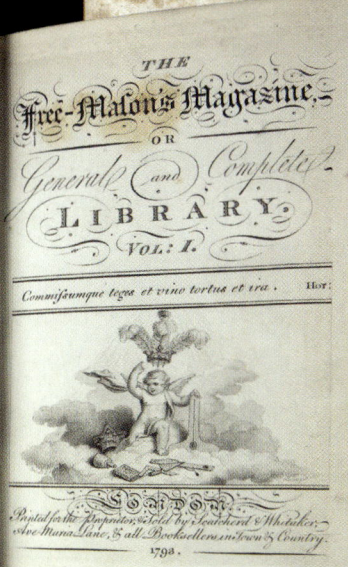

D2: Lodge of Perfect Union: Frontispiece of the Charter, 1800. ➢

The frontispiece of the Charter of the Lodge of Perfect Union was the work of Peter Lambert de Lintot, a French engraver working in London. Only two lodges were formed under the auspices of the Grand Lodge of All England, South of the River Trent. This was a body that existed intermittently during the eighteenth century, mainly based in the city of York. The first lodge was constituted at the Queen's Head Tavern in Holborn, London on 9 August 1779; and the second, the Lodge of Perfect Observance, on 15 November 1779 at the Mitre Tavern in Fleet Street, London with Peter Lambert de Lintot as the first Right Worshipful Master.

D3: Royal Arch Register of the Antients Grand Lodge, 1800. ➢

Frontispiece of the Antients' *Register of Excellent Masters* by Laurence Dermott.

One of the major differences between the Antients and Moderns Grand Lodges was their respective dealings with the degree of the Royal Arch. The Moderns, who established a Supreme Grand Chapter to control the Order in 1766, carried out the degree in separate units known as Chapters, whereas their lodges restricted their activity only to the three degrees of Craft Masonry. The Antients on the other hand performed the Royal Arch, and indeed other degrees of Freemasonry, within the confines of the lodge itself. In 1783 a General Chapter of Royal Arch Masons resolved that the names of these members should be recorded in 'a particular book prepared for that purpose', of which two volumes exist, showing the name and lodge number of the individual and the year of his Exaltation – or more probably the return relating thereto. Some entries were recorded retrospectively, the earliest being Laurence Dermott in 1746, with the last entries dated 1819.

D4: Nine Worthies Collar Jewel designed by Thomas Harper, 1801.

A collar jewel worn by one of the nine members of the committee elected annually to ensure that the highest standards of ritual were maintained throughout the lodges of the Antients Grand Lodge.

Right from the outset at its formation in 1751 the Antients Grand Lodge was concerned to ensure that the ritual of Freemasonry was not altered in any way and was carried out to the highest standard. Indeed, it has even been suggested that this was one of the main reasons for its formation. The Antients Grand Lodge consistently complained throughout its existence about the low standards and negligent attitude to the ritual demonstrated by the Moderns Grand Lodge. So as to ensure that appropriate standards were maintained within their lodges, the Antients formed a committee in 1792 consisting of nine elected senior Masons, who became known as the 'Nine Worthies' or 'Nine Excellent Masters'. The members of the committee were entitled to wear a distinctive silver jewel designed by Thomas Harper. On the obverse of this there is a depiction of working operative masons constructing a building using ropes, ladders and working tools such as a level, a set square, a pick, a trowel, a maul and a chisel; the text reads 'one of the nine Worthies'. On the reverse there is a vivid and detailed engraving of a lodge room, set up for a ceremony of the Royal Arch, rather than the Craft. The jewel is rich in the symbolism of the Royal Arch, including the depiction of a Mason wrenching forth the keystone of the arch of a vaulted chamber, together with an important element from the ritual: *sit lux et lux fuit* – 'Let there be light, and there was light'. The Royal Arch was of considerable importance to the Antients, and it is no coincidence that Thomas Harper took this opportunity of including it as part of a jewel worn by those whose responsibility it was to ensure that the traditions of the Antients Grand Lodge were maintained.

D5: Moira Jewel, 1800.

The jewel, suitably engraved, was presented to Francis Rawdon-Hastings, 1st Marquess of Hastings and 2nd Earl of Moira, at a festival attended by more than 500 people, in recognition of the role played by him in helping to bring together the two Grand Lodges in 1813 and of the service he had given to Freemasonry over a period of some twenty-three years.

Originally valued at £1,500 (£87,500 itm) it was subsequently inherited by a female relative, who had the gemstones re-set in a tiara and the ornamental chain made into bracelets. The jewel shown here has been re-set with imitation stones.

The considerable role played by the Earl of Moira, during his tenure of office as Acting Grand Master, in bringing about the Union has been consistently understated, with much of the credit going instead to the Duke of Sussex, who only became Grand Master during the year of the final agreement in 1813. Likewise, today the important part he played, together with the Duke of Atholl (the Grand Master of the Antients), following the enactment of the Unlawful Societies Act of 1799 is not widely known – this would otherwise have undoubtedly resulted in Freemasonry being proscribed in Britain.

The Unlawful Societies Act of 1799 was passed 'for the more effectual suppression of societies established for seditious and treasonable purposes' and deemed that all societies which required members to take any oath not authorised by law to be regarded as 'unlawful combinations'. Through the intervention of the Earl of Moira and the Duke of Atholl a special exempting clause was inserted in the Act for the benefit of societies 'held under the Denomination of Lodges of Freemasons', provided that they had been 'usually held before the Act' and their names, places and times of meeting and the names of members were annually registered with the local Clerk of the Peace. The section requiring the submission of the Annual Returns from each lodge was not repealed until as recently as 1967.

Francis Rawdon-Hastings (1754-1826) was a member of Britannic Lodge No. 33, London by 1790. He became a Joining Member of Lodge of Antiquity No. 1 (now No. 2) in 1803. He served as Acting Grand Master *[Pro Grand Master in today's parlance]* of the Moderns from 1790 to 1813 during the tenure of the Prince of Wales as Grand Master. He was active in the negotiations to form the United Grand Lodge of England (UGLE) and must have felt some personal disappointment not to have been involved at its conclusion as, in November 1812 on becoming Governor-General of India, he resigned as Acting Grand Master. The Duke of Sussex became Grand Master the next year following the resignation of his brother George Augustus, Prince of Wales, who had become the Prince Regent in 1811.

D6: Augustus Frederick, Duke of Sussex, 1827.

Portrait in oils by J. Naish of Augustus Frederick, Duke of Sussex (1773-1843), wearing the original regalia of the Grand Master of the United Grand Lodge of England.

On his left breast the Duke is wearing the Royal Medal of the Lodge of Antiquity No. 2, consisting of a red ribbon, from which hangs a jewel, surmounted by a gold duke's coronet bearing the coat of arms of the Duke of Sussex and surrounded by a garter, bearing the text *Honi soit qui mal y pense*. He is pictured standing in front of the Grand Master's throne [L1].

The ninth child and sixth son of George III, Augustus Frederick was educated abroad, and being a severe asthma sufferer did not follow his brother William into the navy; he was therefore the only surviving son of George III who did not pursue an army or naval career. A cultured and erudite man with an interest in the arts and sciences, he was a liberal by nature and became involved in Whig politics, particularly concerned with social reform. He married without the consent of the King and contrary to the Royal Marriage Act, not once but twice – first in 1792 to Lady Augusta Murray, whom he had met on a visit to Rome and by whom he had two children; and secondly in 1831 to Lady Cecilia Gore. The first marriage was subsequently annulled. He was Queen Victoria's favourite uncle, and gave her away on her marriage day to Prince Albert. His second wife was made Duchess of Inverness, in her own right, the same year. Augustus Frederick had been created Duke of Inverness in 1801.

Augustus Frederick was initiated into Freemasonry on 20 December 1798 in the Lodge Victorious Truth in the Grand Lodge of Prussia. In England he joined the Prince of Wales's Lodge (now) No. 259 in 1800; the Lodge of Friendship No. 6 in 1806, the Lodge of Antiquity No. 2 in 1808 and Royal Alpha Lodge No. 16 in 1820 – the latter being his personal Lodge and which has retained its Royal connections to the present day. He duly became the Permanent Master of all four lodges respectively in 1881, 1806, 1809 and 1814; offices that he held until his death in 1843.

He had been 'introduced' into the Royal Arch in 1810 and became First Grand Principal of the Grand and Royal Chapter (Moderns) at the same meeting.

He was made Past Grand Master of the Moderns Grand Lodge in 1805, Deputy Grand Master in 1812 and Grand Master in 1813. His brother, Edward Augustus, Duke of Kent became the Grand Master of the Antients Grand Lodge in the same year and when in December of that year the two Grand Lodges came together, largely as a consequence of the work done by the two brothers in general but by the Duke of Sussex in particular, it was the latter who was elected Grand Master of the UGLE and held that office until he died in 1843.

On the formation of Supreme Grand Chapter in 1817 he became its First Grand Principal and also held that office until his death.

The Duke of Sussex had a considerable influence and effect on English Freemasonry, not only during his lifetime but right up to the present day. The English Constitution is one of the very few in the world where the Craft and the Royal Arch are inextricably linked in terms of government and administration.

D7: Bust of the Marquess of Zetland, c.1845.

White Wedgewood, Parian ware bust of Thomas Dundas, 2nd Earl of Zetland as Grand Master, wearing his chain of office. Parian ware is a white bisque porcelain which was invented to imitate marble. It comes in a liquid form, which is then poured into a mould. This enables mass production and it is often used for figurines and busts. The original of this bust was made by the sculptor Thomas Earle (1810-76) in 1846. It was presented to Minerva Lodge No. 250, of which Earle was a member.

Thomas Dundas, 2nd Earl of Zetland, was elected Whig Member of Parliament for Richmond, Yorkshire in 1818, serving until 1830; and again in 1835, serving until 1839. He was also Member of Parliament for York from 1830 to 1832 and from 1833 to 1834.

He was initiated in Prince of Wales's Lodge No. 259 in 1830, where he served as Deputy Worshipful Master from 1837 to 1838. He became a Joining Member of Lodge of Antiquity No. 2 in May 1839, and Royal Alpha Lodge No. 16 in 1843. He served as Provincial Grand Master, Yorkshire North and East Riding from 1839 to 1870; was appointed Deputy Grand Master in 1839; Pro Grand Master in 1840 and Grand Master in 1844, serving until 1870. He died at Aske Hall, Yorkshire, aged 78 on 6 May 1873.

D8: Duke of Atholl, 1901.

John Murray, 4th Duke of Atholl (1755–1830) followed his father, the 3rd Duke of Atholl, as Grand Master of the Antients from 1775 until 1781 and again from 1791 to 1812. He was then succeeded by Edward Augustus, Duke of Kent and Strathearn, to help facilitate the Union of 1813. It is no wonder, given his length of service, that the Antients Grand Lodge is often referred to as the Atholl Grand Lodge. The portrait of the fourth Duke is by Thomas R. Hinks Beaumont (1857-1940) and is a replacement of the original which was destroyed in the fire of 1883 at Freemasons' Hall.

His contribution to Freemasonry was considerable, serving as Grand Master of the Antients for a total of twenty-seven years, and ultimately standing down in favour of the Duke of Kent in 1812, so as to ensure that at the time of the Union there were Princes of the Blood Royal at the head of each of the original two Grand Lodges. He was, with the Earl of Moira, instrumental in ensuring that the Unlawful Societies Act of 1799 did not have a negative impact on Freemasonry in Britain.

D9: Edward Augustus, Duke of Kent and Strathearn, 1813.

The portrait of Edward Augustus, Duke of Kent and Strathearn is by George Henry Harlow (1787–1819), a highly-regarded English portrait painter. The Duke of Kent became Grand Master of the Antients in 1813, when his brother the Duke of Sussex was Grand Master of the Moderns and whom he then proposed as the first Grand Master of the United Grand Lodge in 1813. Edward Augustus, Duke of Kent (1767-1820) was the fourth son of George III and father of Queen Victoria. He spent a considerable time in North America, living there from 1791 to 1800. In 1799 he was appointed a General and Commander-in-Chief of British forces in North America, and promoted to Field Marshal in 1805. He has been credited for his impact on the development of Canada and with the first use of the term 'Canadian' in 1792, when referring to both French and English settlers in Upper and Lower Canada.

He was initiated in 1789 in the *Loge l'Union des Coeurs*, Geneva. He had a keen interest in Freemasonry, serving as Provincial Grand Master for Lower Canada under the Antients Grand Lodge from 1792 to 1797. He was also Grand Master of the Knights Templar from 1804 to 1807 and then Grand Patron from 1807 to 1812, becoming Grand Master of the Antients in 1813.

D10: Articles of Union, 1813.

The agreement bringing together the Moderns Grand Lodge and Antients Grand Lodge to form the present the UGLE was finally concluded with the signing of the Articles of Union on 27 December 1813.

Formal moves to bring the two Grand Lodges together started in 1809 with the establishment of a Special Lodge of Promulgation, composed of representatives from both sides. The original agreement was signed on 25 November 1813 in advance of the meeting of the two Grand Lodges, but became the subject of renegotiation and was amended at the last moment, requiring it to be re-signed on 1 December 1813, before being subsequently formally approved by the two Grand Lodges on 27 December 1813. The Articles consist of twenty-one clauses and the critical amendments can be discerned from handwritten alterations and deletions from the original text, and which mostly related to the Royal Arch and its relationship with the Craft. The position of the Royal Arch was of major significance to the Antients Grand Lodge and had a profound effect on the outcome of the negotiations and the compromise statement that still takes prominence in the current *Book of Constitutions*:

> *Preliminary Declaration*
> By the solemn Act of Union between the two Grand Lodges of Free-Masons of England in December 1813, it was 'declared and pronounced that pure Antient Masonry consists of three degrees and no more, viz., those of the Entered Apprentice, the Fellow Craft, and the Master Mason, including the Supreme Order of the Holy Royal Arch'.

Articles of Union
Between
The two Grand Lodges of Free Masons of England
In the name of God Amen

The Most Worshipful His Royal Highness Prince Edward Duke of Kent and Strathearn Earl of Dublin Knight Companion of the Most Noble Order of the Garter and of the Most Illustrious Order of Saint Patrick Field Marshall of His Majesty's Forces Governor of Gibraltar Colonel of the First or Royal Scots Regiment of Foot and Grand Master of Free and accepted Masons of England according to the Old Institutions The Right Worshipful Thomas Harper Deputy Grand Master The Right Worshipful James Perry past Deputy Grand Master and The Right Worshipful James Agar past Deputy Grand Master of the same Fraternity for themselves and on behalf of the Grand Lodge of Free Masons of England according to the old Institutions being thereto duly constituted and empowered on the one part.

The Most Worshipful His Royal Highness Prince Augustus Frederick Duke of Sussex Earl of Inverness Baron Arklow Knight Companion of the Most Noble Order of the Garter, and Grand Master of the Society of Free and Accepted Masons under the Constitution of England The Right Worshipful Walter Rodwell Wright Provincial Grand Master of Masons in the Ionian Isles The Right Worshipful Arthur Tegart past Grand Warden and The Right Worshipful James Deans past Grand Warden of the said Fraternity for themselves and on behalf of the Grand Lodge of the Society of Free Masons under the Constitution of England being thereto duly constituted and empowered on the other part.

to the said Festival of Saint John which shall be the form to be observed on that occasion

21. A revision shall be made of the Rules and Regulations now established and in force in the two Fraternities and a Code of Laws for the holding of the Grand Lodge and of private Lodges, and generally for the whole conduct of the Craft, shall be forthwith prepared, and a new Book of Constitutions be composed and printed under the superintendance of the Grand Officers, and with the Sanction of the Grand Lodge.

Done at the Palace of Kensington this twenty fifth day of November in the year of our Lord 1813 and of Masonry 5813.

Edward G.M.   Augustus Frederick G.M.

Thos Harper D.G.M.   Walter Rodwell Wright P.G.M. Ionian Isles

Ja Perry P.D.G.M.   Arthur Tegart P.G.W.

Ja Agar P.D.G.M.   J. Deans P.G.W.

In Grand Lodge this 1st day of December 1813. Ratified and confirmed & the Seal of the Grand Lodge affixed — Edward G.M.

D11: 'Sussex Plate': a Silver Candelabrum presented to the Duke of Sussex, to mark his twenty-five years as Grand Master, 1838. ➤

The candelabrum is rich in Masonic symbolism, but of particular interest are the four panels at the base, and none more so than the panel at the rear of the piece. It portrays the scene of the Act of Union between the Antients and Moderns Grand Lodges in 1813, with the two Grand Masters, the Duke of Sussex and the Duke of Kent, and their respective Grand Officers. As far as is known, it is the only artistic depiction of one of the most momentous events in English Freemasonry, and appeared together with a detailed description of the piece in the *Freemasons Quarterly Review* of July 1838.

Subscriptions from thirty-eight Provinces and three military lodges enabled the candelabrum to be designed by H. Sibson and made by Messrs Garrard of Haymarket, London for presentation to the Duke on 27 April 1838. The widow of the Duke of Sussex, the Duchess of Inverness, donated the candelabrum to the Library and Museum of Freemasonry in 1845. It is one of the most striking exhibits in the Museum and almost impossible not to miss, being one of the largest, with the base measuring some 28in by 24in. The Sussex Plate has tarnished very little over time, largely as a result of the microclimate that has formed in its wood and glass case.

D12: Engraving on the 'Sussex Plate': a silver candelabrum presented to the Duke of Sussex to mark his twenty-five years as Grand Master, 1838. ▽

D13: International Compact, 1814.

The Grand Masters of Ireland and Scotland met with the Duke of Sussex in the early summer of 1814 and agreed and signed what became known as the International Compact, which has governed Masonic relations between those countries ever since.

In July 1814, only six months after the signing of the Articles of Union, an historic tripartite international conference was held at Freemasons' Hall, London, involving the Dukes of Sussex, Leinster, and Lord Kinnaird: the Grand Masters respectively of England, Ireland and Scotland. The purpose of the meeting was, as far as possible, to ensure that the three Grand Lodges were 'perfectly in unison in all the great and essential points of the Mystery and Craft'.

The original version of the Articles adopted on 27 December 1813 contained the following:

> ... But this article is not intended to prevent any Lodge or Chapter from holding a meeting in any of the degrees of the Orders of Chivalry, according to the Constitutions of such Orders.

At the Conference, a Compact of eight Articles was drawn up and agreed, which defined pure Antient Masonry and used almost the same wording as that contained in the Act of Union of 1813 – save that all references to the Orders of Chivalry had been deleted!

> It is declared and pronounced that pure Ancient Masonry consists of three Degrees, and no more, viz.: – those of the Entered Apprentice, the Fellow Craft, and the Master Mason, including the Supreme Chapter of the Holy Royal Arch.

What is now known as the 'The Preliminary Declaration' did not appear in the *Book of Constitutions* of the UGLE until 1853, but has appeared in every edition of it since that date.

At a Conference held in Free Masons Hall London on Monday the 27th of June and continued by adjournment to Saturday the 2nd July 1814 and of Masonry 5814.

Present

The M. W. His Royal Highness The Duke of Sussex
 Grand Master of Masons in England.

The M. W. His Grace The Duke of Leinster,
 Grand Master of Masons in Ireland.

The M. W. The Right Hon: The Earl of Donoughmore
 Past Grand Master of the same.

The M. W. The Right Hon: Lord Kinnaird
 Grand Master of Masons in Scotland.

The R. W. The Right Hon. The Earl of Rosslyn
 Past Deputy Grand Master of the same.

The R. W. The Right Hon: Lord Dundas,
 Deputy Grand Master of Masons in England.

The R. W. James Perry, Past Dep: Grand Mar. of the same

The R. W. James Agar. Ditto

The R. W. Thomas Harper Ditto.

The R. W. Arthur Tegart, Past Gr. Warden of the same

The R. W. James Deans. Ditto

The V. W. Willm H. White } Grand Sec^{ys} of the same
The V. W. Edward Harper

His Grace The Duke of Leinster, Lord Kinnaird, The Earl of Donoughmore and The Earl of Rosslyn having been appointed a deputation

from

D14: Royal Arch Breast Jewel designed by Thomas Harper, 1807. ▷

Thomas Harper (1735-1832) was both a prominent Freemason and a successful silversmith, with premises at 207 Fleet Street, London. He first registered his mark, consisting of TH in a plain rectangle, at Goldsmiths' Hall on 27 May 1790.

Many examples of his excellent work survive today, including a number of Royal Arch breast jewels, which are highly sought-after by collectors. He was renowned for making pierced jewels, created by cutting out the metal, as shown in this example of his craft.

Thomas Harper, who was one of the most influential Freemasons of his day, was initiated in 1761 into Lodge No. 24, which at that time met at the Bush Inn, Marsh Street, Bristol. He is known to have spent some time plying his trade as a silversmith in America, where an advertisement in the *South Carolina Gazette* of January 1773 describes him as a working jeweller and goldsmith. He joined a Lodge in Charlestown, South Carolina, where he also joined the Royal Arch in 1770. On his return to England he joined Grand Master's Lodge No. 1 on the roll of the Antients Grand Lodge, in which he enjoyed rapid promotion, being appointed Junior Grand Warden in 1786, Senior Grand Warden from 1787 to 1789, Joint Grand Secretary from 1792 to 1795, Deputy Grand Secretary from 1797 to 1800 and ultimately Deputy Grand Master from 1801 to 1813. He also managed to play both sides against the middle by joining three lodges belonging to the Moderns Grand Lodge: Globe No. 14 (now No. 23) in 1787, serving as Master in 1793 and as Grand Steward in 1796; Lodge of Antiquity No. 1 (now No. 2) in 1792; and Nine Muses Lodge No. 330 (now No. 235) in 1800. Harper was expelled from the Moderns Grand Lodge in 1803, ostensibly because of his refusal to relinquish his dual membership of the Antients Grand Lodge. His twofold membership would have been well known, and certainly no secret, especially given his status as Deputy Grand Master of the Antients and the fact that he was involved in the negotiations for a possible union between the two Grand Lodges. There is every indication that politics and intrigue played their part in his expulsion, which resulted in negotiations regarding the Union being stalled. It is no coincidence that it was not until seven years later, when Harper was re-instated by the Moderns (joining Nine Muses Lodge again in 1810), that negotiations again resumed in earnest. His active involvement as the principal negotiator in the discussions between the two Grand Lodges was crucial and culminated in the Act of Union of 1813, of which he was one of the signatories.

D15: Modern Royal Arch Jewel, 1900. ▽

D16: Grand Registrar's Purse, *c*.1830.

This embroidered bag was originally made to contain the Articles of Union of 1813. It is still carried today by the Grand Registrar into the Quarterly Meetings of Grand Lodge.

The purse is a flat, rectangular bag of dark blue velvet edged with gold lace, with padded embroidery on one side depicting the coat of arms of the UGLE on a round panel.

Originally the Articles of Union were kept in the mahogany Ark of the Masonic Covenant in the Temple of Freemason's Hall. The Ark having been destroyed in the disastrous fire of 1883, a decision was made to have a ceremonial Purse containing the Articles brought into each meeting of Grand Lodge by the Grand Registrar, whose duty it is also to carry it in public processions.

D17: Collar jewel worn by Augustus Frederick, Duke of Sussex as Grand Master, *c*.1820.

This gold jewel is in the form of a pair of Compasses on a section of a circle, framing a radiant All-Seeing Eye in gold and painted enamel.

D18: Apron worn by Augustus Frederick, Duke of Sussex – the first Grand Master of the United Grand Lodge of England, *c.*1817.

The full dress apron of the Grand Master consists of a gold embroidered, blazing sun with a face, surrounded by a border with an elaborate design embroidered in gold and composed of pomegranates, wheat and lotus flowers; padding is used to give a striking three-dimensional effect.

Prior to the Union between the two Grand Lodges in 1813 there were few or no regulations with regard to the design or specification of Masonic regalia or jewels. The design of present-day regalia, including that for a Grand Master, takes its origin from the deliberations of the Board of Works in 1817 and has changed very little since that date.

D19: *Book of Constitutions*: Frontispiece showing Soane's Ark of the Masonic Covenant, 1815.

The illustrated frontispiece to the first edition of the *Constitutions and Regulations* published after the Union of the two Grand Lodges shows Sir John Soane's Ark of the Masonic Covenant, which he designed to store the Articles of Union.

The copy of the Articles of Union, signed and sealed by the two Grand Masters at the Grand Assembly on 27 December 1813, was bound and put in an embroidered case and afterwards placed inside the Ark of the Masonic Covenant. The Ark stood before the Grand Master's Throne, and on it were placed the Volume of the Sacred Law (the Bible) and a set of Square and Compasses. The Masonic Ark was designed specifically for that purpose by Sir John Soane in 1813, shortly after he became a Freemason. It clearly bears no relation to the Ark of the Covenant as described in the Bible; it was designed by him as a mahogany pedestal or cabinet based on geometric lines with an unusual and original equilateral, triangular base, each side some 3ft long; the whole about 4ft high and plainly not meant to be transportable like the biblical Ark. Its entablature was supported at the corners by the three pillars of classical architecture – Doric, Ionic and Corinthian – symbolising respectively Wisdom, Strength and Beauty; and surmounted by a triangular-based dome. Regrettably this magnificent and unique piece of furniture was destroyed in the fire of 1883 and lost for ever.

D20: Arms of the United Grand Lodge of England, 1919.

Grand Lodge has been granted authority by the College of Heralds to have its own coat of arms. From about 1730 the Moderns Grand Lodge adopted as their coat of arms those of the London Company of Masons and the motto 'In the Lord is all our Trust'. The Antients Grand Lodge used arms which bore in the four quarters the devices of a man, a lion, an ox and an eagle and had the Ark of the Covenant as a crest, cherubim as supporters, and the motto *Kodesh L'Adonai* or 'Holiness to the Lord'. The arms of the Antients are another example of the importance that was placed by its members on the inclusion of the Royal Arch as an integral part of Freemasonry as practised by them. The emblems incorporated in the arms form an important part of the symbolism of the Royal Arch degree.

The lion represents strength; the ox, patience and assiduity; the man, intelligence and understanding; and the eagle, promptness and celerity or swiftness. The four living creatures (lion, ox, man and eagle) make reference to the vision of Ezekiel (Ezekiel 1: 1-11) where they are the principal examples of the inhabitants of the four worlds.

The coats of arms of the two Grand Lodges were combined in 1813 at the Union and form the basis of the current coat of arms of the UGLE. A new motto *Audi, Vide, Tace,* meaning 'Hear, See, Be Silent', was adopted.

All three sets of arms were used without any official authority and it was not until 1918 that it was decided to regularise matters by formally petitioning for an official Grant of Arms from the College of Heralds. The request was acceded to and Letters Patent, dated 9 July 1919, were granted. The Grant of Arms formally enabled the existing use of the combined arms of the two former Grand Lodges, with one addition. The application came to the attention of King George V who, by Royal Licence, gave permission for eight lions to be added to the bordure of the shield to commemorate the long connection between the Royal House and Freemasonry in general and the Grand Mastership of his father in particular.

The frontispiece to the current edition of the *Book of Constitutions* illustrates the arms as exemplified in the Grant, in which the description is given in heraldic terms – the *blazon* – that takes on more meaning for those uninitiated into the language of heraldry if translated as follows:

> the shield divided into two coats (*per pale*) one red (*gules*) and the other divided into four (*quarterly*) coloured blue and gold (*azure and or*) on the left side (*dexter*)*, on an inverted V across the centre of the coat (*a chevron*) between three castles coloured silver (*argent*) a pair of compasses extended coloured gold (*of the third – the third colour referred to earlier*), on the right-hand side (*sinister*)* a cross dividing it into four (*quarterly*) coloured silver (*of the fourth*) and green (*vert*) between, in the top left (*first quarter*) a lion in an upright position with its left paw on the ground (*rampant*) coloured gold (*of the third*), in the top right (*second*) an ox walking with its right leg raised (*passant*) coloured black (*sable*), in the bottom left (*third*) a man with hands elevated depicted in his natural colours (*proper*) clothed (*vested*) in green (*of the fifth*) the robe crimson lined with ermine, and in the bottom right (*fourth*) an eagle with wings expanded (*displayed*) also coloured gold (*of the third*), the whole within a border around the shield (*bordure*) of red (*the first*) filled (*charged*) with eight lions walking with their right legs raised (*passant*) and their heads turned to face you (*guardant*) coloured gold (*of the third*) for that part of the coat of arms above the shield (*the crest*), on a wreath of gold and red [*the colours: a wreath generally has six twists – the left one is always a metal, gold or silver, and it alternates with the main or first colour of the coat of arms*] a representation of an ark supported on either side by a cherub depicted in natural colours (*proper*) with the motto over in Hebrew characters 'Holiness to the Lord', and for the figures depicted escorting the shield (*the supporters*), on either side a cherub depicted in its natural colours (*proper*).

* N.B. The blazon is written from the viewpoint of the bearer of the shield.

TO ALL AND SINGULAR

to whom these Presents shall come &c.

Henry Studholme Brodie Lumsden Commander of the Royal Victorian Order Gentleman of the Vice Marshal of the Ceremonies Knight Commander of the Royal Victorian Order Chancellor King of Arms and Charles Harold Elliott Esquire Member of the Royal Victorian Order Norroy King of Arms and Charles Harold Elliott Esquire Member of the Royal Victorian Order Norroy and Ulster King of Arms send Greeting **Whereas** The Most Noble Bernard Marmaduke Duke of Norfolk Knight of the Most Noble Order of the Garter Knight Grand Cross of the Royal Victorian Order Earl Marshal and Hereditary Marshal of England (as by Letter signed unto Us by the Right Honourable Edmund Bernard Talbot (commonly called Lord Edmund Bernard Talbot) Knight Grand Cross of the Royal Victorian Order Deputy Earl Marshal and Acting Earl Marshal of England bearing date the Twenty fourth day of June last signified unto Us) hath pleasingly ordered to grant unto the United Grand Lodge of Antient Free and Accepted Masons of England now known in Common Law, Neither Commerce a chance, either of the said Royal Arms and Armorial to be used and of men effect **And Forasmuch** as (as setteth doth by Warrant under his hand and Sealed according to the Laws of Arms and received in the College of Arms) I have in the said Royal Arms and Armorial to be used and of men effect **And Forasmuch** as (as setteth doth by Warrant under his hand and Sealed according to the Laws of Arms and received in the College of Arms) I have in the said Armorial Bearings and Supporters accordingly to be ancient Office to each of the respective Officers to each Warrant for and hereby to these Presents exemplify the Arms following for the said United Grand Lodge of Antient Free and Accepted Masons of England that is to say Per pale Gules and Azure on a Chevron between three Castles Argent a pair of Compasses extended of the third, sinister a Cross quarterly of the fourth and Or: between in the first quarter a Lion rampant of the third, in the second an Ox passant Sable in the third a Man with hands erected proper vested of the fifth the Robe Crimson lined with Ermine, and in the fourth an Eagle displayed Or of the third, the whole within a Bordure of the first charged with eight Lions passant guardant of the third. And for the Crest On a Wreath of the colours. A representation of an Ark supported on either side by a Cherub proper with the Motto over in Hebrew characters "Kodness to the Lord" By the authority aforesaid I the said United Grand Lodge of Antient Free and Accepted Masons of England do by these Presents grant and assign unto the said United Grand Lodge of Antient Free and Accepted Masons of England the Arms and Crest aforesaid as in the margin hereof are more plainly depicted to be borne and used by the said United Grand Lodge of Antient Free and Accepted Masons of England on Seals Shields Banners or otherwise accordingly to the Laws of Arms. **In Witness** whereof We the said Garter Clarenceux and Norroy and Ulster Kings of Arms have to these Presents subscribed Our names and affixed the Seals of Our several Offices this ninth day of July in the Tenth year of the Reign of Our Sovereign Lord George the Fifth by the Grace of God of the United Kingdom of Great Britain and Ireland and of the British Dominions beyond the Seas King Defender of the Faith and in the year of Our Lord One thousand nine hundred and nineteen.

H. Farnham Burke
Garter

William H. Weldon
Clarenceux

G. A. Atkinson
Norroy

A Cornucopia of Freemasonry

Diane Clements

In 1814 the new United Grand Lodge of England (UGLE) already owned several items of historic and artistic merit. The walls of Freemasons' Hall, designed by Thomas Sandby, the Professor of Architecture at the Royal Academy, were hung with portraits of Grand Masters. It housed an impressive suite of ceremonial furniture made for the Prince of Wales as Grand Master in 1791. In its meetings the Grand Sword Bearer carried a Sword of State dating from the mid-seventeenth century. Both the Premier and Antients Grand Lodges had kept records of their meetings, maintained registers of their members and retained important correspondence. The Articles of Union of 1813 referred to depositing the new Great Seal of the United Grand Lodge 'in the archives'. Within a few years plans were under way for the development of the collection and the creation of a Library and Museum.

The architect Philip Hardwick, the newly-installed Grand Superintendent of Works, put forward a plan in 1838 for the possible use of the recently acquired houses at 62 and 63 Great Queen Street, adjacent to the Hall – 'the room on the ground floor and on one side of the passage in the House No 63 appears to be well calculated for the present purposes of a Masonic Museum and Library'. £100 was provided for the acquisition 'of books, manuscripts and objects of Masonic interest.' In that same year of 1838 a dedicated gallery building in Trafalgar Square was opened to house the new National Gallery.

Despite this initial interest, progress in creating a Library and Museum was slow. One of the junior clerks in the Grand Secretary's office, Arthur Loutherbourg Thiselton, himself a keen collector, spent some time in this first Library and Museum. His obituary in the *Freemason's Quarterly Review* of June 1842 described his work: 'he arranged the few books and manuscripts in the Masonic library, and had the contributions to this department been ever so extensive, he would have been delighted to have regulated them; as it was, he considered the office of curator as disgraceful, having nothing to do'. By 1847 only half of the original grant had been spent and an inventory listed 279 books on Freemasonry and other subjects, a series of printed *Lists of Lodges* and calendars dating back to 1723, some Court Directories and six atlases. At the same time the first Library regulations were proposed, including regular opening times, readers being required to sign a Visitors' Book and a restriction on books leaving the Library. Some of these regulations remain in force in the Library and Museum at Great Queen Street today.

It was the appointment in 1887 of the Grand Tyler, Henry Sadler, as Sub-Librarian which inaugurated a period of major change for the Library and Museum. Although the Grand Secretary was still ex officio Librarian and Curator, Sadler's salary was increased and opening hours were extended. Sadler was an excellent choice. He organised and collected archive material and used this as the basis for much of his own research. He was eventually also a member of Quatuor Coronati Lodge No. 2076, the premier Lodge of Masonic research, formed in 1884. The Masonic historian Robert Freke Gould said of Sadler '… scarcely a single Masonic book would have been written without the author being assisted by him'. Sadler retired as Grand Tyler and was appointed full-time Librarian and Curator in 1910 but died just a year later.

Sadler's period coincided with the growth in an evidence-based Masonic history, supported by the collection of Masonic artefacts and books. Lists of donations to the Library and Museum started to appear in the *Quarterly Communication* from 1893. The collections continued to grow and could be displayed properly for the first time in a further new extension of Freemasons' Hall created by Henry Florence in 1900.

Outside London, several Provinces began to develop their own Museum and Library collections. A Masonic exhibition at the Guildhall in Worcester was held in 1884 on the occasion of the Provincial Grand Lodge meeting. It involved 'many hundreds of Books, Medals and Curios' borrowed from nearly 150 Brethren. The catalogue was written by local Freemason and collector George Taylor. He subsequently organised a Masonic Week at Kidderminster in March 1886, the centrepiece of which was the display of his own collection of books and objects. These were purchased by the Province to form the basis of its Library and Museum, so that the local Brethren would have 'an excellent opportunity to become acquainted with the eventful past of our beloved fraternity'. In Manchester, the President of the Association for Masonic Research there, J.O. Manton, gave the formation of a Masonic Library and Museum as one of the reasons for starting the Association.

In 1919 plans for redeveloping the Great Queen Street site were announced. The rules for the architectural competition held in 1925 for the design of the Masonic Peace Memorial included instructions to provide for space for a substantial Library and Museum incorporating a gallery, two Librarians' rooms, a workroom, two strongrooms, a large museum space with good lighting and a separate reading room. By this stage the Library and Museum was clearly seen as an important feature of the new building. Ashley and Newman's winning design placed the Library and Museum on the first floor of the building, on the same level as the ceremonial areas, giving it a unique prominence and status.

The collections at Great Queen Street were to be given additional importance by the publication of a three-volume catalogue compiled by the then Librarian and Curator, Algernon Tudor Craig. Wide publication seems to have been an aim, and volumes were purchased by many overseas Grand Lodges, Provinces and non-Masonic libraries, but work on the final volume was only completed in 1938 and so distribution was curtailed by the outbreak of war in 1939. At this time the Library and Museum collections at Great Queen Street were stored away in safes and strongrooms in the building.

The establishment of the collections over many years and their integration with Grand Lodge's own archives has resulted in an extraordinary richness in the Library and Museum collections which are illustrated in this volume.

Alongside the porcelain, silver and gem-encrusted jewels are items of ephemera such as the comprehensive collection of lodge Summonses that stretches back as far as 1766 [E1] [E2] [E3] [E4] [E5] [E6] [E7] [E8] [E9] [E10]; as well as articles often created by members themselves and made from everyday materials such as bone, horn, shells, metal [E11] and wood. These were often made from materials that referred to the name or membership of the lodge, or were appropriate in some way to the person who acquired and gifted the item to the lodge. Freemasonry proved central to the building and cohesion of the British Empire and there are many objects, books and documents with imperial connections. Jewels for lodges throughout the British Empire reflected the type of members and the locations of lodges. Their imagery often highlighted the lodge name. Atbara Lodge was named after a city known as Sudan's 'Railway City' [E12]. United Dooars Lodge in Bengal had links to a tea plantation [E13].

The collections also reflect the social history of 300 years. Although English Freemasonry has always remained apolitical, lodge jewels often reflect issues and events of contemporary relevance. The cause of Polish nationalism was a popular one in the mid-nineteenth century. In 1846 the Founders of Polish National Lodge included several supporters of this cause and the Lodge was granted special permission to use the Polish white eagle, the emblem of Poland, on their Members' and Past Masters' jewels [E14]. Rose of Denmark Lodge No. 975 is just one of many English lodges named after royal events, in this case the marriage of the Prince of Wales to Alexandra of Denmark [E15]. The extensive collection of jewels held by the Library and Museum from English Constitution lodges across the world enables trends in sentiment and lodge self-image to be plotted. By way of example, at the turn of the nineteenth century it became very popular for Masons to wear multiple jewels – to such an extent that ultimately it became necessary to wear miniatures rather than normal-size jewels, on account of the lack of space and the weight! [E16] The designs of jewels for lodges formed towards the end of the 1939-45 war did not focus on victory but highlighted the peace and harmony [E17] [E18] [E19] which victory brought and included images of doves [E20], of peaceful countryside and sunrise [E21].

In the post-war period the Library and Museum collections continued to grow with many donations and occasional acquisitions. In the mid 1980s the Librarian and Curator, John Hamill, played a significant role in Grand Lodge's communications function and the development of 'openness'. This included encouraging greater access to the Library and Museum, and the tours by the general public and academic researchers. Grand Lodge took the opportunity in the late 1990s to restructure the Library and Museum, which had until then been a department of Grand Lodge, instead creating a Charitable Trust and placing the Grand Lodge collections on long-term loan to it. This 'separation' from Grand Lodge enabled the Library and Museum to play a more active role in the library and museum sector generally and also to work towards achieving accreditation, the nationally-agreed standard for museums in the UK, and to apply for external funding – almost unknown amongst Masonic charities. In 2007 the work of this team and all its predecessors was recognised when the collections were awarded 'Designated' status as collections of national and international significance. The development of an online catalogue and several digitisation projects made the collections much more accessible and supplemented a continuing programme of temporary exhibitions.

The Library and Museum of Freemasonry in London has served as a tremendous role model for the formation of similar establishments throughout the country. Many Masonic Halls both large and small have vibrant Museums and Libraries within them which are open to the public. Whilst none can compete with London in terms of size and resources, they nevertheless house important Masonic treasures of local interest which are often unique.

E1: Lodge Summons – Turk's Head, 1766.

A lodge Summons is a classic example of ephemera: an item that is important or useful for only a short time, not meant to have lasting value and usually discarded after use. The word 'summons' is derived from the Latin verb *summonere* – to warn or advise. The first record of a Freemason being initiated in England is that of Elias Ashmole on 10 October 1646. Ashmole subsequently recorded in his diary, some years later on 10 March 1682: 'About 5H:p.m. I rec[d] a Summons to appear at a Lodge to be held next day at Masons Hall London.'

From the earliest days of Freemasonry lodges have issued Summonses to advise members of a forthcoming meeting. Originally, a lodge was often known by the name of the tavern in which it met. The design of the Summons has always been a matter for individual lodges. The means of production has changed over time but has always reflected the character and history of a lodge. Many lodges invested in an engraved copper plate with the date, time and place of meeting being inserted individually by hand. The Masonic symbolism contained on each Summons varied greatly. Initially it would have been the responsibility of the lodge Tyler – a paid factotum – to deliver the Summons by hand; a task subsequently taken over by the postal service and most recently by email.

E2: Lodge Summons – King's Head Tavern – Friendly Lodge No. 466, 1796. ▷

Constituted in 1790 as Friendly Lodge No. 557, it was renumbered as No. 466 in 1792 and No. 521 in 1814 before lapsing in about 1815. Between 1793 and 1798 the Lodge was meeting at the King's Head Tavern in High Holborn, London. In the early days of Freemasonry a lodge was often known by the name of the tavern in which it met.

E3: Lodge Summons – Bedford Lodge No. 205, 1813. ▽

Constituted in 1766, the Lodge is believed to have operative origins.

E4: Lodge Summons – St George's Lodge No. 164, 1815.

By any stretch of the imagination the Lodge may be described as peripatetic, having had no less than thirty meeting places since its constitution in 1765.

E5: Lodge Summons – Royal York Lodge of Perfect Friendship No. 243, 1821.

The Lodge, which met in Bath, was erased by Grand Lodge in December 1824, following what was described as internal discord.

E6: Lodge Summons – Lodge of Honor and Generosity No. 274, 1822.

Warranted in 1767 but not named until 1789, the Lodge was numbered 274 in 1814, when it was meeting at the Horn Tavern, Doctors Commons, London. It met at three other taverns before going to the Bunch of Grapes, Little St Martin's Lane in 1822, when this Summons was issued. It is now No. 165.

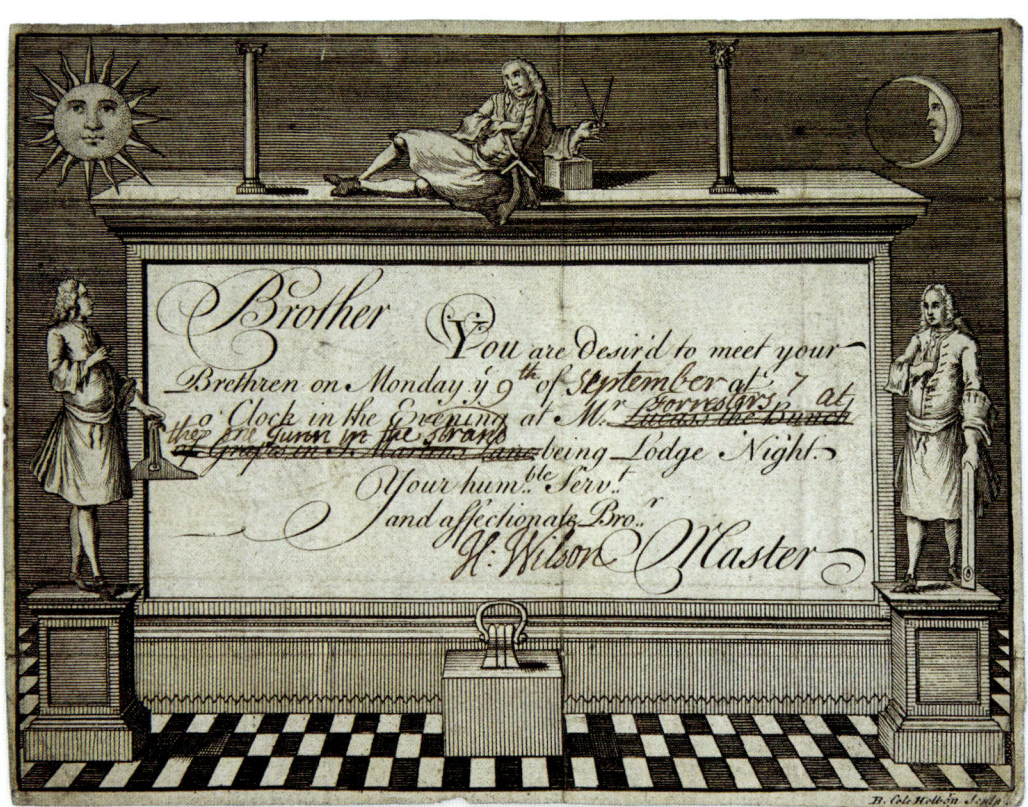

E7: Lodge Summons – Grand Master's Lodge No. 1, 1824.

Grand Master's Lodge No. 1 was the most senior Lodge on the roll of the Antients Grand Lodge. In 1813, at the Union between the Moderns and Antients Grand Lodges to form the United Grand Lodge of England (UGLE), it was decided that the enumeration of lodges on the new combined roll should be done on the basis of allocating numbers in order of seniority, alternately one from each of the two former Grand Lodges. The Lodge of Antiquity – the most senior of Lodge of the Moderns – 'lost' in the ballot to determine which was to be No. 1. Despite being older than Grand Master's Lodge (the Lodges being constituted in 1691 and 1759 respectively), it became Lodge of Antiquity No. 2.

E8: Lodge Summons – St John the Baptist Lodge No. 53, 1825.

In 1814 the Lodge was numbered No. 53 and met at the Globe Tavern in Exeter. Now numbered No. 39, it currently meets at Freemasons' Hall in Exeter.

GRAND MASTER'S LODGE, No. 1.

Designed & Engraved by B. W. Alexander and Presented by him to the Grand Master's Lodge March 15. 1824.

Brother

You are requested to attend the Masonic Duties of this LODGE, at Free Masons Tavern, Great Queen St. on Monday the 21st day of June, ins.t at four o'Clock in the Afternoon punctually

By Order of the Worshipful Master

T. Crew Secretary

To ballot for Initiation of Richard Hervè Giraud of N.o 7, Furnivals Inn — Solicitor, proposed by the W. Master seconded by Brother Pain

E9: Lodge Summons – Lodge of Peace and Harmony No. 82, 1826.

Currently numbered No. 60, it is one of the nineteen lodges that annually nominate a Grand Steward; as indeed are Grand Master's No. 1, Antiquity No. 2, and Globe Lodge No. XXIII.

E10: Lodge Summons – Globe Lodge No. XXIII, 2003.

Globe Lodge was constituted in 1723 and took its name from the tavern in which it met. It was one of the few lodges in the English Constitution to have their number in roman rather than arabic numerals. This is a very busy Summons which abounds in Masonic symbolism, and goes back to the earliest days of the Lodge. The only details that needed to be changed from meeting to meeting were the date, time and place of meeting, which were inserted individually by hand. Note the use of the words 'Yours Affectionately' in the salutation – still in use by members today, as is the original design of the Summons. The original engraved copper plate having been long lost and the quality of the printed version having deteriorated, the summons was completely re-drawn – replicating the original design – by Dr Archie Walls, a member of the lodge, in 2003. It was then electronically scanned and digitised. An excellent example of how an old and successful lodge can adapt and be able to combine tradition with new technology.

E11: Gavel used by Ad Astra Lodge No. 3808, 1918.

Ad Astra Lodge No. 3808 was formed in 1917 as a Lodge for Masons serving in the Royal Air Force. It ceased to meet in 2000. This gavel is made from the alloy duralumin (aluminium and copper), salvaged from the wreck of the first German airship shot down over Cuffley in Hertfordshire during the First World War in September 1916.

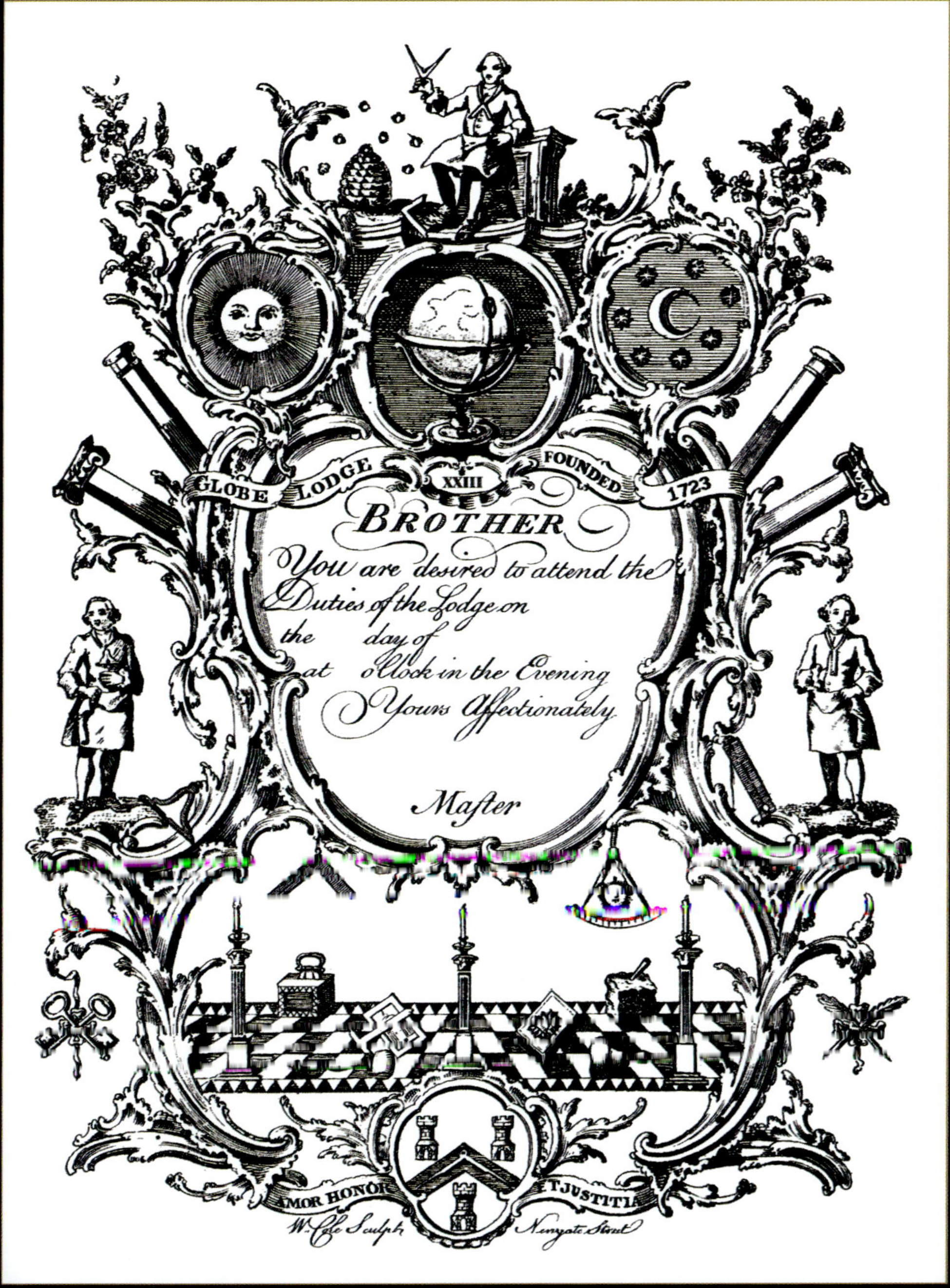
GLOBE LODGE
XXIII
FOUNDED
1723
BROTHER
You are desired to attend the
Duties of the Lodge on
the day of
at o'Clock in the Evening
Yours Affectionately
Master
AMOR HONOR ET JUSTITIA
W. Cole Sculpt
Newgate Street

ZEPPELIN L21
CUFFLEY
SEPT 3RD 1916

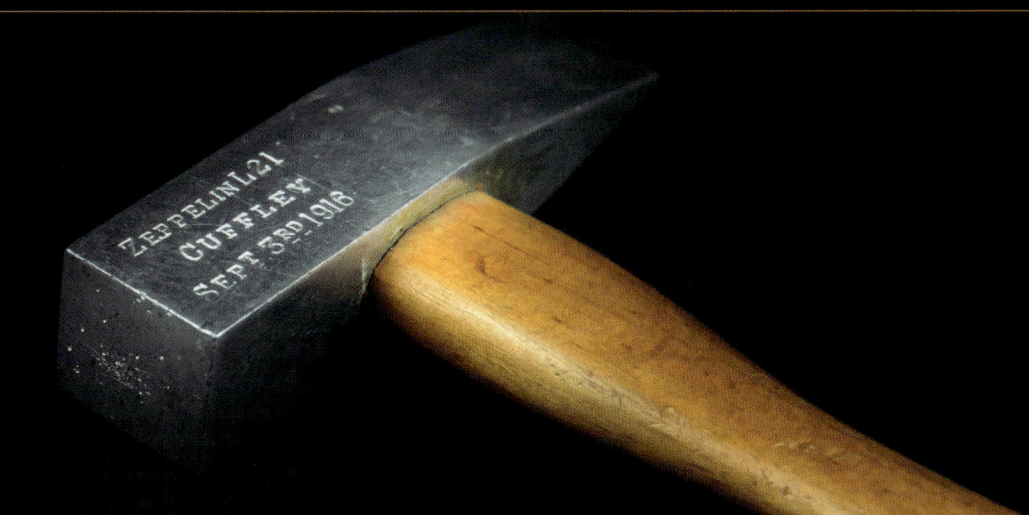

E12: Founder's Jewel – Atbara Lodge No. 3407, 1909. ▽

Atbara Lodge was founded in Atbara, Sudan's 'Railway City', in 1909 but closed in 1955 because of falling numbers.

General Charles Gordon (1833-85) was originally based in Atbara where, amongst other things, he was involved in the development of Sudan's railway system from 1873 to 1876. In February 1884 he returned to the Sudan to evacuate the Egyptian forces in Khartoum. The city almost immediately came under a siege that lasted nearly a year and culminated in General Gordon and his troops being massacred in January 1885. The statue that features on this jewel originally stood in Khartoum, but is now located outside Gordon's School in Woking, Surrey.

E13: Founder's Jewel – United Dooars Lodge No. 3351, 1909. ▽

The jewel depicts the Lodge's link with the tea trade, with a depiction of a tea plantation in front of a backdrop of mountains. The Lodge originally met in Jalpaiguri, Bengal and now meets in Calcutta.

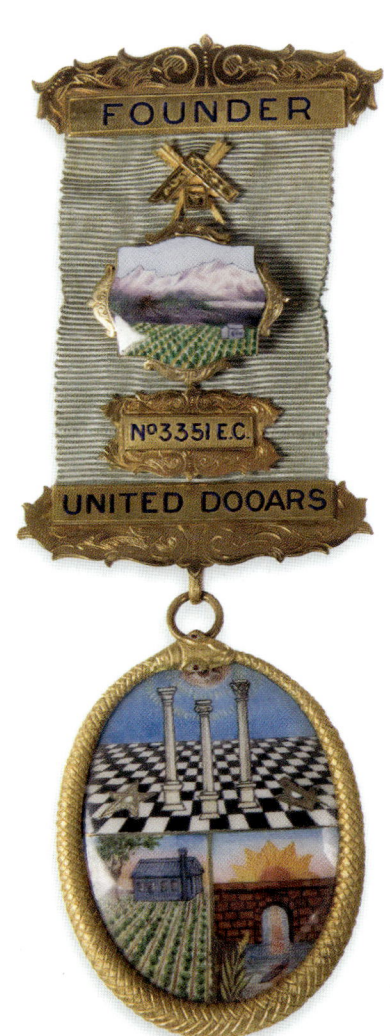

E14: Member's Jewel – Polish National Lodge No. 534, 1846. ▷

Originally numbered No. 788, the Lodge was founded by Polish exiles who sought asylum in England following political unrest in Poland. Lodge member's jewels are comparatively rare in Freemasonry and require special permission to be granted by the Grand Master. The authority for members of Polish National Lodge to wear their distinctive jewel takes the form of an annotation to the Lodge Warrant. The jewel consists of the Polish white eagle – the emblem of Poland – in sterling silver, suspended from the ribbon of the *Virtuti Militari*, the highest Polish military decoration. Members who have given distinguished service to the Lodge are granted the right to wear a similar jewel – known as the Commander's White Eagle – with a golden crown, suspended from a collarette.

E18: Founder's Jewel – Ringway Lodge No. 6024, 1945. ▸

The Founders of the Lodge had a connection with Manchester Ringway Airport, as indicated in the jewel which belonged to the first or Primus Master. In 2007 it closed, to amalgamate with Mapesbury Lodge No. 4084.

E19: Founder's Jewel – Tranquillus Lodge No. 5912, 1943. ▸▸

The jewel belonged to the first Immediate Past Master.

E20: Founder's Jewel – Serenity Lodge ◂ No. 5917, 1943.

The Lodge was founded during the middle of the Second World War – the dove is symbolic of the desire for peace.

E21: Past Master's Jewel – Riddlesdown Lodge No. 6107, 1945. ◂

The Lodge was warranted in May 1945 and the jewel features a simple country scene with rolling green fields and a rising sun on the horizon.

E15: Past Master's Jewel – Rose of Denmark Lodge No. 975, 1910. ▸

The Rose of Denmark Lodge No. 975 was named after the wife of the Prince of Wales, who was Danish. In its early years the Lodge met at various venues in south-west London. The jewel consists of an 18 carat gold rose cast in high relief, with a clear gemstone set at the centre of the flower; it is surrounded by a gold laurel wreath and topped by a ducal coronet in gold and red enamel.

E16: Bladon Miniatures, *c.*1910. ▸▸

A collection of seventy-two miniature jewels formerly belonging to Henry Bladon, a Freemason and manufacturer of Masonic regalia in London. During the Victorian era it became the custom for Freemasons to wear jewels to demonstrate not only their various Masonic achievements but also their membership of Masonic Orders beyond the Craft. The enthusiasm for doing so became such that the only way of adequately achieving this was by wearing miniatures.

Henry (Harry) Bladon took over the family jewellery business in Clerkenwell when his father Joseph retired in 1894. Although the partnership with Frederick Humphries was dissolved in 1897, the company traded as Bladon & Humphries until 1910, when it became Bladon & Co.; it continued to manufacture and retail Masonic jewellery and regalia until Harry's death in 1948.

Henry Bladon was born in 1867 and, having been proposed into the Duke of Cornwall Lodge No. 1839 by his father, was initiated on 13 September 1890. He combined business with pleasure by becoming what can only be described as a very enthusiastic and conscientious Freemason. He joined Roll Call Lodge No. 2523 in 1895 and was a Founder of Victoria Diamond Jubilee Lodge No. 2675 in 1897, of which he was Master in 1901. Over the next twenty years he became a member of twelve lodges, helped found nine, and was Master of seven. As a Provincial Officer in Middlesex and Surrey, he was part of the Consecrating Team on a large number of occasions, resulting in him becoming an Honorary Member of some twenty lodges. Awarded London Rank in 1911, he first became a Grand Officer in 1916. In addition he was very involved in other Masonic Orders, including the Royal Arch, Mark, Royal Ark Mariners, Knights Templar and the Ancient and Accepted Rite.

E17: Founder's Jewel – New Era Lodge No. 5991, 1944. ▸

The Lodge is aptly-named, given that it was constituted in the final years of the Second World War. It is quite usual for a jewel to bear the emblem of the lodge office held by the Founder – in this case the Senior Warden.

Regalia such as medals are regularly worn by Masons. These are known in Masonic circles as jewels. The jewels are mostly issued to celebrate some form of Masonic anniversary; for example, once a Master has completed his year in the Chair he is usually awarded a Past Master's breast jewel to wear in perpetuity. The form of the jewel varies, but normally incorporates the lodge logo or motif. Jewels may also be struck to celebrate the founding of a lodge and, at the other end of the scale, to commemorate the centenary or even bicentenary of a lodge. Some of the jewels are pieces of exquisite workmanship and, until the Second World War, were often made of solid gold.

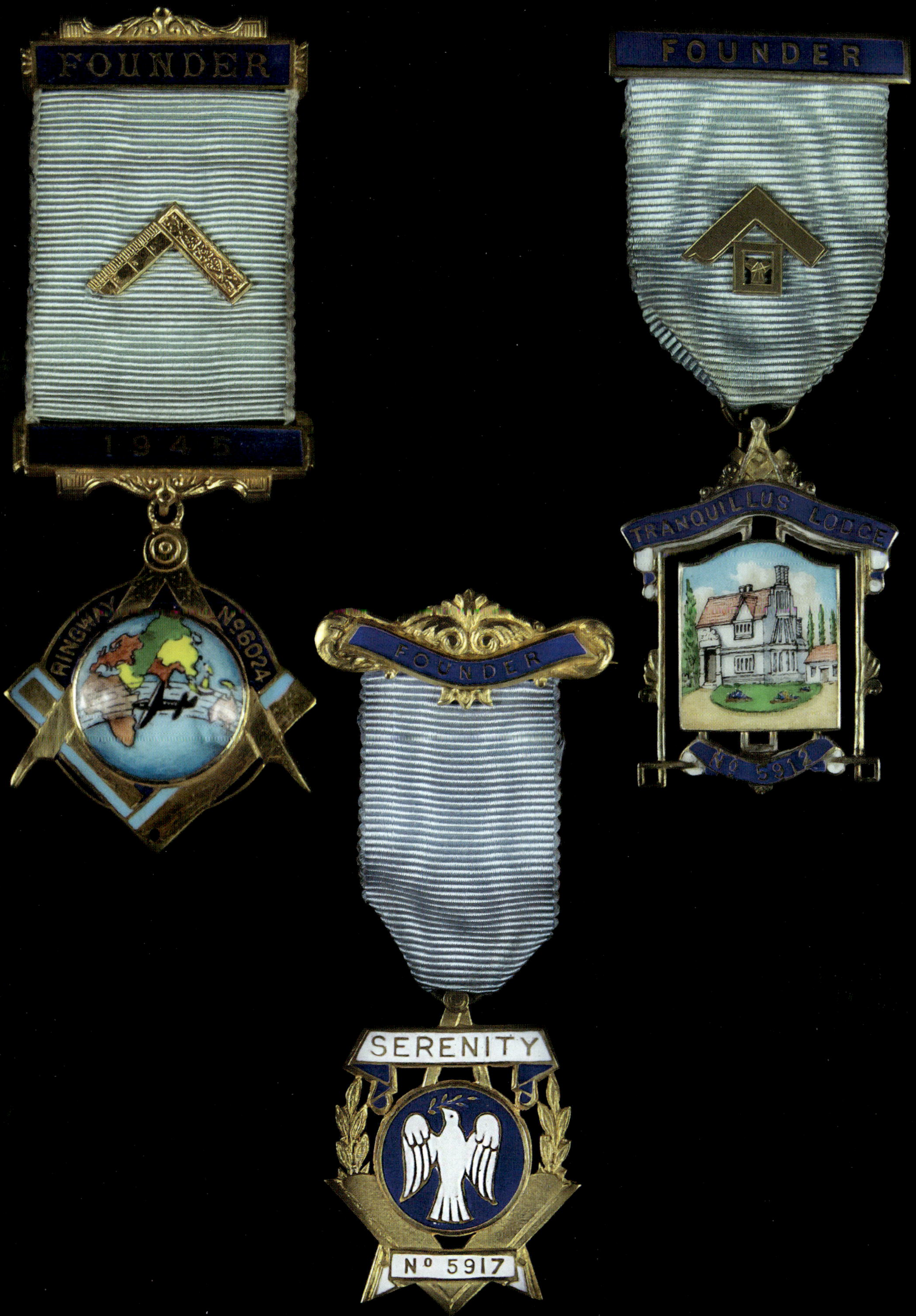
FOUNDER
1945
RINGWAY
Nº 6024
FOUNDER
TRANQUILLUS LODGE
Nº 5912
FOUNDER
SERENITY
Nº 5917

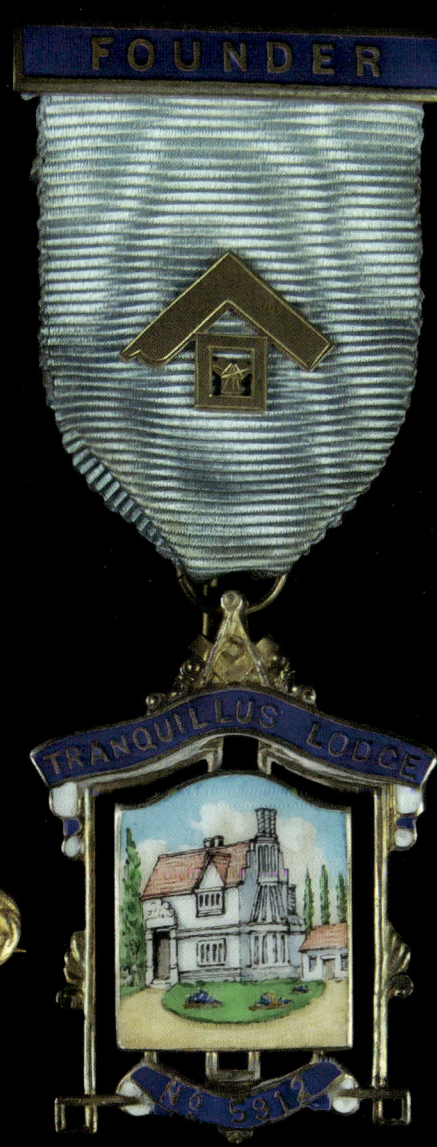

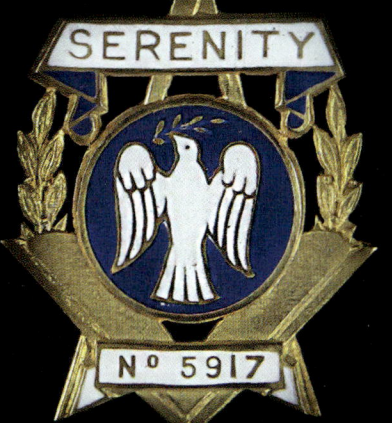

My Cup Runneth Over

Richard Gan

Many Masonic Halls throughout the country have excellent Museums and Libraries that are open to the general public. Although none have the resources to match those of the Library and Museum of Freemasonry in London (L&M of F) they do nevertheless house Masonic treasures, many of local interest and often unique. Very few, if any, employ full-time, qualified staff and the majority are run by extremely enthusiastic and gifted individuals who give freely of their time. A number have striven for and achieved Accredited Museum status through Arts Council England. The L&M of F is a tremendous role model and provides active support, assistance and advice wherever and whenever possible. The Masonic Library and Museums Group, to which many Provincial Museums and Libraries belong, meets on a regular basis twice a year, giving the opportunity for an interchange of ideas.

The title of this chapter is 'My Cup Runneth Over' – in testimony to the abundance of Masonic treasures that flourish and overflow from the cornucopia found in London. Limitation of space prevents anything other than a snapshot which provides a flavour of what is to be found around the country. The contact details and locations of the featured museums in Bristol, Derbyshire, Essex, Hertfordshire, Leicestershire, Northumberland, Nottinghamshire, West Lancashire and Worcestershire are to be found on page 296.

Since the beginnings of Freemasonry itself individual Masons have been avid collectors of Masonic treasures. Masonic jewels and postage stamps with a Masonic theme are two subjects that continue to have a great appeal to individual collectors. This is reflected in the fact that there are two national organisations which cater for the needs of collectors: the Jewels of the Craft and the Masonic Philatelic Club, both of whom publish regular, first-class magazines. The sheer quality and beauty of craftsmanship of the various jewels [F1] [F2] [F3] [F4] [F5], together with the range of philatelic subjects [F6] [F7] [F8] available, are amply illustrated here and help explain why so many Freemasons find them of such interest.

Bristol is the only city to have a Provincial Grand Lodge in its own right – London being a Metropolitan Grand Lodge – and other than Jersey in the Channel Islands is the only Province where all Masonic meetings are held under one roof. The Province also differs in that lodges use a ritual claimed to be that used before 1813 and which is certainly very different to that adopted elsewhere after the Union of 1813. Members have to keep their own handwritten copy, as there is no official printed version. It is not surprising that there are many unique items in the Museum which reflect Bristol's history, both social and Masonic, such as the scrimshaw carved by a French prisoner of war during the Napoleonic Wars [F9], and the Master's hat [F10] [F11], together with oddities which the Museum has accrued, such as a coffee pot presented to the father of a Lewis whilst Master of a lodge in Lincolnshire [F12].

The Library and Museum of the Provincial Grand Lodge of Derbyshire Freemasons were established in 1907. The Library consists of more than 3,000 volumes, and is currently involved in helping to record and catalogue the books and papers of the distinguished Freemason Revd Neville Barker-Cryer, who left his extensive library and papers as a legacy to Tyrian Lodge No. 253 in recognition of both his membership and the affection in which he held the Lodge. Much of the Masonic history of Derbyshire is revealed within the Museum collection, which has been built up over many years from the donations of a succession of Freemasons. As might be expected there are many excellent pieces of Crown Derby porcelain in the collection [K18]. There has always been a close association between the Dukes of Devonshire [F13] and the Province, a connection for which the members have held a close affection [F14]. The respect in which certain individuals are held is illustrated by the generosity of presentations made to them [F15].

Although only established in 2006, amongst the aims of the Essex Provincial Library and Museum is raising the awareness of Freemasons and members of the public to the rich history and development of Freemasonry. The ability of Provincial Museums to bring to light items of local interest is demonstrated by the linking of the Masonic apron and Grand Lodge Certificate belonging to Samuel Lancaster [F16] [F17].

The Hertfordshire Provincial Museum is housed in the Provincial Headquarters. The collections started to be put together in 2008. A Provincial Archive and Library has been established, to enable research by both members and historians. The collection is extremely varied. The Masonic jewel collection numbers in excess of 6,000 items, largely as a result of the receipt of a generous legacy from John Gandy. He was a prolific collector and a founder member of The Jewels of the Craft, who bequeathed over 3,000 jewels and 1,500 artefacts to the Museum [F18] [F19] [F20] [F21] [F22]. Over the years Hertfordshire has had many members who have achieved high rank and distinction, not just within the Craft but also in society at large. One of the more prominent and successful was Sir Thomas F. Halsey, who was a Member of Parliament and served both as Provincial Grand Master for Hertfordshire and Deputy Grand Master [F23].

The Library and Museum at Leicester contains a very fine collection of rare books and artefacts. The Museum was founded around 1870 in the original Masonic Hall at Halford Street and transferred to the present building in 1910. Associated with the Museum is the Library, with a wide collection of books and pamphlets relating to various aspects of Masonic history as far back as the early eighteenth century. The core of the collection was assembled by John T. Thorp, a Past Master of the Lodge of Research No. 2429 (Leicester) and of Quatuor Coronati Lodge No. 2076. Other Masonic historians, such as Hughan, have contributed pieces to the collection. All these collections were originally the property of the Lodge of Research but have since been transferred to the Province to form the nucleus of its Library and Museum. In addition to the expected pieces such as regalia and jewels, there are collections associated with a wide variety of Masonic activities. There are items of porcelain, pottery, glassware, and of course the well-renowned 'Leicester Table' [F24].

The Library and Museum in Northumberland is in the process of being re-located to the new Provincial office in Gosforth, where no doubt the unique 'Wooler' Master's Chair will take pride of place [F25].

Housed in a dedicated area of the Masonic Hall in Nottingham, the Masonic Museum and Library houses the heritage collection of pottery, porcelain, glass, silver, furniture, jewels and regalia. Many of these highly-decorated items, from the eighteenth century to the present day, are engraved, painted or enamelled with Masonic symbols. The Museum also displays the different ranks, offices and branches of Freemasonry and explains its symbolism, charities and traditions. From time to time temporary exhibitions portray stories from the history of Freemasonry and specific aspects of Masonic life. Visitors are welcome to use the Library and archives for reference: these contain a comprehensive collection of books and manuscripts on many facets of Freemasonry in England and associated topics, in particular records of Nottinghamshire Masonry as well as other parts of the world. Family records are of particular importance to those researching their ancestors and Masonic archives can often answer many questions on family history. The items illustrated here not only demonstrate the depth and quality of the collection, but also the importance of ensuring that items of local context and interest are also included [F26] [F27] [F28] [F29][F30][F31].

The Warrington Museum of Freemasonry is housed in the Warrington Masonic Hall, which was purpose-built in 1932 and opened in September 1933. It receives support, advice and formal mentoring from Warrington Museum and Art Gallery, part of Culture Warrington.

The collection includes regalia, books, jewels, pottery and glassware from 1599 onwards. The range of objects is continually expanding, with the Museum being in a position to accept loans and donations from individuals and other Masonic Halls.

Warrington has a strong connection with Freemasonry. Elias Ashmole became the first recorded Initiate in an English Lodge when he was made a Freemason in Warrington in 1646. The celebrated antiquary subsequently established the Ashmolean, England's first public museum at Oxford, in 1683. The various pieces from the collection illustrated here all have a very strong local connection and demonstrate the importance that Museums have in ensuring that Freemasonry is seen as an integral part of the community [F32] [F33] [F34] [F35] [F36].

The Masonic Museum and Library in Worcester first opened its doors in 1887. Its purpose, according to its founder George Taylor, was to educate. As he said, 'It is most remarkable how few brethren there are who comprehend the extent of Masonic literature and its attendant objects.' Today the Museum extends its education to the public at large, being open to all for individual visits on a regular basis and at other times by special arrangement for groups. Since its inception, the collection of artefacts, books and documents has grown and it is now considered one of the finest Masonic collections in the country. The exhibits include a selection of engraved glass, much of it from the nineteenth century, and a very large display of ceramics, including jugs, dishes and tankards, many of which are decorated with Masonic symbols and date from the late eighteenth and early nineteenth centuries. Other items in the collection are Masonic curiosities such as trivets, horse brasses, meerschaum pipes, unusual gavels and assorted Masonic bric-a-brac. Antique regalia, including pictorial and hand-painted aprons, some dating from eighteenth century France, are to be found together with a number of unusual items of lodge furniture. An accredited Museum, the very extensive collection may be browsed online at www.worcestermasonicmuseum.co.uk. The choice as to which items to include here from such an important and wide-ranging collection has not been easy. Two pieces have been used to illustrate themes elsewhere in the book: the Hogarth Jewel [A4] and the Jewel of the Nine Worthies [D4]; in addition one item of particular local interest included here is the Provincial Grand Master's Collar Jewel belonging to John Dent [F37].

As has been shown, this section more than justifies the title 'My Cup Runneth Over' in demonstrating the sheer breadth and quality of Masonic treasures that are accessible in the many Masonic Libraries and Museums which exist throughout the country. It has only been possible to feature a very small number of them and to include a few items from each of those collections; but in doing so it has shown the part that Provincial Museums have to play in bringing the history of Freemasonry alive and tangible in a local context.

F1: Chapter Jewel belonging to Francis Lambert, 1821.

The silver jewel was made by Charles Rawlings and is engraved 'Francis Lambert Exalted in the British R A Chapter Dec 3rd 1821.'

This extraordinary and unique jewel is composed of two main elements:

The inner part is a Royal Arch Chapter Jewel made in hallmarked silver dating from 1821, in the style of Thomas Harper, and which originally belonged to Francis Lambert;

The outer part, also in silver, was added later by his widow and is engraved: 'This Jewel Badge and sash were presented to George Lambert by his Mother Jan 1st 1847 having been used by his late father. / Exalted in the Royal York Chapter of Perseverance No 7 Febry 23rd A.D. 1847 A.L. 5608.'

Francis Lambert was born in 1778, apprenticed as a silversmith when a boy to a Mr Wesley in The Strand, and later to a Mr Clark. By 1800 he had set up his own business in Piccadilly which became so successful as to attract patrons such as Queen Victoria, the Prince of Wales and many other members of the Royal family. He eventually set up in partnership with Charles Rawlings who, following the death of Francis Lambert, carried on the business until Lambert's son George took over.

George Lambert was apprenticed to the Goldsmith's Company in 1837 and held the office of Prime Warden in 1887, being one of very few apprentices to have attained that distinction. When he died in 1901 he left an estate to the value of £114,847 (£11.3 million itm).

F2: Pierced Jewel, St Georges East York Militia Lodge No. 356, 1796.

This fine and rare jewel is engraved: 'James Elliott St Georges East York Militia Lodge No 356 0ct 24th 1796.' James Elliot, a sergeant in the Artillery, was aged 30 when initiated in 1796. He came from Brighton, as did nine other soldiers who were members of the Lodge. The Lodge was warranted in York in 1782 as No. 442, renumbered in 1792 as No. 356, and as No. 460 at the Union in 1813. One of the most active military Lodges formed in Yorkshire, it ceased working in 1829.

F3: Pierced Silver Jewel belonging to Christopher Fenton, *c.*1814.

The jewel, which has a silver hallmark, was hand-cut from a flat piece of silver and hand-engraved with the Latin motto: *Virtute et Silentio – Amor Honor et Justitia*.

Bro C.E. Fenton was initiated in the Lodge of Antiquity on 22 January 1812. This piece was probably designed to double both as a decorative jewel, and also to illustrate Masonic symbols to other Brethren.

F4: Member's Jewel, *c.*1830. ▽

The jewel shows the progress from Junior Warden through Senior Warden to Master. Made from silver with paste stones, some 2in in diameter, it would have been worn as a breast jewel.

F5: Silver Pierced Jewel, *c.*1790. ▷

A superbly engraved member's breast jewel, packed with Masonic symbols.

F6: Anti-Masonic Serbian Postage Stamps, 1942.

Philately provides yet another example of the very different types of Masonic treasures available to collectors. Two sets of stamps are shown here from two ends of the spectrum – one distinctly hostile to Freemasonry, the other more sympathetic.

In 1942 Serbia issued four stamps to commemorate an Anti-Masonic Exhibition which opened in Belgrade in October of the previous year. The stamps show Serbia crushing what it perceived as a plot for world domination by an evil axis of Freemasonry, Communism and Judaism.

This is in stark contrast to the celebratory commemorative stamps issued by Honduras, France, Luxembourg and Brazil.

F7: Six Commemorative Masonic Postage Stamps, 1938–78.

Honduras – Exterior of the Masonic Temple in Tegucigalpa, 1938; Honduras – Interior of the Masonic Temple in Tegucigalpa, 1955; France – Bicentenary of the Grand Orient of France, 1973; Luxembourg, 175th Anniversary of the Grand Lodge of Luxembourg, 1978; Brazil – Sesquicentenary of the Grand Orient of Brazil, 1973; Brazil – 50th Anniversary of the Grand Lodge of Brazil.

F8: Victory 3d. Postage Stamp, 1946.

The 3d. Victory Postage stamp issued in 1946 is full of Masonic symbolism. King George VI, himself an enthusiastic Freemason, is depicted facing east, looking directly at a dove with an olive branch, which was officially adopted as the Deacon's jewel and badge of office at the Union of 1813. Also depicted is the Square – the collar jewel worn by the Master of a lodge – together with the Compasses, positioned as they would be during the ceremony of the Second Degree. The trowel and brickwork are also of Masonic significance. Whilst the Victory stamp was not issued as a Masonic stamp, but rather to commemorate the end of the Second World War and the return to peace and the reconstruction that was to follow, the Masonic symbolism it contains cannot be entirely coincidental.

Bristol
F9: Scrimshaw carved by a French Prisoner of War during the Napoleonic Wars, *c*.1795. ➤

Scrimshaw carved with Masonic symbols by a French prisoner of war during the Napoleonic Wars.

Bristol
F10: Master's Hat: St Paul's Lodge No. 6400, *c*.1830. ▽

Although only warranted in 1946, the Lodge continues the tradition in Bristol where the Master of the Lodge wears or carries a bicorn or cocked hat during the procession in and out of lodge. The hat is shown here with its original storage case.

Bristol
F11: Master's Storage Box St Paul's Lodge No. 6400, *c*.1830. ▽

Bristol
F12: Silver Coffee Pot presented to F.J. Sawby, 1892.

Silver coffee pot engraved:
'Presented to
W.Bro. FJ Sawby
by Brethren of the Yarboro Lodge No. 422 Gainsboro
to commemorate the birth of a
Lewis
during his year as Worshipful
Master
November 1892'.

Derbyshire

F13: Apron of the Provincial Grand Master for Derbyshire, *c.*1938. ➤

This apron belonged to Edward William Spencer Cavendish, 10th Duke of Devonshire, the Provincial Grand Master of Derbyshire (1938-47). Traditionally this apron has been passed into the care of every succeeding Provincial Grand Master since that time. The Duke was elected as Grand Master in 1947, a position he held until his untimely death in 1950.

F14: Devonshire Casket, *c.*1947.

The Devonshire Casket holds a historic significance for many Derbyshire Brethren. It was commissioned by the Province to commemorate the election of The 10th Duke of Devonshire as Grand Master in 1947. Sadly His Grace suffered a serious heart attack in November 1950, resulting in his death. Hence this beautiful, impressive object was never presented.

For many years after, the casket was displayed in the Provincial Library. However, in 1990 a massive fire engulfed the Masonic Hall, destroying part of the upper floor containing the Provincial Offices and Library and resulting in the loss of many important documents, books and artefacts. At the height of the fire the floor collapsed except for a small section of Library floor. It was on this section of floor that the casket, inside its protective case, was standing. Amazingly, unscathed and intact, both casket and glass case survived.

Derbyshire
F15: Lodge of Repose Loving Cup, 1933.

Royal Crown Derby Loving Cup presented to W Bro Thomas Ryley in 1933 to commemorate his fifty years' membership of the Lodge of Repose No. 802. He was their first Initiate to reach this significant milestone. W Bro Ryley held the office of Provincial Grand Treasurer in 1911.

Invoice

Invoice No.	249757
Invoice Date	28/03/18
Order No.	195663
Order Ref	Mail
Order Date	20/03/18
Page	1 of 1

Lewis Masonic
Heritage House
52-54 Hamm Moor Lane
Addlestone
Surrey
KT15 2SF

Phone: 01932 834959
Fax: 01932 845220
Email: sales@lewismasonic.co.uk

Order & Track Deliveries Online: www.lewismasonic.co.uk

Invoice To
B V Ashworth
7 HARTLEY CLOSE
CHARLTON KINGS
CHELTENHAM
GL53 9DN

Deliver To
B V Ashworth
7 HARTLEY CLOSE
CHARLTON KINGS
CHELTENHAM
GL53 9DN

Delivery Free Delivery
Phone 01242 241702

SKU	Description	Ordered	Unit RRP	Unit Price	Sub Total	Sent	To Follow
9780853184058	Beyond the Craft (6th Edition)	1	£12.99	£12.99	£12.99	1	0
Y83402	Compendium of Masonic Prayers & Graces	1	£5.99	£5.99	£5.99	1	0
9780853184966	Freemasonry and Fraternal Societies	1	£12.99	£12.99	£12.99	1	0
9780853185314	The Treasures of English Freemasonry 1717 - 2017	1	£45.00	£45.00	£45.00	1	0

Payment received with thanks. Credits for returns will only be issued provided a return has been duly authorised and the product received in good condition.

Lewis Masonic is a trading name of Ian Allan Publishing Ltd, a company registered in England & Wales, company number 400981. VAT registration number GB 207 5323 87. Registered office: Terminal House, Station Approach, Shepperton, Middlesex TW17 8AS. All orders are subject to our standard terms & conditions of business, a copy of which is available on request.

Sub Total	£76.97
Delivery	£0.00
VAT (incl)	£0.00
Total	**£76.97**

B V Ashworth
7 HARTLEY CLOSE
CHARLTON KINGS
CHELTENHAM
GL53 9DN

DSP249757

From: Lewis Masonic, Heritage House, 52-54 Hamm Moor Lane,

Essex
F16: Grand Lodge Certificate belonging to Samuel Lancaster, 1813. ➤

A Certificate presented to Samuel Lancaster and dated 11 February 1813, whilst he was a member of Union York Lodge meeting at that time in Colchester, Essex.

Union York Lodge was originally a military travelling lodge established in 1792, attached to the 2nd Regiment of West York Militia, under the Irish Constitution, with the number 626. The Lodge appears to have joined the Moderns Grand Lodge in 1811, becoming No. 634 in 1814 and was finally erased in 1829.

Essex
F17: Hand-Decorated Apron belonging to Samuel Lancaster, c.1813. ▽

An apron, hand-decorated with Masonic symbols, which belonged to Samuel Lancaster.

The Certificate and apron are both in the possession of Angel Lodge No. 51, which was established in 1736 and met at the Three Cups Hotel, High Street, Colchester. It was named the Angel Lodge in 1819.

The light shineth in darkness, and the darkness comprehendeth it not.

To The Right Worshipful.

Nº 626.

THE Master, Wardens, and other Officers and Brethren of all Regular Lodges of the Ancient and Honourable Society of Free and Accepted Masons.

WE, The Master, Wardens, Secretary, and Brethren of the Respectable Lodge, known by the name of the UNION YORK (English Constitution) held in Colchester, Essex,

DO hereby Certify that our Worthy Brother Samuel Lancaster was under due & regular Tradition, made an E. App. Past F.C. and raised to the sublime _____ and as such we do recommend him to the Brethren of all Regular constituted Lodges, to be admitted by them after due examination, to the said part of the friendly Mystery, and sacred ceremony thereof which belong to him; and that no improper use may be made hereof, our Brother, has subscribed his name under the seal of our Lodge, so that by causing him to write his name, a judgment may be had whether this Certificate be his own.

GIVEN under our Hands and Seal of the Lodge this 11th Day of February and of Masonry ____

S. Lancaster

J. Layton R.W.M.

_____ Secretary

Hertfordshire
F18: Selection from the John Gandy collection of nearly 600 Founders Jewels, 1900-30. ➢

John Gandy was a prolific collector and a founder of The Jewels of the Craft, who bequeathed over 3,000 jewels and 1,500 artefacts to the Province of Hertfordshire. His speciality was Founder's Jewels.

Hertfordshire
F19: Founder's Jewel: Cassiobury Lodge No. 3234, 1907. ⱴ

Cassiobury Lodge No. 3234 has met in Watford since it was constituted in 1907, and celebrated its centenary in 2007. The Jewel is part of the extensive collection bequeathed by John Gandy.

Hertfordshire
F20: Founder's Jewel: Caldwell Lodge No. 3201, 1907. ⱴ

Caldwell Lodge No. 3201 has met in March, Cambridgeshire since it was constituted in 1907, and celebrated its centenary in 2007. The Jewel is part of the extensive collection bequeathed by John Gandy.

Hertfordshire
F21: Past Master's Jewel, 1803. ➢

A silver Past Master's quadrant collar jewel of 1803, not engraved, but made by a Mr Atkins of Aldersgate Street, London. Mr Atkins was a witness at the Old Bailey at the trial of a man who robbed him in the street of his handkerchief, the judge saying, 'That as you did not steal his money or watch I will be lenient, and sentence you to four years hard labour'.

Hertfordshire
F22: Shaving Bowl, *c.*1820. ➢

A shaving bowl, approximately 200 years old, with Masonic symbols.

Hertfordshire
F23: RMIB Steward's Jewel presented to Sir Thomas F. Halsey, 1912. ➢

This 1912 Royal Masonic Institute for Boys Steward's Jewel, embellished with the initials TFH set with sapphires, garnets and seed pearls, was presented by the members of the Province of Hertfordshire to the Festival Chairman, Sir Thomas Frederick Halsey.

Sir Thomas Frederick Halsey, 1st Baronet (1839–1927), was a politician who sat in the House of Commons as a Conservative from 1874 to 1906. He took an active interest in all aspects of life in Hertfordshire – as Justice of the Peace; Deputy Chairman of the St Albans Quarter Sessions; after retiring from the Hertfordshire Yeomanry he joined the county Territorial Force Association, becoming its Chairman; and in 1908 was appointed a Deputy Lieutenant of Hertfordshire.

A very active Freemason, he was initiated in Apollo University Lodge No. 460 in 1861 and became a Joining Member of Westminster and Keystone Lodge No. 10 later the same year. He joined Watford Lodge No. 404 in 1863, Berkhampstead Lodge No. 504 in 1872, Grand Master's Lodge No. 1 in 1913, and was the Founding Master of Hertfordshire Masters' Lodge in 1920. He served as Provincial Grand Master for Hertfordshire from 1873 to 1923 and as Deputy Grand Master from 1903 until 1926.

Leicestershire
F24: Leicester Masonic Table, *c.*1825.

A *pietre dure* (literally 'hard stone') marble table, showing a depiction of King Solomon's Temple. The table has been dated from the early to mid nineteenth century. It is octagonal in form – a square upon a square – and its border depicts various jewels of office in marble slices. The central picture is of two Pillars and the entrance of the Temple, all of which stand on a chequered pavement.

It seems the table, known to be one of a small number made, may have been commissioned by English Masons resident on Malta with either the army, navy, mercantile or government in the early years of the nineteenth century. It was then shipped to England where it was fitted with its current base. The table was probably part of the furnishings of a stately home. Quite how it passed to a suburban house in Nuneaton, where it was until sold to the Museum in Leicester via an auction sale, still remains a mystery.

Northumberland
F25: 'Wooler' Master's Chair, *c.*1806.

The Master's Chair, which originally belonged to All Saints Lodge, Wooler, Northumberland, is decorated with Masonic symbols and the inscription *Sit Lux et Lux Fuit* – 'Let there be Light and there was Light'.

All Saints Lodge was originally warranted by the Moderns Grand Lodge in 1762 but was erased in 1775. In 1802 it was constituted under a Warrant from the Antients Grand Lodge as No. 189, and was subsequently re-numbered as No. 231 in 1814, No. 161 in 1832 and No. 138 in 1863. It met at the Black Bull Inn and the Anchor Inn, both in Wooler, Northumberland, before moving to the Sun Inn from 1806 until it handed in its Warrant in 1866. It is thought that the artwork on the Chair may have been the work of one of the Dalziel brothers, who were active Freemasons and engravers during the period when it is believed the chair was made.

Nottinghamshire
F26: Master's Chair, *c*.1760. ▶

It is thought that this Chair is after a design by Thomas Chippendale (1718-79) and there are designs very like it in his pattern book published in 1754, *The Gentleman and Cabinet-Makers Director*. The chair is a good example of the English rococo style *c*.1760, with its tall back and fluted, moulded and slightly out-turned uprights joined by a serpentine cresting rail, crisply carved in solid mahogany. At the top is scrolling leafage in rococo form, demonstrating the asymmetrical effect of this style. The carving includes Masonic emblems and of particular interest are the arms, terminating in clenched fists springing from cuffs, carved as pleated linen, probably in the manner of the second half of the eighteenth century. The chair is 5ft to the cresting rail, just over 2ft wide and the seat is some 21in above the floor – so many a smaller Master would need a footstool on which to rest his feet.

Nottinghamshire
F27: Warden's Chair, *c*.1840. ◀

The chair is early Victorian, probably one of a pair, and constructed in a substantial form with a rectangular outline. The overall black appearance of the mahogany has been achieved by a process of staining and polishing, known as ebonising. The whole chair is raised on massive acanthus-carved, cabriolet legs with claw and ball feet. The arms terminate in leopards' heads and the chair is 4ft 10in high and just under 2ft wide.

Nottinghamshire
F28: Limoges Enamels, *c*.1780. ➢

These two rare Masonic, Limoges enamelled panels date from the last quarter of the eighteenth century, are decorated with Masonic emblems, and each is 2in high. Such enamels were produced at Limoges in central France, the enamel being applied on a copper base, with a high survival rate as a result. They would have been worn as pendants, possibly hung from a ribbon, and were decorated on both sides. The Arms of the Moderns is depicted in a central cartouche.

Nottinghamshire
F29: Three Graduated Jugs, *c*.1790. ➢

A set of three graduated jugs for the Festive Board, elaborately gilded in the style of the Derby porcelain factory of the early nineteenth century. The jugs range in height from 6.5in to 5.5in and 4.5in. The jugs are profusely decorated with Masonic symbols and each on the front bears the name 'George Wildgoose Croydon'. Research has shown that a person of that name was initiated into the Patriotic Lodge No. 245 on 11 March 1784. The Lodge was established by the Moderns Grand Lodge in 1783, and numbered initially as No. 245 and subsequently after 1792 as No. 206. The Lodge met at the Greyhound Hotel in Croydon High Street. It appears that Wildgoose was a land surveyor and died on 26 February 1806, aged 61. The jugs could have been presented to him perhaps when he became Master of his Lodge.

Nottinghamshire
F30: Two Ceramic Masonic Figures after the Meissen original modelled by Johann Joachim Kändler, *c*.1774.

Hard-paste continental porcelain pieces from the late nineteenth century. One is a man in a tricorn hat and Masonic apron, holding a ruler. The figure is 9.5in high and has a pug dog on a pedestal. The figure of the lady in a full crinoline is 8.5in high and has a pug dog beneath her skirts.

The pug dogs are probably a reference to the Order of the Mopses, created in the 1730s by a number of German Catholics at a time when the Pope excommunicated Freemasonry. People invented their own ceremonies and a dog was chosen as a symbol because it signified fidelity. It is thought the founder of the organisation had a fondness for pug dogs and the name Mopses was chosen as a corruption of the German word for a pug dog *Mops*. The Order spread through Germany, the Netherlands, Austria, Flanders and into France. A significant difference between the Order of the Mopses and Freemasonry was that the Mopses did not swear an oath – as it was this act that led to excommunication by the Pope. The other major difference was that Mopses had both male and female members. In fact, there were two Masters of each lodge – or Grand Mopses as they were known – one of whom was a man and the other a woman, and they took it in turn to rule a lodge at six month intervals.

Nottinghamshire
F31: Thomas Wildman's Chain, 1822.

Colonel Thomas Wildman, then the Provincial Grand Master for Nottinghamshire, founded the Royal Sussex Lodge No. 402 in 1829. Wildman, a former school fellow of the poet Lord Byron, purchased Newstead Abbey from him in 1816. Wildman was a great friend of the Duke of Sussex, who often used to visit him at the Abbey.

The chain follows a traditional format of serpentine roping; six panels with initials GR (*Georgius Rex*) and stars and suspended from a chain; and a round badge with the word Nottinghamshire and encircling a Square and Compasses with acanthus leaf decoration. It is engraved on the reverse 'Thomas Wildman Esq, appointed Provincial Grand Master 30th April, AL5827 AD 1823.' The silver gilt is hallmarked London 1822 and there is an 18 carat duty mark and the maker's initials JA, which have not been identified.

West Lancashire
F32: Georgian Masonic Chairs, *c.*1790.

A set of three Masonic chairs, made from mahogany, with hand-painted panels, manufactured in the style of Thomas Chippendale. The chairs, which have been recently restored, were originally purchased by the Lodge of Lights No. 148, which was warranted in 1765. Unfortunately there is no record of the original purchase – the earliest sets of Minute Books were lost when the Lodge box was broken into and items stolen, during the time that the Lodge met at Linghams Coffee House, Horsemarket Street, Warrington.

F33: Early Lambskin Apron, *c.*1815.

A shaped, lambskin apron with the remains of a narrow border of red silk. There are printed Masonic emblems in black on the apron.

Beneath the apron is an illuminated description describing its provenance, which reads:

Marquis of Lorne Lodge No. 1354 Leigh Lancashire

I, the undersigned, do hereby certify that the apron enclosed in this frame was given to me by Bro Tatnai Radcliffe, of West Leigh, who stated that it had been given to his father by Peter France, of West Leigh, a private soldier in the British Army, who was engaged at the Battle of Waterloo, Sunday June 18th 1815, and who took the apron from the body of an officer lying dead upon the field of battle.

October 1880
James Jackson
PM 148 and 1354

Marquis of Lorne Lodge, No. 1354.
Leigh, Lancashire.

I, the undersigned, do hereby certify that the Apron enclosed in this frame was given to me by Bro. Tatnai Radcliffe, of West Leigh, who stated that it had been given to his father by Peter France, of West Leigh a private soldier in the British Army, who was engaged at the Battle of Waterloo, Sunday, June 18th 1815, and who took the Apron from the body of an officer lying dead upon the Field of Battle.

October, 1880.

F34: Commemorative Jewel, 1827.

A silver gilt, plate jewel made by Thomas Harper, depicting a scroll with a key and quill in saltire, with the lettering 'Lancashire' on the obverse and 'Western Division' on the reverse. The jewel bears the mark of Thomas Harper, who was over 90 when the jewel was made.

The Province of Lancashire was divided into the Eastern and Western Divisions in 1826; it is thought that this jewel was commissioned to commemorate the event.

F35: First Degree Tracing Board, 1864.

The Tracing Board was painted in oil on canvas by Henry Woods RA whilst he was a student at Warrington School of Art. Restored and reframed in 1907, it was donated to the Lodge of Lights No. 148, of which the artist's father was a member, by John Hesketh, a fellow student of the artist and himself a member of the Lodge.

Henry Woods was born in Warrington in 1846 and died in 1921 in Venice, Italy; he was renowned as one of the leading Neo-Venetian school of artists. He was also a member of the Royal Academy.

F36: Past Master's Collar Jewel, 1866. ▷

A Past Master's hallmarked collar jewel of unusual design – a circular, cast and engraved roundel with an engraved wheat and acacia design (indicating Grand Rank), the centre being a Set Square with a border and the 47th Proposition of Euclid suspended below.

This jewel was made for Gilbert Greenall, later Sir Gilbert Greenall, 1st Lord Daresbury, who was initiated into the Lodge of Lights No. 148 in 1850 and was Master in the centenary year 1865. The following year he was appointed and invested as Senior Grand Warden of the UGLE.

Worcestershire
F37: Provincial Grand Master's Collar Jewel belonging to John Dent, 1792.

John Dent (1761-1826) was an English banker – a partner in Child's Bank – and a politician – Tory Member of Parliament for Lancaster – who served as the second Provincial Grand Master (PGM) from 1792 to 1826. His appointment was based on patronage, which was not unusual at the time, and he was very much an absentee PGM; his duties were carried out locally by at least two Deputy Provincial Grand Masters during his tenure.

The Craft of Symbolism

Hugh O'Neill

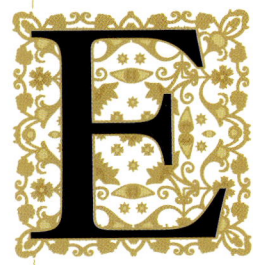*mpty the glare of Symbol and of Sign*
Unless th' internal import thro' them shine

Couplet inscribed on the inside bound cover of William Preston's *Syllabus* by Bro John Sherwood, initiated 18 January 1812 into Lodge of Antiquity No. 1 (now No. 2).

The above couplet makes it perfectly clear that Masonic knowledge seemed to have been as lacking at the time of the Union as it appears to be today in 2016. Herein it is hoped to address that lack to some extent.

First, it should be made clear that in no way can this be an exhaustive treatment of Masonic symbolism, nor could any such claim be made by any writer, as what is represented by any particular symbol is, and must inherently be, within the mind of the recipient and coloured by one's own personal experiences. What however it is hoped to do is to bring forward for both the Masonic and non-Masonic reader some commonly-held explanations, as well as reveal some less usual thoughts. In this endeavour we will look at symbols we encounter in the Degrees of Craft Freemasonry – also appropriately termed 'Symbolic Masonry' – under the English Constitution from the beginnings through the last 300 years up to the present day. During that time some symbols have made only brief appearances, while others have been with us from the outset, and still more have come into use at various times and remain in current use today. Although under the present English Constitution the Holy Royal Arch is included within pure ancient Freemasonry, we will here concentrate our focus on the three Craft Degrees, after an initial skirmish around symbolism in more general terms.

Symbolism in General

As defined by the Oxford English Dictionary, the word 'symbol' has a received meaning as an object regarded by general consent as naturally typifying or representing or recalling something by possessing analogous qualities, or by association in fact or thought. In brief, then, a symbol can be shorthand for something else. However, its meaning may overlap those of 'emblem', 'metaphor' or 'allegory'. By example and in our special context the overlaid and combined symbolic image of a Square and Compasses tends to call into our minds the general subject of Freemasonry. Further, it is probably true to say that the same tendency occurs in any person of whatever nationality or persuasion they may be, in any part of the civilised world. It is, then, a symbol widely recognised by general consent.

Within our lodges the use of symbolism is paramount in the transferring of ideas and concepts from the more versed members to Candidates for any of the Degrees or to the members generally. Indeed symbolism plays an integral part in the formation, or Consecration, of every new lodge **[G1]**. However, the import of a particular symbol depends very much upon the context within which it is used. There is, of course, no dogmatically fixed meaning for each and every one of them. For example, a pair of Compasses will at one time signify the seriousness of an undertaking and at another the limits of a person's attainments. A Square on its own and worn appended to a collar **[G2]** indicates the wearer to be Master of his lodge. In another context it would remind us to regulate our life and actions. A rather beautiful presentation 'jewel' **[G3]** would identify its wearer as a member of the then Wellington Lodge No. 707, Chepstow, sometime after 1820, doubtless named after the military hero of Waterloo, but it would carry no ritualistic signification at all.

The early catechism *Dialogue between Simon and Philip* (*c*.1725-40) records both the older cruciform and the later rectangular forms of a lodge, which include several symbolic items in diagram form as well as in the text and notes. As this and other early catechisms (most of which appear to be Exposures and so their accuracy cannot be relied upon) bear strong resemblances to each other and to other sources, we can be reasonably sure that the use of symbolic items was already well established by this time and an essential part of the 'work' of lodges. The conferral of the original two Degrees was a relatively brief affair, with much of the time being spent on working lectures by question and answer round the dining table, illustrating the import of the Degrees by reference to those symbols. In order to assist with these explanations, symbolic outlines (the 'lodge') would be drawn on the floor or, later in that century, physical objects would be used there or on the table. During the second half of the eighteenth century painted fabric floor cloths ('floorings') were being used and in some instances portable *pietra dura* (inlaid marble) 'lodge' designs. Several of these latter still exist in both Private Lodge Museums and in our Grand Lodge's Museum of Freemasonry.

One such 'Master's Tablet' **[G4]** depicts from left to right:

In the upper half: Square; Compasses with one point within a circle; rough ashlar beneath; two smooth ashlars, one with a lewis; Volume of the Sacred Law; pencil; Plumb rule.
In the lower half: Mosaic pavement; two grand parallels; draughtsman's building plan, within which are depicted a mound and three groups of five; Jacob's Ladder of three rounds.
The two halves are separated by a draughtsman's square, with the whole being surrounded by a tessellated border.

In this context we could say the symbols shown remind us that the Square regulates our actions; the Compasses keep our conduct within due bounds; the Point keeps us from straying; the rough ashlar represents our untutored self; the smooth ashlar our educated self, ready and useful; the lewis supports us in old age; the Volume of the Sacred Law is the Divine plan and revealed will of the Great Architect of the Universe; the pencil says that our words, thoughts and actions are recorded by Him to whom we must give an account; the Plumb rule represents our upright intentions; the pavement the joys and sorrows of this world; the grand parallels which were at that time the two Saints John but now, since the 1813 Union, relate to Moses and Solomon; the plan of the Temple is within each of us; the mound is the grave of our inevitable destiny; the three groups of five are those who went to search for that which was lost; Jacob's ladder connects this world with the heavenly mansions by the virtues of faith hope and charity.

As implied already, events connected with the first Temple, built by King Solomon about 1,000 years BC, are used as an allegory for the construction of our own individual internal 'temple' – the care taken to avoid 'pollution'; the very special place within us for the Holy of Holies and the Shekinah; the winding stair as a symbol of upward progress through education and of the intricate windings of this mortal life; absolute fidelity even in the face of the direst consequences **[G5] [G6] [G7] [G8]**.

Symbolism in the Degrees

The symbols displayed, or rather hidden in full view, on the Degree or Trestle Boards – more commonly called Tracing Boards – these days are worthy of further consideration. Generally accepted as the most beautiful in execution, clarity and detail are those produced by Josiah Bowring, of which there are but twelve sets extant in the world. Depicted here is the set belonging to Lodge of Honor and Generosity No. 165, painted in 1819. Bowring's earliest known single 'lodge' board, covering all the Degrees, was painted in 1796 and belongs to the Lodge St George No. 200, SC, Bermuda. All the others are in sets of three and were the forerunners of what was to follow, particularly in the use of perspective; earlier ones by John Cole and John Browne being somewhat two-dimensional. Later boards produced to John Harris's designs show, to some tastes, rather grandiose Georgian architectural elements. It is well worth exploring the symbolism contained in Bowring's First, Second and Third Degree boards, drawn largely from William Preston's *Illustrations of Masonry* **[G9]**.

First Degree

[G10] What particularly strikes the attention are the three prominent columns with the initial letters W, S and B on their bases, standing for Wisdom, Strength and Beauty. To us, the capitals at the top, in the Ionic, Doric and Corinthian orders, are symbols for those virtues whereby the wisdom to contrive is balance by the strength to support, thus creating a beautiful edifice worthy of adornment. Central to the arrangement is Jacob's Ladder, explained above, with female symbolic figures for Faith, Hope (with an anchor) and Charity (with children). On Bowring's earlier boards, dating from before the omission of overtly religious emblems, the first figure holds a Christian cross. The Ladder rests on the open Volume of the Sacred Law (VSL), signifying that requirement in order to ascend to the immortal mansions, symbolised by the firmament containing an irradiated All-Seeing Eye, the sun and the moon, with seven stars representing the seven planets then known. Suspended from the Ladder by a thread is a key, symbolically the tongue of good report hanging in a brother's defence and which does not lie. The Square and Compasses properly set upon the VSL completes the Three Great Lights of Freemasonry mentioned above. The two grand parallels are now tangentially combined with the circle of eternity and its centre from which as Masons we cannot err. In the background are two ashlars, rough (with the tools an apprentice would need) and smooth as described above, while in the foreground is the true tracing board on which the Master lays out his designs. At the foot of the columns are the three jewels which are movable to new officers at the Installation of a new Master; the Square symbolising the guide to all his actions, the Level to symbolise the use of equal measures in assisting the Master in ruling his lodge and the Plumb rule to symbolise the integrity of those same measures. There is yet a final symbol to which we will here turn our attention: another pair of Compasses on the pavement before the Master's column of Wisdom in the 'east', with a gold dot at one of its points. On Bowring's earlier 1811 board, those Compasses and the accompanying dot are shown at the foot of the board in the 'west', as that was then the location for a Candidate taking his Obligation. By 1819, after the Union, the Candidate was taking his Obligation in front of the Master in the 'east', hence the movement. The remaining two gold dots at the foot, one on the border and one outside, complete the symbolism of the 'perfect points of entrance', reference to which has all but disappeared from our various lodge rituals. That explanation is given in William Preston's First Lecture, Section I, clause 2 and may be summarised thus: 'of, at and on' – 'having come of one's free will and accord, knocked at the door of the Lodge and obligated on the point of a sharp instrument'. So, those three gold dots are important symbols, unique to Bowring's boards and have been found on no others.

Thus the symbolism depicted on the First Degree board is quite deep and complex, certainly worthy of considerable contemplation.

Second Degree

The board illustrated **[G11]** is in the same set as the first above. Again, pillars are prominent and the overall design appears simple but belies the symbolic complexities beneath the surface view. The Palladian structure containing a mosaic-floored chamber is what might be expected, guarded by a Junior and a Senior Warden. But the staircase, unusually in this design, goes the 'wrong' way – or does it? In more conventional designs in general use today, the stairs are shown to spring from the left side of the picture ascending anti-clockwise. Biblically we are told that the opening was in the south side of the Holy Place. That means ascending from the south, anti-clockwise toward the west. Now, the Temple had the Holy Place at its west end. When lodge rooms were first laid out, church practice was followed in that they were oriented with the Holy Place at the east end; the reverse of Solomon's Temple. So, our movement now becomes from the north towards the east. This can be justified in a symbolic sense, as the winding stair can represent to us the intricate windings of this mortal life, springing from the north, whence we commenced our Masonic journey in the First Degree, towards the east whence all wisdom emanates. As to the image on this unusual Second Degree board, where the stairs ascend in a clockwise direction, there was undoubtedly confusion in the minds of designers and of those who commissioned the paintings. It should also be noted that many boards of this Degree, including this one, have no cardinal points marked in the border as do others of the First and Second, presumably so that Brethren would not feel constrained when arranging the board for use in their lodge. However, using the symbolism just given, it matters not which way the stair turns, only that it winds.

This board by Bowring has at its foot a scenic illustration of part of the Traditional History expounded during the conferral of the Degree and is not alone in possessing this feature.

Third Degree

In this 1819 design **[G12]** one sees a mixture of pre – and post-Union symbols. Aaron's rod in bud (Numbers 17: 8) was a symbol of God's authority for the tribe of Levi to hold the priesthood. In lodges and in society generally to this day, certain officers carry rods as symbols of the authority vested in them. The pot of manna is symbolic of divine or spiritual nourishment. Neither of these two elements has survived into Masonic rituals today and hence is not shown on modern boards. The acacia was associated in ancient Egyptian mythology with the tree of life and for us can symbolise the hope of life eternal. Apart from the obvious emblems of mortality, other symbols shown have already been described but one can see here for the first time an instrument called a skirret, the etymology of which is uncertain and which symbolises that our conduct in life should not deviate from what is laid down in the VSL and exemplified by the Tables containing the Ten Commandments. Five points of behaviour towards one another are appropriately linked in a circle of fellowship. The three figures '5' refer to the three groups of five who went to search for that which was lost. What lies behind the closed door of the porchway or entrance, through which we must all of necessity travel, is hidden from the view of our mortal eyes.

In conclusion, whilst symbolism is a fundamental element of the ritual of Freemasonry, it is true to say that with the passage of time – as it is in many aspects of modern life – the meaning of esoteric Freemasonry has waned somewhat for the majority of Masons. Yet, even this brief introduction illustrates how much the symbolism of Craft Freemasonry has to offer to the deep-thinking and contemplative Mason.

G1: Silver Gilt Cornucopia and Ewers, 1852.

The set of silver gilt vessels are used in the ceremony for the formation, known as the Consecration, of a new lodge and in the laying of a Foundation Stone for a new building. The former ceremony involves the scattering of corn, the pouring of wine, the sprinkling of oil and the strewing of salt – emblematically to symbolise, respectively: abundance and plenty; joy and gladness; peace and harmony; and fidelity, hospitality and everlasting friendship.

The ewers and cornucopia were purchased in 1852 from Lambert & Rawlings, together with two columns and ivory mauls, at a cost of £194. 14s. 6d. (£2,000 itm). George Lambert was a Freemason who was made Grand Sword Bearer in Grand Lodge in 1881, and was Prime Warden of the Goldsmiths Company in 1887. The firm of George Lambert started up in 1819 and closed in 1916. The makers' marks are those of Charles Thomas Fox and George Fox, silversmiths, who made a number of pieces for Lambert & Rawlings.

G2: John James Howell Coe, c.1819. ▸

Portrait in oils, by an unknown artist, of John James Howell Coe, who served as a Grand Steward in 1819. He is shown wearing the distinctive red apron of a Grand Steward and the collar and jewel of the Master of Peace and Harmony Lodge No. 82 (now No. 60), in addition to a very ornate Past Master's jewel and one indicating that he is the Past Principal of a Royal Arch Chapter.

G3: Wellington Lodge Jewel, 1820. ▾

The jewel takes the form of an oval pendant 3.5in high, and features a Square and Compasses design around the letter G, with a sunburst above and a set of steps below. On the reverse is the inscription dated 31 July 1820: 'To Bro Henry Smith, Junior Warden of the Wellington Lodge, Chepstow No. 707. This medal is presented as a token of respect for his great assistance in promoting the welfare of the lodge'.

Wellington Lodge No. 707 was formed in 1818 and no doubt named after the military hero of Waterloo. It met originally at the Beaufort Arms, Beaufort Square, Chepstow and then from 1820 at the Bell Inn in Chepstow. It enjoyed only a short life as a Lodge, closing before 1837 due to lack of members. The only known surviving document of the Lodge is a list of its sixteen members in 1819, which includes Henry Smith, whose occupation is given as auctioneer.

G4: Master's Tablet, *c*.1800. ➤

Tracing Boards take their origin from the earliest days of Freemasonry when a lodge board was drawn either on the table around which the Brethren sat or else on the floor of the lodge room. The lodge board would consist of the various Masonic symbols, usually drawn in chalk specifically for that evening's ceremony or illustrating some aspect of the Degree. At the end of the evening it was normally part of the role of the Tyler of the lodge to make sure the design was cleaned up and cleared away so that it would not be seen by those not qualified to do so. By the late 1700s other methods were being used that avoided the need for the designs to be re-drawn on each occasion, including floor cloths and symbolic tablets for placing on the Master's pedestal. After the Union between the two Grand Lodges in 1813 Tracing Boards were introduced, which were not only more manageable but also ensured some level of consistency in terms of design.

G5: *King Solomon's Temple*: Robert Sayer, *c*.1760. ◀

Robert Sayer (1725-94) is first recorded as a print seller in 1748. He purchased stock from print sellers and engravers such as John Senex (in 1755) and John Rocque (in 1762) and became a leading figure in the print, map and chart business.

King Solomon's Temple and its innermost and most sacred part – the Sanctum Santorum, in which was housed the Ark of the Covenant, containing the tablets given to Moses by God – were built both as a testament and a physical demonstration of man's faith in God. The construction of the Temple and the events surrounding it play a significant part in Masonic ritual, combining elements from the Old Testament with Masonic tradition. It is not surprising therefore that King Solomon's Temple forms a significant feature in Masonic literature and art, especially in the early years of Freemasonry. Artistic licence is combined with the use of measurements and details contained in the Bible in an attempt to reconstruct the Temple in scale models and in paintings or engravings. The engravings were later widely reproduced as transfer prints on ceramics.

G6: *An Accurate Description of the Grand and Glorious Temple of Solomon* by Jacob Juda Lyon: Frontispiece – a reprint of the 1675 publication, 1778. ▽

G7: *Orbis Miraculum or The Temple of Solomon portrayed by scripture-light…* by Samuel Lee, 1659. ▽▷

G8: *The Builder's Dictionary*: Frontispiece, 1734. ➤

'The Builder's Dictionary: or, Gentleman and Architect's Companion ... containing the theory and practice of the various branches of that useful and noble art requisite to be known by masons ... Being a work of great use, not only to artificers, but likewise to gentlemen, and other, concerned in building'. The frontispiece shows two gentleman architects.

G9: William Preston: *Illustrations of Masonry*, 1772. ⌄

The bookplate from the first edition with the arms of Charles, 12th Viscount Dillon (1745-1813), Deputy Grand Master of the Moderns Grand Lodge at the time of publication.

To Face the Title.

To build, to plant whatever you intend
To rear the Column or y^e Arch to bend
To Swell the Tarras or to Sink y^e Grot
In all, let Nature never be forgot.
                                        Pope.

G10: Craft First Degree Tracing Board by Josiah Bowring, 1819.

A set of Tracing Boards for the First, Second and Third Degrees of Craft Freemasonry by the painter Josiah Bowring (1757-1832), on loan from the Lodge of Honor and Generosity No. 165.

Tracing boards take their origin from the earliest days of Freemasonry when a lodge board was drawn either on the table around which the Brethren sat or else on the floor of the lodge room. The lodge board would consist of the various Masonic symbols, usually drawn in chalk specifically for that evening's ceremony or illustrating some aspect of the Degree. At the end of the evening it was normally part of the role of the Tyler of the lodge to make sure the design was cleaned up and cleared away so that it would not be seen by those not qualified to do so. By the late 1700s other methods were being used which avoided the need for the designs to be re-drawn on each occasion, including floor cloths and symbolic tablets for placing on the Master's pedestal. After the Union between the two Grand Lodges in 1813 Tracing Boards were introduced, which were not only more manageable but also ensured some level of consistency in terms of design.

G11: Craft Second Degree Tracing Board by Josiah Bowring, 1819.

G12: Craft Third Degree Tracing Board by Josiah Bowring, 1819.

Freemasons' Hall, London

Dr James Campbell

Freemasonry had flourished in England for a long time before it saw any need for its own buildings. Lodges met in hired rooms in taverns. The Grand Lodge of England was founded on 24 June 1717 with just four lodges and it met for the first time in a room in the Goose and Gridiron Tavern in St Paul's Churchyard [A12]. Many of the first Grand Officers and Grand Masters were drawn from members of the aristocracy and this led to an initial surge in membership and an increase in the number of lodges in the early eighteenth century. The Sword still used by Grand Lodge today was presented by one of these aristocratic Grand Masters, Thomas Howard (1683-1732), 8th Duke of Norfolk, who was installed in 1730 [H1].

By 1730 the original four lodges had increased to sixty-one and by 1768 there were over 400 lodges, 130 of which were in London. In the 1750s the first Grand Lodge suffered from poor management. Attendances at Quarterly meetings fell off. The Grand Master and Grand Secretary threatened lodges that failed to send a representative with expulsion and indeed expelled a number of lodges. The result was a good deal of ill-feeling, which helped to bolster the number of lodges and Freemasons breaking away and joining a new rival Antients Grand Lodge, which had been formed in 1751. The 1760s saw increasing attempts by the first Grand Lodge to stem the tide. Having a prestigious building was one way to raise the standing of the older Grand Lodge and distinguish it from its newer rival. Another problem was simply one of size: by the 1760s it was becoming increasingly difficult to find places large enough for the Premier Grand Lodge to meet. Taverns were fine for the lodges themselves but no longer big enough for the Quarterly meetings.

The idea for a building for Grand Lodge was first mooted in 1768 but nothing much was done until Robert Edward Petre (1742-1801), 9th Baron Petre, became Grand Master in 1772. He appointed a Hall Committee to look into the problem. It met for the first time on 12 May 1773 and subsequently decided that Grand Lodge should acquire premises in Covent Garden. They purchased 61 Great Queen Street, a substantial house with a garden and coach-house behind. The whole site was 44ft wide (13.4m) and 200ft deep (60.9m). The next problem was who should design the Hall. As there were no previous purpose-designed Halls, there were no precedents to draw on. Grand Lodge chose as their architect the first Professor of Architecture at the Royal Academy, Thomas Sandby (1723-98), and he became the first and only person to bear the title Grand Architect.

Thomas Sandby's Freemasons' Hall

Sandby's Freemasons' Hall was completely hidden from the street, in the garden behind the house. This Hall no longer survives: it was demolished when the current Freemason's Hall was built in the 1920s, but it occupied the space currently taken up by the room that lies alongside the Connaught Rooms Grand Hall and is used today for drinks receptions before Quarterly Communications.

The Hall that Sandby built was entered through a modest side door off the street, down a long passage and then up three short flights of stairs. The element of surprise must have been considerable. Raised above a basement, it consisted of a huge, single, first floor room, 78ft (24m) long, 43ft (13.2m) wide and 58ft (17.8m) high. The Hall was illustrated in Pugin's *Illustrations of the Public Buildings of London* (1825) in which it was described as an 'elegant and finely proportioned room, and both in architectural character and decoration … strictly appropriate to the purpose for which it was designed.' [K7] [K8].

Sandby's Hall became a popular venue not just for Masons but for all sorts of meetings including those of the Royal Humane Society, the Academy of Ancient Music and numerous charity events. The Hall was officially dedicated in a meeting open to non-Masonic visitors on 23 May 1776, with an elaborate ceremony accompanied by music especially composed for the occasion [H2].

The Hall was paid for by a tontine and by selling medals. Two rather special medals are preserved in the Museum [H3]. The first belonged to Sandby, the architect of the Hall, while the second belonged to Chevalier Ruspini, the founder of the Masonic School for Girls. A tontine was a popular form of raising money at the time. Donors paid £50 to take part and nominated a person (themselves or more typically a child) to receive an equal share of £250 divided amongst all the nominated people each year. Thus as the numbers of nominated people gradually died, a greater share of the £250 went to each of the remainder. Ann Ellis, the last surviving nominee, was aged 2 when she was nominated and was 89 when she died in 1869, having received the whole sum for the last few years of her life.

Thomas Sandby's New Freemasons' Tavern

The house in front of the Hall was knocked down in 1788-89 and the Freemasons' Tavern built in its place. The Grand Lodge rented this and its successors to a series of landlords over the next 150 years with varying degrees of success; eventually after substantial alterations converting it into the New Connaught Rooms as they exist today. This building acted as the public front to the Hall. It contained private dining rooms for hire for meetings and of course supplied the food for dinners held in the Hall. All external traces of this building were removed in the subsequent re-buildings of the Hall in the nineteenth century, but luckily various images survive to show us clearly what it was like at the time [H4] [H5].

Sir John Soane's Temple

The Union of the Antients and Moderns in 1813 provided not only a cause for celebration, but also the need for an expansion of the current premises. The Antients Grand Lodge had never had its own Hall so it was obvious where the alteration should be made. A number of plots behind the buildings to the east of Sandby's Hall were purchased. The chosen architect for the extension was Sir John Soane (1753-1837), who had become Professor of Architecture at the Royal Academy. The choice of Soane appears to have been through the direct intervention of the Grand Master, the Duke of Sussex. Soane was not at the time a Freemason, but this was hastily rectified. He was initiated in November 1813 and immediately promoted to Grand Superintendent of Works, a rank entirely invented for him (Sandby, already a Freemason, had been given the unique title of Grand Architect in a similar way). Soane was first engaged in minor alterations, but additional properties were purchased enabling the building of a new extension with a new kitchen and hall above in 1828-31. Sandby's Hall was retained and was used as the banqueting hall and for larger meetings, but Soane's room was reserved entirely as a lodge room and quickly became known as 'the Temple' [H6]. Despite the fact that it has been much praised by architectural historians ever since, Soane's Temple was not popular with Freemasons. It was impractical for working the new, more elaborate ritual and they disliked its idiosyncratic, novel style, in every way preferring Sandby's more traditional rectangular hall.

Soane also designed the Ark of the Masonic Covenant, a triangular pedestal that sat in front of the Grand Master's Chair in 1813 and contained the Articles of Union of the two Grand Lodges. This was a rather wonderful piece of design, typical of Soane's style. It was sadly lost in a later fire [H7].

Philip Hardwick's alterations

Soane had barely been buried when in 1838 plans were put forward for alterations and extensions to the Temple he had so carefully designed. The alterations were made by Philip Hardwick (1792-1870), who was a Freemason and had succeeded Soane as Grand Superintendent of Works. A prolific architect, Hardwick's best surviving work is the Goldsmiths' Hall in Foster Lane, London. In Great Queen Street, he added an extra bay and an apse to lengthen Soane's Hall, making it more suitable for the new ceremonies. Even then, Freemasons continued to dislike the room and the premises as a whole. By the 1850s there was a growing feeling that the piecemeal nature of the present Hall, which by then included the public house (the Freemasons' Tavern) and a hotel (the Bacon Hotel), was unsatisfactory and not befitting the dignity of the institution. They resolved to rebuild the whole complex, retaining Sandby's Hall and the Bacon Hotel, but demolishing all the other buildings, including Soane's temple, by then mutilated. A competition was held in 1863 to choose an architect. The surprise winner of the competition was the young Frederick Pepys Cockerell (1833-78).

Frederick Pepys Cockerell's Hall

Cockerell's design was deceptively simple. The front part of the building, including Sandby's Freemasons' Tavern, was demolished and a new building created behind a classical, three-bay façade. The entrance and Sandby's Hall were created using Portland stone. An eastern bay in a more modest style contained the grand staircase and a new dining hall where Soane's Temple had been. The building committee had initially been uncertain about appointing Cockerell, who was only 30 at the time and a young and untried architect, and they asked for testimonials. Sydney Smirke wrote 'that there is no young member of the profession more likely to produce a fine and original work of art than Mr F. Cockerell.' Cockerell's design reversed the move of the Masonic meetings from Sandby's Hall to Soane's Temple. Now the meetings were held in Sandby's Hall and the members moved to the new banqueting hall to eat. Cockerell's dining hall is still in use today as the main Banqueting Hall of the New Connaught Rooms. It contains no Masonic decoration, perhaps because it was always seen as a room that could be hired out to non-Masons [H8].

The building was completed in 1869. The work had been paid for by money left over from the tontine for Sandby's building, but now the building fund was entirely depleted and there was no money left to fund the inauguration. The solution was to call for Stewards, who in return for funding the celebration would each receive a jewel [H9].

Fourteen years later in 1883 a dramatic fire swept through Sandby's Hall, gutting its interior and destroying the fine paintings that lined the walls. At this point the possibility of building a new Hall in the Adelphi was first discussed. However the insurance only covered reinstatement, so this is what was done. Sir Horace Jones, Freemason, and Architect and Surveyor of the City of London, who was responsible for the design of Smithfield, Billingsgate and Leadenhall markets, was the Grand Superintendent of Works at the time and oversaw the reconstruction. In the decades that followed Grand Lodge managed to acquire more of the houses on the same side of the street, which became offices; and to make minor alterations to the Tavern, which was renamed the Connaught Rooms in 1909, before the First World War halted further development.

Ashley and Newman's Hall

On 27 June 1919 an Especial Grand Lodge was held in the Albert Hall to celebrate the end of the First World War. The then Grand Master, the Duke of Connaught, was too ill to attend but expressed a wish for a 'perpetual Memorial' in the form of a new Grand Lodge building. A Committee was formed and in 1920 an appeal was launched in the national newspapers to raise £1 million. The money was entirely from Freemasons, who were given special jewels to wear in honour of the money donated [H10]. On Saturday, 8 August 1925 Olympia hosted the largest banquet ever held for 8,000 Masons to celebrate the success of the appeal. Photographs of the banquet were published in all the leading newspapers.

While fundraising progressed, the Committee, aided by the Grand Superintendent of Works Alexander Burnett Brown, investigated sites. Grand Lodge had managed to acquire the remaining sites along Great Queen Street in 1920, so that it now owned a substantial part of the whole block, including the corner with Wild Street. However the Committee were still not sure that Covent Garden was the most appropriate site and considered moving to the Adelphi, an option that had been considered before. In the end there were concerns over the securing of the freehold and they decided to stay put. The Committee then turned to the question of the selection of an architect. The building was going to be substantial, so it was decided that it should be the subject of an international architectural competition, to be overseen by the Royal Institute of British Architects (RIBA). The rules required three judges. The Grand Superintendent of Works was one; Walter Crane, a Freemason architect was chosen as the second; the selection of the third assessor was left up to the RIBA. The Grand Superintendent of Works reported to the Building Committee at the meeting on 19 September 1924 that 'The President of the RIBA had nominated as Assessor Sir Edwin Lutyens RA [not himself a Freemason] who, though at present in India, would, it was understood, accept the appointment'.

The judges unanimously selected the winning scheme and at the Hall Committee meeting on 4 May 1926 the sealed envelope was opened to reveal the name of the winning practice [H11]. Ashley and Newman had entered into partnership in 1907 when they won an architectural competition for extending Birmingham Council House. They were moderately successful, designing banks, factories, hospital extensions and houses. They were not a large practice and work on the Peace Memorial Hall and its subsequent extensions sustained the office for the next decades.

The Building Completed

Demolition of the remaining building on the site began in March 1927 and on 14 July 1927 the Foundation Stone was laid by means of an electrical relay from a special Masonic meeting held in the Royal Albert Hall. The construction was carefully recorded in photographs at every stage and the complete Clerk of Works' diaries for the project are preserved in the Library at Great Queen Street **[H12]**.

The structure was a steel frame with an external skin of Portland stone **[H13] [H14] [H15] [H16]**. Building proceeded quickly and by 1931 the first six Lodge Rooms were completed at the rear of the building and accommodation provided for the staff. The first lodge meeting was held on 15 September 1931. Work then began on demolishing the Victorian offices. In the process Sandby's Hall was found to be unsafe and had to be demolished. The new building was officially dedicated on 19 July 1933. On 22 July 1933 *The London Illustrated News* devoted a special issue to the building with an architectural appreciation written by A. Trystan Edwards FRIBA (1884-1973), an architectural critic and writer.

The Masonic Peace Memorial becomes Freemasons' Hall

At the outbreak of the Second World War the optimism expressed in the title 'Masonic Peace Memorial' in 1933 seemed tragically misplaced and the name was quietly dropped. Today it is known simply as Freemasons' Hall. The building, an outstanding example of art deco architecture, is frequently featured in films. It remains an important symbol of the United Grand Lodge of England, an institution that has survived for 300 years.

H1: Sword of State of the United Grand Lodge of England, 1735.

The ceremonial Sword is carried in front of the Grand Master by the Grand Sword Bearer in meetings of Grand Lodge.

The Sword is reputed to have been found lying across the body of Gustavus II Adolphus, King of Sweden (1611-32) at the Battle of Lützen in November 1632. It came into the possession of the eighth Duke of Norfolk who in 1730, during his term as Grand Master, presented it to the Grand Lodge. The silver gilt hilt and mounts on the scabbard were made in 1730 by George Moody, the first Grand Sword Bearer of Grand Lodge and armourer to George I and George II; they were restored by Wilkinson Sword in 1964.

H2: Ode and Anthem composed for the Dedication of the Temple at Freemasons' Hall, 1776.

The music was specially composed for the event by John Abraham Fisher. Although the idea for a Hall had been put forward in 1768, the site was not purchased until 1774. The Foundation Stone was laid in 1775 and the Hall was officially dedicated at a ceremony on 23 May 1776. Non-Masonic visitors (male and female) were admitted to join in parts of the event.

H3: Freemasons' Hall Medal, 1780.

Designed by Lewis Pingo, these medals were issued to Freemasons who lent money to help pay for the first Freemasons' Hall (Sandby's Hall) in Great Queen Street. These two particular jewels were presented to Thomas Sandby and Bartholomew Ruspini respectively. Sandby was the architect of the Hall and Ruspini the founder of the Masonic School for Girls.

The cost of building the Hall had been estimated at £6,500 but the final cost was more than double this figure, finishing at £15,000 (£1.5 million itm). To help pay this debt, Grand Lodge asked its members to lend them an interest-free sum of £25, to be repaid when possible. Lodges could also subscribe to the scheme and in total eighty-two individuals and twenty-six lodges contributed, raising a total of £2,700. In return, the lenders received this commemorative medal, known as the Freemasons' Hall Medal. The amount raised through the provision of medals was not sufficient and hence a variety of other methods were employed to raise the balance of the necessary finance. One of the most successful, and a popular means at the time, was a tontine – which was in essence a lottery, where subscribers paid an agreed sum into the fund. As members died, their shares devolved to the other participants. On the death of the penultimate member the capital passed to the last survivor.

H4: Freemasons' Tavern, 1783.
Watercolour by John Nixon (1760-1818).

The building of a dedicated Freemasons' Hall was first put forward in 1768. In 1774 the premier Grand Lodge acquired two houses and a garden in Wild Court, Great Queen Street. The Freemasons' Coffee House operated in part of the rear house and in 1779 it was transferred to the front house and converted into the Freemasons' Tavern. A plan prepared by Thomas Sandby (1721-98), the Grand Architect (but seemingly carried out by William Tyler) resulted in the rebuilding of the Tavern between 1788 and 1789 with Freemasons' Hall built behind it – where the garden had been, with no street frontage.

H5: Earthenware Dish showing the Freemasons' Tavern, 1820.

The transfer print based on the watercolour by John Nixon shows Freemasons' Tavern in 1789.

The earthenware dish is part of a dinner service, almost certainly commissioned for use within the Tavern by Jackson Cuff (1779-1848), who was the innkeeper at Freemasons' Tavern from 1808 to 1845.

H6: Watercolour of Sir John Soane's Hall, showing the Ark of the Masonic Covenant, 1828.

A painting by the English artist Joseph Michael Gandy (1771-1843), who was noted for his original paintings illustrating Sir John Soane's architectural designs. Sir John Soane (1753-1837) is probably the most famous architect to have been involved in the design of Freemasons' Hall. He was responsible for adding another Hall, completed in 1831, alongside the one designed by Sandby, with whom he coincidentally shared the distinction of being a Professor of Architecture at the Royal Academy. Soane also designed the Ark of the Masonic Covenant, here depicted – with artistic licence – apparently at the front of the painting on the Senior Warden's pedestal, rather than in front of the Grand Master's throne, presumably on the basis that if it had been placed in its intended position it would not have made the same impact in the picture.

Sir John Soane enjoyed a meteoric career in Freemasonry. Initiated, passed and raised in the three Degrees of Freemasonry all in one day on 25 November 1813, he was able to witness on 1 December 1813 the Duke of Sussex, the Grand Master of the Moderns, being 're-made' as an Antient Mason so as to enable him to attend the Installation of his brother the Duke of Kent as the Grand Master of the Antients. At the meeting of Grand Lodge on 27 December, when the Act of Union was formally approved, Soane was appointed as the inaugural Grand Superintendent of Works, a post he held until his death in 1837.

H7: Reception of HRH The Prince of Wales as Past Grand Master, 1869.

The painting, by Sigismund Rosenthal (1813-84), shows the scene when Albert Edward, Prince of Wales (later Edward VII, 1841–1910) was invested as Past Grand Master in December 1869, having been initiated the previous year in Sweden.

Freemasons' Hall, designed by Sandby, continued in use until the 1920s, having been rebuilt after a fire in 1883. The painting offers a rare contemporary view of the interior, and shows Soane's Ark at the bottom of the steps.

Also worth noting is the statue of the Duke of Sussex in the alcove behind the throne [A11]. It was installed there in 1846 and sculpted by Edward Hodges Bailey, best known for the statue of Nelson on the top of Nelson's column in Trafalgar Square. The statue survived the fire of 1883 and is now situated in the corridor leading to the old Board of General Purposes meeting room.

H8: Cockerell's Freemasons' Hall, 1869.

Cockerell's Hall was completed in 1869. The symmetrical façade conceals a more complicated plan behind. Sandby's Hall was behind the left hand side of this main façade and this section still remains today. The much less grand façade beyond it on the left was also new, and was the Tavern with the Banqueting Hall behind. It replaced Soane's Temple. This facade still survives, much altered behind, as the Connaught Rooms. The building on the far left in the background was the Bacon Hotel, which was largely untouched by Cockerell but later demolished to make way for Mark Masons' Hall which occupied the site from 1899-1939.

H9: Freemasons' Hall Steward's Jewel, 1869.

Presented to Bro Albert W. Woods. The obverse features the bust of the then Grand Master, Thomas, 2nd Earl of Zetland; and on the reverse an illustration of the new Hall. The inauguration ceremony of the second Freemasons' Hall took place on 14 April 1869, attended by 127 specially-appointed Stewards who paid a fee of six guineas for the privilege and who each received this commemorative jewel bearing the scheme's design.

The first Freemasons' Hall proved to be too small and in the 1820s another Hall was built alongside Sandby's, designed by Sir John Soane. When the third Freemasons' Hall was completed in 1869 to the designs of Frederick Pepys Cockerell (1833-78), it incorporated Sandy's original Hall, but sadly Soane's Hall was demolished.

H10: Silver Hallstone Jewel, *c*.1920. ➤

Presented to Bro T.A. Fox of Lodge of Charity No. 4431. The jewel was designed by Bro Cyril Spackman, whose design was chosen in a public competition.

At an Especial meeting of Grand Lodge in 1919, the Grand Master, the Duke of Connaught and Strathearn, suggested that a new Headquarters for English Freemasonry be built as a permanent memorial to over 3,000 Masons who had died during the First World War. As in previous cases, it was decided to raise funds to finance the new building by means of subscription from individual members, lodges, Provinces and Districts. The Masonic Million Memorial Fund was established in 1920. For contributions over a certain amount, a Hallstone jewel was awarded to individual members – in silver for a contribution of 10 guineas, and gold for one of a 100 guineas.

A lodge donating an average of 10 guineas (£375 itm) per member was awarded a gold version of the jewel, to be worn on a collarette by the Master. A Province or District which donated an average of 500 guineas per lodge was awarded a gold and enamel version, to be worn on a collarette by the Provincial or District Grand Master.

The official description of the Hallstone design reads: 'The jewel is in the form of a cross, symbolising Sacrifice, with a perfect square at the four ends, on the left and right, squares being the dates 1914-1918, the years in which the supreme sacrifice was made. Between these is a winged figure of Peace presenting the representation of a Temple with special Masonic allusion in the Pillars, Porch and Steps. The medal is suspended by the Square and Compasses, attached to a riband, the whole thus symbolising the Craft's gift of a Temple in memory of those brethren who gave all for King and Country, Peace and Victory, Liberty and Brotherhood'.

H11: Freemasons' Hall – the winning competition scheme by Ashley and Newman, 1927. ▽

The current Grade II* listed building was built to a design, chosen in a public competition, by architects Henry Victor Ashley (1872-1945) and F. Winton Newman (1878-1953). Initially known as the Masonic Peace Memorial, the name was changed to Freemasons' Hall at the outbreak of the Second World War in 1939.

H12: Freemasons' Hall – Clerk of Works' Diary, 1928-29.

A remarkable and fascinating record of the day-to-day work carried out on site throughout the construction of the building of the Masonic Peace Memorial.

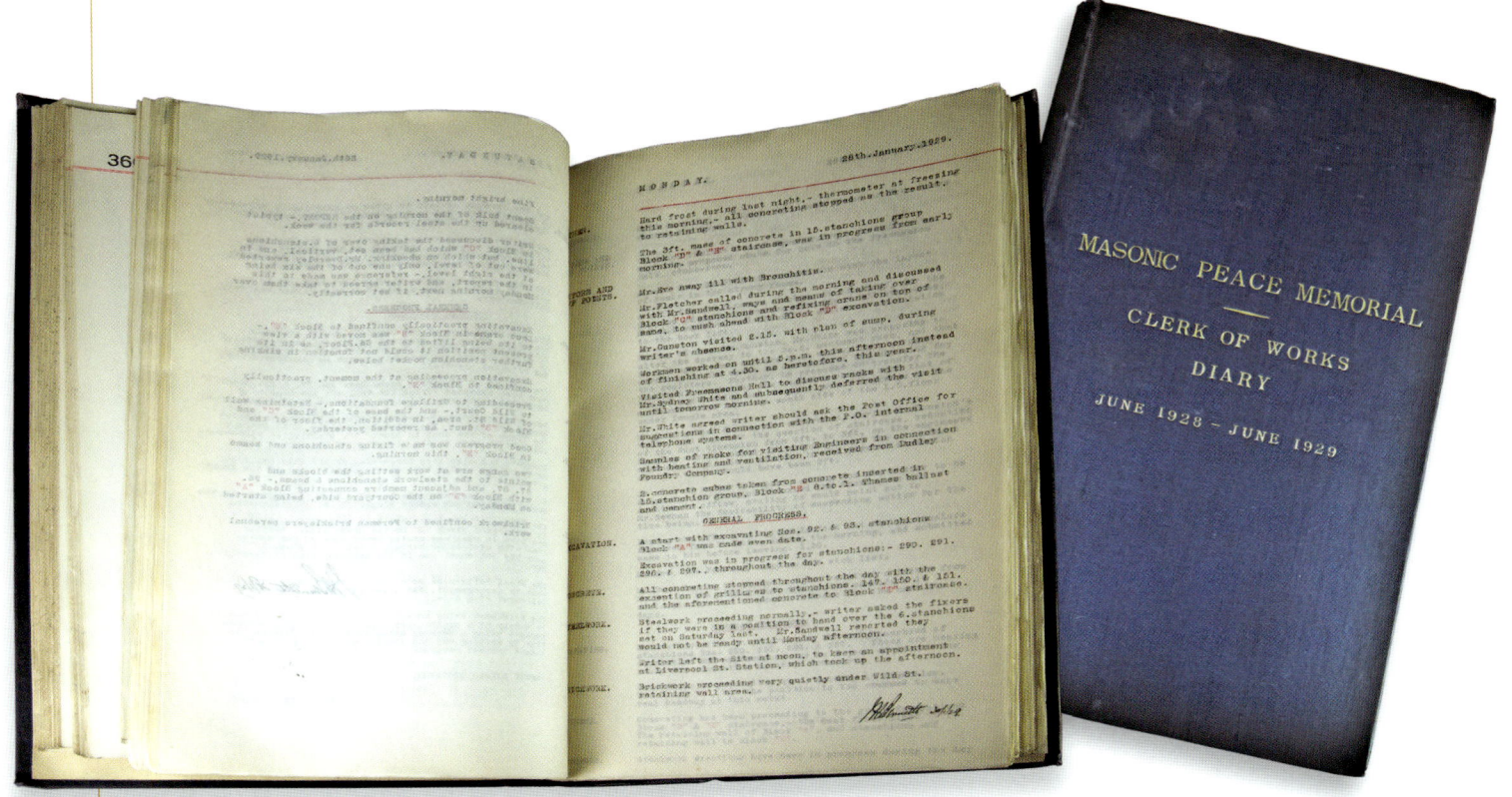

H13: Freemasons' Hall during construction (i), 1928-29.

A photographic record was made during the building of the Masonic Peace Memorial between 1927 and 1933.

Regular photographs were taken of the work as it progressed, providing a fascinating glimpse into the construction process. As these photographs clearly show, Freemasons' Hall is a steel frame building.

H14: Freemasons' Hall during construction (ii), 1928-29. ▽

The steel frame was errected first and the external walls were built afterwards, faced in Portland Stone.

H15: Freemasons' Hall: The Grand Temple, 1928-29. ◁

The steel frames were then covered in concrete to produce a fireproof, load-bearing structure. The marble that covers the Temple interior is a thin veneer. This view clearly shows the balconies on each side of the main Hall.

H16: Freemasons' Hall: The Dais in the Grand Temple, 1928-29. ▷

A workman lays the marble steps leading up to the platform that holds the Grand Master's throne. The craftsmanship exhibited in every detail of the building is a tribute to the dedication of the skilled workmen involved.

English Freemasonry Overseas

Dr James Daniel

Once Freemasonry became formalised in the British Isles with the establishment of Grand Lodges in England (1717), Ireland (1725) and Scotland (1736) it quickly spread overseas. Its first propagators in British colonies and on the continent of Europe in the early eighteenth century were British emigrants, traders, soldiers and sailors on the one hand and foreign visitors to British lodges on the other. From the lodges they established overseas has grown a host of Grand Lodges all over the world.

The speed of the expansion of lodges under the Grand Lodge of England into British colonies is exemplified by the decision in 1734 of a young printer in Philadelphia to reprint 'for the use of the brethren in North America' Anderson's *The Constitutions of the Free-Masons*, a book originally published in London, England, in 1723 [J1]. The printer was none other than Benjamin Franklin (1709-90). Franklin had been initiated in Philadelphia and as the Master of his Lodge in 1734 he wrote to the Provincial Grand Master for New England, Henry Price, to request a formal 'Deputation or Charter' from him, as the representative of the Grand Master of the Grand Lodge of England, to confirm the authority of the Philadelphia Lodge annually to elect its own Master and Wardens. Price, a tailor, was born in London in 1696 and initiated into a lodge there in 1730 before business took him to Boston. Price's request to be appointed as Provincial Grand Master had been granted in 1733 and he filled that office at various times until his resignation in 1769 [J2]. As British Freemasonry spread throughout Britain's thirteen colonies on the east coast of North America and Canada, the 'home' Grand Lodges appointed Provincial Grand Masters to establish Provincial Grand Lodges to superintend their lodges in those territories; some of these were taken there by British regiments, sent to America to protect British interests from the French and then to repress the rebels in the War of Independence (1775-83). Britain lost that war and the British Grand Lodges also lost their remaining Provincial Grand Lodges in America which then became Grand Lodges in their own right.

While Franklin was in England (1757-75) he tried to reconcile the differences between Britain and her American colonies, or, as he later put it in a letter to Lord Howe in 1776, 'to preserve from breaking that fine and noble China vase, the British empire'. He would surely have prized the Ch'ien Lung porcelain punch bowl [J3] that is decorated with Masonic symbols and dates from about 1776. Freemasonry was fashionable in Europe and Freemasons quickly developed a taste for distinctive costumes, badges and decorative objects. The representation of two Freemasons with a terrestrial globe [J4], a Meissen ceramic from about 1744, not only exemplifies this development but suggests that the subjects are discussing how far Freemasonry had already spread around the world. The ceramic figure **[J5]** from the same factory and produced at about the same time, is wearing similar clothes and an identical apron, but he is distinguished by the Master's jewel suspended from his neck on a blue ribbon; that the index finger of his right hand is raised to his lips suggests that he is reminding his Brethren of their obligation to preserve the 'secrets' of Freemasonry.

Franklin, a member of the Congressional Committee of Secret Correspondence, travelled to Paris in 1777 with a commission from Congress to secure French backing for the American Revolution. Franklin's Commander-in-Chief during the war was another Freemason, George Washington (1732-99) **[J6]**. He had been initiated in Fredericksburg, Virginia, and is shown in this portrait as the first Master of Alexandria Lodge in Alexandria, Virginia, founded in 1788. It is possible that the book on the pedestal is the 'George Washington Inaugural Bible' on which he took his Oath of Office at his Inauguration as the first President of the United States in 1789. If so, it has since been used at the Inauguration ceremonies of several of his successors. When he laid the Foundation Stone of the Capitol building in Washington with Masonic honours, he is said to have worn 'a splendid apron made by the wife of the Marquis de Lafayette' – evidence of the American/French Masonic connection.

At the outset of the American War of Independence Boston, Massachusetts was held by British troops, including the 38th Regiment of Foot and its travelling (Irish) Lodge No. 441. Prince Hall (1748-1807), a freed slave and community leader working there as a leather dresser, and fourteen other men of African descent, were initiated in that travelling Lodge in 1775. The Regiment soon had to evacuate Boston, however, so Hall established a new Lodge and, once the war was over, he petitioned the Grand Lodge of England for a Warrant. His Lodge finally received its Warrant (dated 1784) and was entered on the register in London as African Lodge No. 459 – the last lodge in the USA to be warranted by a British Grand Lodge; which Hall acknowledged with a letter of thanks to his Grand Master, HRH Henry Frederick, Duke of Cumberland **[J7]**. Neglected thereafter by England and rejected by the white lodges in Boston, Hall formed additional lodges and eventually the 'African Grand Lodge' was established. Today there are 'Prince Hall' Grand Lodges in most of the American states, sharing the territory amicably with the original state Grand Lodges.

Meanwhile, in Europe, France suffered its own revolution (1789-99) and thereafter much of the European world and its overseas territories became engulfed in the Napoleonic Wars (1803-15) in which Napoleon pitted his forces against an array of European powers, including Britain. French Freemasons established their first Grand Lodge in 1733 (the first in continental Europe) and lodges proliferated throughout France. In 1766 a French exile called De Vignoles even established a Lodge in London, *Loge L'Immortalité de l'Ordre*, which worked under the aegis of the Premier Grand Lodge until the early 1770s. It is possible that the fragment of the jewel **[J8]** is from De Vignoles' own jewel as it bears the date 1767, when he completed his year's Mastership of the Lodge. Two items have been selected to represent French Freemasonry at the turn of the century. First, a cup and saucer **[J9]** decorated with a red Phrygian-style cap or *bonnet rouge*, symbolising liberty, and fasces and a level, both closely associated with the French Revolution. Secondly, a French Masonic apron **[J10]**, hand-coloured in about 1805 with a design influenced by Napoleon's Egyptian campaign in 1799. The figures on the two pedestals represent Prince Joseph Bonaparte (Emperor Napoleon's older brother, appointed Grand Master of the Grand Orient of France by the Emperor to monitor French Freemasonry) and his Masonic deputy, Jean-Jacques-Régis Cambacérès, the author of the Napoleonic Code of civil law and later the first Duke of Parma.

Gibraltar was a key British stronghold during the French Revolution and the Napoleonic Wars. The 18th Regiment of Foot was stationed there from 1784 and in 1789 one of its officers presented a Bible [J11] to the Regiment's Lodge (warranted with the number 315 by the Grand Lodge of Ireland). At this time, Scottish and Irish military lodges in Gibraltar were required to submit to the authority of the Provincial Grand Lodge of Andalusia. This body had suspended Lodge No. 351 for one year in 1792 for not paying its rent and Provincial dues. The Lodge left Gibraltar the following year with its Regiment to assist royalists in the siege of Toulon (France), having failed to settle its debts. Perhaps the Masonic authority in Gibraltar also impounded the Bible, for it was later transferred to the Lodge held in the 100th Regiment of Foot (Gordon Highlanders) No. 3, which the Province formed and warranted in 1796 and whose Warrant is to be found in the front pocket of the Bible.

These were turbulent times indeed, yet individual Freemasons were still travelling all over the world, despite the war, some in ships like the *William & Anne*, clearly identifying its owner as a Freemason by the flag flying from its mast [J12]. These travellers proved their Masonic credentials with the personal Certificates issued to them by their Grand Lodge. Frank Abell, for example, was initiated in 1799 in a Lodge in Wapping, just downstream from London, which included over 250 mariners in its membership. His Certificate is endorsed by the lodges he visited on his travels – in 1802-19 – some in today's Germany, and in 1820 an English one established in St Thomas in the then Danish West Indies in 1819 [J13].

It is estimated that over 122,000 French prisoners of war were incarcerated in Britain during this period (1793-1815). Some were Freemasons who made and traded souvenirs of Masonic interest from easily available items like wood, bone, hair and card [J14] [J15]. *Plus ça change*: for, nearly 150 years later, British Freemasons held as POWs by the Japanese in Changi Prison, Singapore, fashioned badges ('jewels') from scrap metal for the Officers of the Prince of Wales Lodge No. 1555 which met clandestinely in the camp [J16]. In 1945, after their meeting place was looted and its contents removed to Germany for an anti-Masonic exhibition, Jersey Freemasons made Officers' jewels from paper [J17]. The final example is that of an apron made from a handkerchief during the siege of Ladysmith, South Africa, in 1900 [J18].

The decorated apron sent in c.1778 to Ghulam Hussainy in Arcot, India, (Umdat-ul-Umara, and later the 9th Nawab of the Carnatic), by the Duke of Manchester, Grand Master of the Grand Lodge of England, was distinctly of a superior class. Britain had mortally damaged French interests in the subcontinent with its victory over the French forces at the Battle of Plassey in 1757, and the future Nawab's Initiation in Trichinopoly in an English lodge in 1775 was another cause for celebration. In his letter of thanks and Loyal Address of 29 September 1779 to the Grand Master (written in Persian on Indian paper and attached to an illustrated English translation on parchment) [J19] he stated that 'he considered the title of an English Mason as one of the most honourable he possessed.' Umdat-ul-Amara is the first documented Indian Freemason and it took until 1836 before the first Indian was appointed as a Grand Officer of the Grand Lodge of England, namely the Moolavie Mahomed Ismael Khan, Past Senior Grand Warden. There had been British lodges in India since the 1720s but the first Lodge specifically 'Founded for the reception of native gentlemen', Lodge Rising Star, Bombay, was warranted in 1843 by the Scottish Grand Lodge's Provincial Grand Master there, Dr James Burnes, the Lodge's first Master. The 'Burnes Medal' [J20], struck to commemorate the Lodge's foundation, has those words on its rim and, on the reverse, representations of Burnes' two Wardens, 'clothed in the full dress of their community'. A replica of the Burnes Medal was among the many gifts presented to the Prince of Wales (later King Edward VII), the Grand Master of the United Grand Lodge of England (UGLE), when he visited India in 1875-76. He also received a Loyal Address from the District Grand Lodge of Bengal, presented in a splendidly decorated silver and gold casket **[J21]**.

The Prince had been initiated in Stockholm in 1868 in the presence of the King of Sweden. The Grand Lodge of England's oldest formal connection with a foreign Grand Lodge is indeed with the Grand Lodge of Sweden and dates from 1799, and the Prince was one of the first foreign dignitaries also to be made a member of the Swedish Order of Charles XIII. Lord Ampthill, Pro Grand Master and Viceroy of India, received his insignia as a member of that Order in 1932 **[J22]** as did Grand Master Lord Scarborough in 1966. It was therefore appropriate that in the year 2000 the King of Sweden conferred the same honour upon our present Grand Master, HRH The Duke of Kent.

J1: *Book of Constitutions, 1734.*

Benjamin Franklin's reprint of Anderson's *Constitutions* of 1723: the first Masonic book published in America.

Benjamin Franklin (1706-90) was one of the Founding Fathers of the United States of America, signing both the *Declaration of Independence* and the Constitutions of the United States. A printer, author, philosopher, scientist and statesman, Franklin was also a Freemason. He was initiated in 1731 into St John's Lodge in Philadelphia. Elected Grand Master of the Grand Lodge of Pennsylvania in June 1734, he was elected for a second time in 1749.

Following the outbreak of the American War of Independence in 1775 Franklin was sent to Paris to gain French support for the American cause. He joined the *Loge des IX Soeurs* (Lodge of Nine Muses), Grand Orient of France, in 1777; assisted in the Initiation of the philosopher Voltaire in 1778; and became Master of the Lodge in 1782. Franklin was one of the nine Freemasons who signed the *Declaration of Independence* and one of the thirteen Freemasons who signed the Constitution of the United States.

Three years after his Initiation an advertisement appeared in his newspaper *The Pennsylvania Gazette* on 9 May 1734, giving notice of the publication of a reprint of James Anderson's 1723 *Constitutions of the Free-Masons* by B. Franklin, priced at 2s. 6d. or 4s. for a bound copy. The book is a fairly accurate reprint of Anderson's 1723 *Constitutions*, but without the ornate frontispiece.

Franklin's accounts show that at least 127 copies of this book were printed – less than 20 copies are known today. The Library and Museum of Freemasonry owns two copies. The provenance of one of the copies donated in 1939 by the photographer and collector Wallace Heaton can be traced to what is thought to be the original owner – Luke Vardy, who had been initiated into St John's Lodge, Boston in 1736.

J2: Letter from Henry Price, Provincial Grand Master of New England, to Thomas French, Grand Secretary, Moderns Grand Lodge, 1769.

In his letter Price, whilst retaining his appointment with jurisdiction over all North America, offers his resignation as Provincial Grand Master and recommends John Rowe as his successor, stating that when he returns to London later in the autumn he will explain in detail his resignation to Grand Lodge.

Henry Price (1697-1780) was born in London, England. He was apprenticed as a tailor and became a member of the Merchant Tailors' Livery Company in 1719. Initiated as a Freemason in London, business took Price to Boston in America, where in 1723 he opened his first shop on King Street. Another shop followed and such was the success of his business that he was able to retire by 1750. In 1733 he established the first lodge in Boston and was appointed as Provincial Grand Master of New England but resigned in 1736. During interregnums between the appointments of future Provincial Grand Masters he served on a number of occasions as Acting Provincial Grand Master; the last time being in 1769 when he recommended John Rowe as his successor.

Boston N. England 3 June 1769

Right Worshipfull Sir,

I here acknowledge the Receipt of yours dated November 29. 1768, which came to hand the 27th April Ult: inclosing the Design of our Most Worshipful Grand Master, His Grace the Duke of Beaufort, of getting the Antient Society of Masons Incorporated: this noble and high Intention of his Graces cannot fail exciting Joy in the Minds of the Brothers; and if accomplished, of giving the Craft its former Lustre. I have laid your Grand Committee's Regulation before our Provincial Grand Lodge for their Approbation, whereupon they chose a Committee for that purpose. I shall forward every thing that is necessary to the other Provincial Grand Lodges on this Continent upon the like Occasion; the Society being Incorporated must have a good Effect, and be pleasing to every good Brother.

  Dear Sir, it would be tedious to explain the matter of my resigning as Provincial Grand Master: I recommended our Right Worshipful Brother John Rowe Esqr. to be Provincial Grand Master of New England: but you cannot find that I ever gave up my own Appointment over all North America; this by the Blessing of God I shall explain to you, and all our Right Worshipful Brothers, face to face in London some time in the Fall, as my Business will then call me home. I assure you Sir that I always had, and still retain the Interest of Masonry at Heart: I have divers things of consequence to advise of relative thereto, which cannot be so well communicated by the Pen, as in Person: then we may settle the Provincial Grand Masters and rank the Lodges properly. I acknowledge the tender regard, that his Grace, and the Honble Charles Dillon our Rt. Worshipful D.G.M. have for the Brotherhood in America; and therefore conclude with high Esteem for and Brotherly Duty to his Grace, the Honble Charles Dillon, and the Rt. Worshipful Brothers of the Grand Lodge of Masons in England.

  I have the Honor to be with all due Respect, Right Worshipful Brother

   Your Affectionate and Obedient
    Humble Servant,

     Henry Price

Rt. Worshipful Thomas French
 Grand Secretary

J3: Ch'ien Lung punch bowl, decorated with Masonic symbols and the arms of the Moderns Grand Lodge, 1760.

Ch'ien Lung [Quianlong] (1711–99) was the regnal title of the fourth Emperor of the Ch'ing [Qing] Dynasty; his given name was Hung-li. A market for Chinese porcelain already existed in the Western world, with Western producers copying Chinese designs and finding a market for so-called 'Chinoiserie'. This led to a market for imported Chinese porcelain with various styles and patterns. The Ch'ien Lung pottery era spans from 1736 to 1795 and is marked by a widely diverse range of painted porcelain using enamels and gilding, incorporating elements from numerous styles but leaving large areas free of decoration. Large bowls and dishes in particular were produced in vast quantities and were widely used as dinnerware in Europe. The decoration on the sides of this bowl are taken from a print dated 1753 by William Tringham, a London-based engraver, print seller and publisher. The Latin phrase *Hic labor, hoc opus* may be translated as 'Here is labour, here is toil', while *Pulsant aperietur* may be translated as 'Knock and it will open'.

J4: Meissen Ceramic Group of two Freemasons, *c.*1744.

The group is composed of two male figures, one seated and one standing, with a globe of the earth on a pedestal in front. The standing figure is wearing a brown frock coat with a repeated diamond pattern, a tricorn hat and a white apron; he holds a pair of compasses in his left hand above the globe and the other hand is raised with an extended finger.

Porcelain started to be made at Meissen, near Dresden in Germany, in 1710, shortly after the first European hard-paste porcelain had been developed. Gathering an assemblage of artists and artisans to produce its wares, Meissen rapidly established itself as one of Europe's top porcelain manufacturers and in 1720 introduced the now-famous crossed swords trademark to protect its products. Initially the pieces made at Meissen copied the Chinese porcelain with which it was competing, but then it developed its own baroque and rococo styles, becoming especially famous for various ranges of figurines modelled by Johann Joachim Kändler (1706-75), who had become the chief *Modelmeister* in 1733.

J5: Meissen Ceramic Figure of a Freemason, *c.*1745.

A male figure, wearing a light blue frock coat, tricorn hat and a Freemason's apron, stands in front of a tree stump and beside a pedestal. His right hand is raised, with one finger to his lips; the other is over the pedestal, holding a Set Square.

J6: George Washington, 1899.

This portrait by Robert Gordon Hardie was commissioned by the pharmaceutical entrepreneur and Freemason Henry Wellcome in 1899 to commemorate the centenary of Washington's death.

George Washington (1732–99) became a Freemason in Fredericksburg, Virginia at the age of 20 in 1752. Following the end of the War of Independence in 1783, a Lodge was formed in Alexandria, Virginia near his home Mount Vernon, and Washington accepted the invitation to become the first Master of Alexandria Lodge No. 22. Freemasonry was clearly important to Washington – when in April 1789 he was inaugurated as the first President of the USA, he took the oath of his office on the Bible of the St John's Masonic Lodge No. 1 of New York; and in September 1793 when as President he laid the cornerstone for the US Capitol, it was in a Masonic ceremony.

J7: Letter from Prince Hall, Master of African Lodge No. 459, 1785.

Letter of thanks from Prince Hall (1748-1807), Master of African Lodge No. 459, Boston, Massachusetts to Henry Frederick, Duke of Cumberland, Grand Master of the Moderns Grand Lodge.

In the United States the issues of slavery and subsequent widespread racial segregation resulted in Freemasonry developing along parallel, segregated lines.

Having been rejected by white lodges in Boston, Mass. in 1775, Prince Hall (his first name was Prince) and some other free black men were initiated into the travelling army Lodge No. 441 of the Irish Constitution. When the army left Boston in 1776, Prince Hall and his Brethren were given the authority to continue their Masonry as African Lodge No. 1. On 29 September 1784 the Moderns Grand Lodge of England issued a Warrant to this Lodge, now numbered African Lodge No. 459.

African Lodge contributed to the Grand Lodge Charity Fund until 1797 and was in correspondence with Grand Lodge until 1802, when communication ceased and contact between the two was lost. In 1797 African Lodge, with no authority from England, formed two Lodges: African Lodge No. 459B to meet at Philadelphia in Pennsylvania, and Hiram Lodge (without a number) to meet at Providence, Rhode Island. At the formation of the UGLE in 1813, the rolls of both the Moderns and Antients Grand Lodges were combined into one. African Lodge was omitted from the register, but not formally erased. What is now known as the Prince Hall Grand Lodge of Pennsylvania was formed in 1815. African Lodge was refused recognition by the Grand Lodge of Massachusetts in 1827, and declared itself to be an independent Grand Lodge. After a number of attempts to form a National African Grand Lodge, the term 'Prince Hall Grand Lodge' was adopted in the 1840s.

All Prince Hall Grand Lodges are descended from what is now the Prince Hall Grand Lodge of Massachusetts and most of the States in the United States of America have a Prince Hall Grand Lodge.

J8: Jewel of *Loge L'Immortalité de L'Ordre*, 1767.

A circular jewel in two sections. The front section is enamel in a silver mount, hand-painted, with a woman seated on a chequered pavement, holding a set square and plumb line in one hand and a staff and snake in the other. Around her are Masonic emblems: beehive, plan, level, maul, globe and plumb rule. The reverse of the jewel is silver and inscribed with the date 1767.

This rare jewel is believed to be the centre of a Past Master's jewel from a short-lived and controversial Lodge, which met at the Crown and Anchor Tavern on the Strand in London. The Lodge had been established by a French exile called De Vignoles in 1766 for European Masons in London. It worked under the Moderns Grand Lodge and carried out its ceremonies first in French and later in German. It was a most expensive Lodge to join – the Initiation fee was £15. 9s. (£2,000 itm). Members included the cross-dressing diplomat and spy Chevalier d'Eon. The Lodge appears to have ceased to meet in the early 1770s. The date of the inscription is an indication that the jewel may well have belonged to De Vignoles himself.

Boston September 22 1784

May it Please your Royel Highness. Permit us your Humble Brethren of the African Lodge to Return your Royal Highness the Wordens and the Brethren of the Grand Lodge under your Royel Highness Charge our Humble thanks for your goodness to us in Granting us a Charter from your venerble and Honrable Lodge for which we Pray Almighty god Ever to Bless and Preserve till time shall be no more; and from time to time Grant your Royel Highness and that Noable socity that you may allways mentain that Blessed Spirit of our Ever Blessed Grand Master Jesus Christ who thou he stiles himself King of Kings and Lord of Lords yet he is not ashamed to call the true Members of his Fratenity his Beloved Bethren; and such a condisen spirit as this your Royel Highness with the Grand Lodge hath abundently menefested to us in Honring us your onworthi members of the Chrast with a charter. this your Beneverlence to us will not only be Recued by us with Love and gratend but will Convence the Blind World that true Masonry hath something in it Divin and Noble and Diffuses universal Love to all mankind; and now may it Please your Royel Highness; we shall allways make it our Study to keep our selves whithin the bounds and Lemites of our nobel Constitu- tion and under your Wise Derections as our Parent Grand Lodge we shall always Cheefully obay your Deretions which you may from time to time be pleas'd to send us; I shall for my Part as long as I shall have this Honor of setting the cheer shall alwayse in desor to give those bretherns as shall be most bennefechel there Light and Knowledg: & after wishing your Royel Highness and all your Elusterus Faameley all the Blesing of Prence hear Below: you may Rain as Kings and Priest in the World above and may the Grand Lodge Keep such a Lodge hear that they Keep a Everlasting above for ever more; is the earnest Wheeh and Prayer of your Humble and obedent Servent and Brother
Prince Hall

J9: Cup and saucer in Sèvres porcelain, 1794. ▽

The designs are closely associated with the French Revolution: the Cap of Liberty, or *bonnet rouge*, the fasces and the level represent Liberty, Fraternity and Equality.

The *Manufacture Nationale de Sèvres* has historically produced some of the most sought-after ceramics in the world. The factory was originally started in Vincennes, an eastern suburb of Paris, in 1740, moving to Sèvres in the far west of Paris in 1756; it still produces porcelain today.

The marks indicate that this piece has been painted by Jacques François Micaud and gilded by Chauvaux Le Jeune. The Sèvres factory archives show that it was fired in May 1794 and the model was called *tasse étrusque à bandeau*.

J10: French Napoleonic Apron, *c.*1805. ▷

A French, hand-coloured Masonic apron. The design is influenced by Napoleon's Egyptian campaign. On the two pillars are Joseph Bonaparte (brother to the Emperor) and Cambacérès (author of the Napoleonic Code), two leading Freemasons of the period.

J11: Bible presented to the Lodge of the 18th Regiment of Foot No. 351 [Irish Constitution], 1787.

The Bible was presented in 1789 to the Lodge by William Mourgue, an officer in the Regiment.

The 18th Regiment of Foot was stationed in Gibraltar from 1784 until 1793. At this time, Scottish and Irish military lodges in Gibraltar were required to submit to the authority of the Provincial Grand Lodge of Andalusia. This body had suspended Lodge No. 351 for one year in 1792 for not paying its rent and Provincial dues. The Lodge left Gibraltar the following year with its Regiment to take part in the siege of Toulon, having failed to settle its debts.

The front pocket of the Bible originally presented to Lodge No. 351 contains the Warrant of Lodge No. 3 of the 100th Regiment of Foot (Gordon Highlanders), issued by the Provincial Grand Lodge of Andalusia on 15 December 1796. It seems likely that the Bible was transferred to Lodge No. 3 following the rather ignominious departure of Lodge No. 351.

The Warrant is stained (possibly with red wine) and there is a ribbon with the seal of the Provincial Grand Lodge in Gibraltar. It reads:

> Lodge No. 3. John Vincent Esqr. Prov Grand Master ... We ... in ample form assembled ... in the Province of Andalusia and masonical jurisdiction thereunto belonging with the approbation and concent [sic] of the warranted lodges held in the town and garrison of Gibraltar ... do hereby authorise, and impower [sic] our trusty and well beloved brethren viz: The Worshipful Charles Erskine Cournal [sic] of the 100 Regt one of our Master Masons ... to hold and form a lodge of free and accepted masons in the 100th Reg' of Foot in the Garrison of Gibraltar or elsewhere throughout the world upon the first Monday of every calendar month and on all seasonable times & lawful occasions & in the said lodge when duly congregated to admit & make Free Masons according to the most ancient & honourable custom of the Royal Craft ... Given under our hands & the seal of our Grand Lodge in Gibraltar the 15th of Decr. 1796 and in the year of masonry 5796 John Winter Provl. Grand Secretary Andalusia John Vincent P. G. M Wm. ...

Travelling military lodges greatly helped in the early expansion of lodges overseas. The four home Grand Lodges of England – the Moderns (1717), Ireland (1725), Scotland (1736) and England, the Antients (1751) – all issued travelling Warrants to regiments of the British Army. The first to do so was the Grand Lodge of Ireland as early as 1731. Whereas normally a Grand Lodge would grant a Warrant to enable a lodge to be held in a particular town or locality, the Warrant granted to a regiment enabled it to hold meetings wherever the regiment happened to be stationed. The primary purpose of the Warrant was to allow the Initiation of members of the regiment; however it also allowed for the Initiation of local civilians if 'no other Lodge was available'. This was very often the case and it meant that when the regiment eventually moved off, the civilians who remained behind took over and were granted a Warrant to hold a lodge permanently in their own right. Military lodges contributed particularly to the spread of Freemasonry in America and India. It is estimated that some 500 lodges were formed worldwide in this way. The only remaining travelling Warrant in existence today is that of Lodge Glittering Star No. 322, originally granted to the 29th Regiment of Foot (now known as the Worcestershire and Sherwood Foresters Regiment) by the Grand Lodge of Ireland in 1759. As a travelling Lodge it does not have a home base as such, but continues to meet in various locations in the United Kingdom as the guest of local lodges.

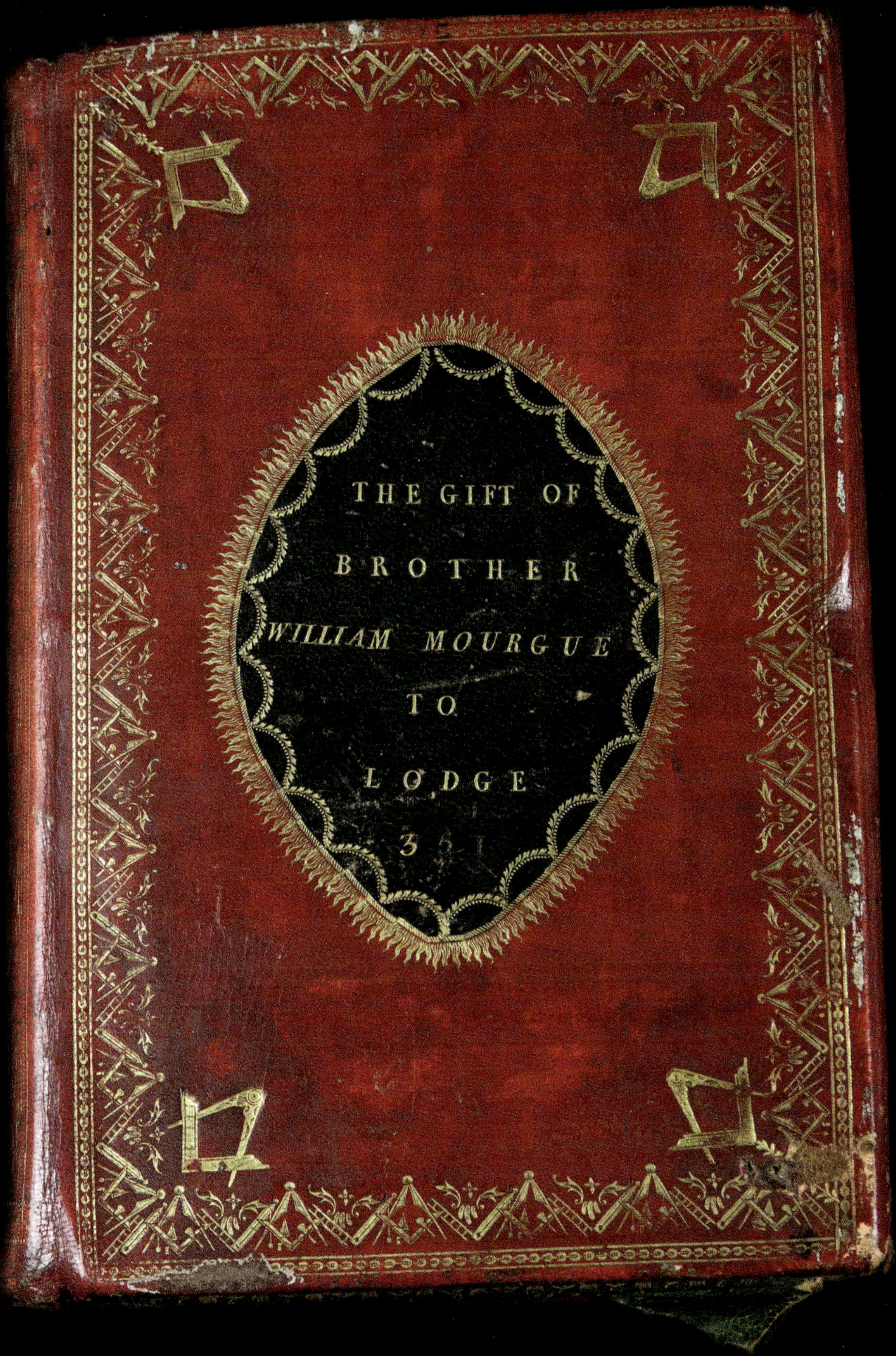
THE GIFT OF
BROTHER
WILLIAM MOURGUE
TO
LODGE
361

J12: Masonic ship: the *William & Ann* of London, 1855.

Flying from one of the masts is a flag with a Masonic Set Square and Compasses. Masonic flags were often flown from ships whose captains did not have a coat of arms but were Freemasons.

The ship shown in the painting is believed to be pictured lying off the coast of Genoa. The *William & Ann* was built in 1759 as a warship, but from the 1780s it began acting variously as a trade, transport and whaling ship. In 1856 she was bought by William Sutton Magub, whose name can be seen at the base of the painting. The *William & Ann* was badly damaged in a hurricane off the coast of Madeira in 1858, and so fell out of service.

J13: Lodge Certificate of Frederick Abell, 1799.

The Certificate was issued by the Dundee Arms Lodge in 1799.

The Lodge was established in 1723 by the Moderns Grand Lodge and met at the Ship, Bartholomew Lane. In 1770 it was named the Dundee Arms Lodge No. 9, re-numbered as No. 18 in 1832, and renamed the Old Dundee Lodge in 1835.

Having taken his Third Degree every Mason, having been registered, receives a Certificate. The new Mason is informed during the presentation that it constitutes a Masonic Passport and should be taken with him when he visits another lodge to prove his membership. On being raised to the Third Degree in 1799, Frederick Abell was issued by the Lodge with a Certificate signed by the Master, Wardens, Secretary, Treasurer and – for good measure – a Past Master of the Lodge. Bro Abell appears to have made good use of his 'Masonic Passport'. His visits are recorded to Hamburg, Amsterdam and even St Thomas in the Virgin Islands: 'Harmonic Lodge, St. Thomas, Virgin Islands, West Indies 4 May 1820 These are to certify that Brother Frederick Abell visited this lodge this day. James Miller, Master'.

J14: Jewel made by a French Prisoner of War during the Napoleonic Wars, *c.*1800.

The jewel takes the form of an oval, hand-painted card encased within a brass-coloured metal frame, onto which are attached Masonic symbols made from paper, metal and metal thread. A domed, glass covering is over the plaque, all contained with a silver-coloured metal horizontal pin on the back. The reverse contains a hand-painted watercolour depiction of a scene with Noah's Ark and some Royal Arch symbols in the foreground.

Given the number of French prisoners of war interred in England during the period of the Napoleonic Wars (1803-15) – in excess of 100,000 – it is not surprising that the Freemasons amongst them formed their own lodges within the camps and made the necessary equipment and regalia required from whatever materials were to hand.

To the Right Worshipful Grand Master,
Deputy Grand Master, Grand Wardens, & the rest
of the Grand Officers, of the Antient & Honourable Society
of Free & Accepted Masons, Greeting —

This is to certify that Fred.^k Abell
being well recomended to us & by us strictly examined, has
been initiated into the three Degrees of Masonry
and as such was by us admitted a Member of our Lodge
at the Dundee Arms Wapping, we therefore recommend
him (after due Examination) to your Friendship & Protection
Given under our Hands & Seal of our Lodge
aforesaid this 10th Day of Jany 1799

By Order of the Master   Powell M

John Rowe Sec.^y   Dobson S.W.

                                      James Herbert J.W.

                                      Jack Hurley P.M.

                                      Richd Francis Treas.

By Order of the Grand Lodge, 21 July 1755 every Certificate granted
to a Brother of his being a Mason, is to be Sealed with the Seal of Masonry, signed
by the Grand Secretary for which five Shillings shall be paid to the Use of the General
Fund of Charity —

J15: Wooden Workbox made by a French Prisoner of War during the Napoleonic Wars, *c.*1800. ➤

A wooden box in the form of a book with a hinged lid and covered in applied straw. The inside of the hinged lid is hand-painted with Masonic symbolism.

In the latter half of the eighteenth and the early part of the nineteenth centuries, when England and France were periodically at war, considerable numbers of captured French prisoners of war were brought to England. In the period 1803-15 over 100,000 prisoners were interred. To keep occupied and to make money, the prisoners often fashioned items from whatever materials were to hand, including figures and models from paper, bone, wood and straw. Many prisoners were Freemasons and not surprisingly made items with a Masonic content.

J16: Jewels made by English Prisoners of War during the Second World War, 1943. ▽

Collar jewels for twelve lodge officers made by W Bro John Richard Skipper, whilst a prisoner of war in Changi Jail, Singapore, from material salvaged from a bombed bus. Over 3,000 civilians were imprisoned from 1942 until 1945, many of them Freemasons. The jewels were used by the members of the Royal Prince of Wales Lodge No. 1555, which met clandestinely in the prison.

J17: Jersey Provincial Grand Lodge Jewels made from Calico, 1945.

Following the liberation of Jersey after the Second World War, Freemasons there had to improvise Masonic regalia.

In June 1940 German forces invaded the British Channel Islands and a few months later in January 1941 the Masonic Temple in Jersey was looted and the contents despatched to Germany for an anti-Masonic exhibition. After the island was liberated in May 1945 a meeting of Provincial Grand Lodge was scheduled for 16 August, but only a few Brethren (who had hidden their Masonic regalia) could produce an apron to wear. To ensure that everybody was suitably attired, old sheets and second-hand linen were collected, cut up and painted to make aprons. These particular Provincial apron roundels were made from calico fabric and hand-painted.

J18: Apron worn at a Meeting during the Siege of Ladysmith, 1899.

The apron is made from a cream, cotton handkerchief with one corner folded to form a flap. On the point of the flap is a Set Square and Compasses in ink, enclosing the date 1899, with the word 'Ladysmith' above.

The apron was worn by Bro Lieutenant Colonel John Henry Lang Sims at a meeting of the Klip River County Lodge No. 2401 during the siege at Ladysmith, Natal which took place between 2 November 1899 and 28 February 1900. There are many instances of lodge meetings taking place whilst under enemy fire during the Boer Wars.

J19: Loyal Address: To the Duke of Manchester, Grand Master, 1778. ▶

Loyal Address, comprising a letter on very fragile Indian paper, written in Persian, and attached to an illuminated English translation on parchment. It is from Ghulam Hussainy, eldest son of Muhammad Ali Wallajah, 8th Nawab of the Carnatic, to George Montagu, 4th Duke of Manchester, Grand Master of the Moderns Grand Lodge, and is dated at Madras, India.

The first documented Initiation of an Indian national was that of Ghulam Husain Ali Khan (1748-1801), in 1775. The event was reported at Grand Lodge in London the following year. Grand Lodge responded by sending Ghulam, the future 9th Nawab of the Carnatic, a decorated apron and finely bound *Book of Constitutions*; he in turn sent this Loyal Address.

The Nawabs of the Carnatic (also referred to as the Nawabs of Arcot) ruled the Carnatic region of South India between about 1690 and 1801. The capital was at Arcot in the present-day Indian state of Tamil Nadu, which included Madras. Ghulam later presented a diamond sword to the Prince of Wales, the future King George IV and Grand Master from 1790; receiving in return a personal letter and portrait of the Prince. All this helped to ensure that at the time the anglophile Nawabs of the Carnatic remained resolutely loyal to British rule.

J20: Burnes Medal, 1843. ◀

Medal commemorating Dr James Burnes, who founded the Rising Star of Western India Lodge No. 342, Bombay under the Scottish Constitution on 15 December 1843. It was the first lodge in the sub-continent to accept Indians as members. The maker of the medal was Benjamin Wyon (1802-58), a medallist in London, who was trained by his father Thomas Wyon and who in 1831 became Chief Engraver of Seals.

Bro Dr James Burnes (1801-62) was a medical officer in the East India Company and first came to Bombay in 1821. A Scottish Freemason, he became Provincial Grand Master for Western India under the Scottish Constitution in 1838.

Maneckji Cursetji, a Parsi and prominent business man, having been rejected as a Candidate by Lodge Perseverance No. 546 under the English Constitution on the grounds that he was an Indian, undaunted and persistent became a Mason in France. On his return to Bombay he applied to become a Joining Member of Lodge Perseverance but was again rejected. At that point thirty Brethren, including nineteen from Lodge Perseverance itself, petitioned Bro Dr James Burnes, as Provincial Grand Master, for a Lodge expressly for the admission of Indians into the Craft.

When the Lodge was consecrated on 15 December 1843, with Burnes as its first Master and Cursetji as Secretary, four Indians were proposed for Initiation, a Parsee and three Muslims. At their Initiation, and for the first time, in addition to the Bible the Volumes of the Sacred Law included the Zend-Avesta, the Koran and later the *Bhagavadgita*. The Lodge was extremely successful and still flourishes today. Ironically Lodge Perseverance transferred its allegiance from the English to the Scottish Constitution in 1862 and it too is still working in Bombay as Lodge Perseverance No. 342 [SC].

Whilst one cannot condone the social mores, customs and practices of 170 years ago, one must recognise that it is through the inspiration of Freemasons such as Burnes, Cursetji and others like them that Freemasonry is today open to all men regardless of race, colour or creed.

Translation
To the Right Worshipful His Grace the DUKE of Manchester
Grand Master of the Illustrious and Benevolent Fraternity of Free and Accepted MASONS
under the Constitution of England and to the Grand Lodge thereof
Much honoured Sir and Brethren
Union of Councils and Interests with the British Nation
Sovereign Ruler of the Universe
initiated
Sir John Day
Umdit ul Omrah
unfeeling Brother
Father of All
Omnipotent and Merciful GOD
Your highly honoured and affectionate
BROTHER
Madras
29th Novr 1778
Umdit ul Omrah Bahauder

FOUNDED FOR THE RECEPTION OF NATIVE GENTLEMEN
DEC. 15. 1843

J21: Casket in silver with gold and diamond chip decoration, 1875.
Presented to HRH The Prince of Wales, later Edward VII, Grand Master, by the Freemasons of Bengal.

This silver and gold casket was presented to the Prince of Wales in Calcutta, on the first Royal visit to India in 1875. It contained an illuminated scroll bearing a Loyal Address. On the lid are the Prince of Wales' feathers; his chain of office as Grand Master of the United Grand Lodge of England; to the left, his collar jewel as Grand Master, and to the right his jewel as First Grand Principal of the Royal Arch. The sides of the box are decorated with the Working Tools of the Craft and Royal Arch Freemasonry, and ornate scrollwork.

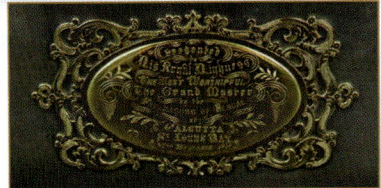

J22: The Order of King Carl XIII of Sweden, 1930.
Presented to Lord Ampthill, Pro Grand Master 1908-35.

The Swedish Masonic rite, which is practised in the Scandinavian countries of Sweden, Norway, Denmark, Iceland and Finland, consists of eleven degrees that are taken consecutively and it is restricted to those professing the Christian Trinitarian faith. The Order is fully recognised by the United Grand Lodge of England and there exists a protocol whereby visiting rights are accorded to English Freemasons, enabling them to witness the various Swedish degree ceremonies depending on which degree they have attained in England. Thus the first three degrees of the Swedish Rite are taken as the equivalent of the English three Craft degrees; whilst the Royal Arch of England is equivalent to the 6th degree of Sweden. To attend the 10th degree in Sweden an English Mason would need to have achieved the 32nd degree of the Ancient and Accepted Rite (Rose Croix) or the Chair in the Order of the Red Cross of Constantine. The Swedish 11th degree (Commander of the Red Cross) is the equivalent of Grand Rank, and as such is extremely restricted, with only members of the English 33rd degree being able to attend as visitors. Even more rare is the Swedish '12th Degree' or 'The Royal Order of King Charles (Carl) XIII of Sweden', established in 1811 by King Carl. It is a civil order conferred on Freemasons holding the 11th degree, with the number limited to thirty-three – this is partly explained by the fact that from 1774 up to 1997 all Grand Masters belonged to the Royal House. King Carl XVI Gustaf is the High Protector of the Swedish Order of Freemasons.

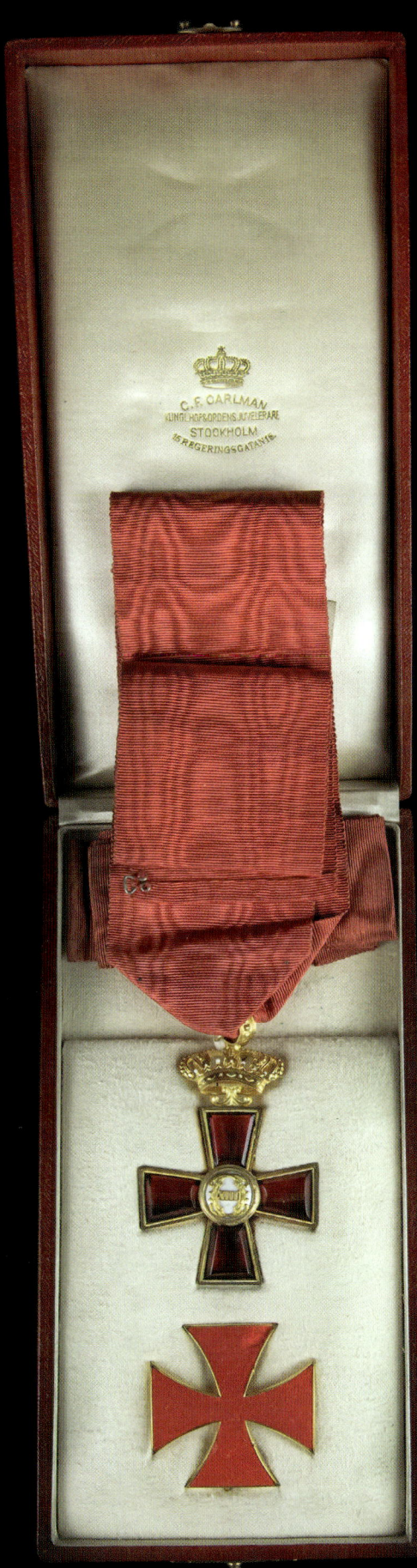

Freemasonry and Charity

Dr John Reuther

Charity may be considered the very essence of mankind and first appeared within the family unit. Charity, as currently interpreted, was practised in the early Christian Church. In the medieval monastic communities *charité* was practised. Archbishop Lanfranc founded two hospitals in Canterbury based on this principle: St John's Hospital for the infirmed and another nearby for victims of leprosy, whilst in 1130 Bishop Henry of Blois established St Cross Hospital near Winchester for: 'Thirteen poor men, feeble and so reduced in strength that they can scarcely or not at all support themselves without other aid'. Travellers can still receive there the Wayfarer's Dole, bread and a horn of ale. St Francis of Assisi, founder of the Franciscans, took vows of poverty based on receiving charity from those to whom he preached.

A secular form of charity was practised by the City Guilds, which had been created in the great cities of Europe to maintain the standards and discipline of their trade. Help was accessible to their members throughout their lives: from their education at their guild school to the alms houses for their aged colleagues. In times of hardship alms could be given, prayers could be read for their sick and after death masses were said for their souls in their Guild church.

Freemasonry has been defined as a child of the Enlightenment but equally it could be argued that the Age of Enlightenment was a child of Freemasonry. Whatever, it cannot be denied that many of these charitable individuals were practising Freemasons. In 1772 William Preston published his book on the symbolism and moral significance of the First Degree in Freemasonry, in which he portrayed the Craft as an influence on the moral character of mankind. He stated:

> To relieve the distressed is a duty incumbent on all men, but particularly on Freemasons, who are linked together by an indissoluble chain of sincere affection. To soothe the unhappy, to sympathize with their misfortunes, to compassionate their miseries, and to restore peace to their troubled minds, is the great aim we have in view. On this basis we form our friendships and establish our connections.

In the early years of Grand Lodge tokens were often presented for deeds of merit. These frequently took the form of those worn by civil dignitaries or within Livery. Such is the case of a pendant jewel presented to Thomas Marriott Perkins by the Sea Captains' Lodge in 1757. The medal is 13cm high, made of silver gilt and enamelled and surmounted by an anchor. It is richly adorned with Masonic symbols and engravings. Perkins had been a member of the Lodge before travelling to the Mosquito Coast and Jamaica where he remained until 1770 **[K1]**.

Shortly after the formation of Grand Lodge, the office of Treasurer, later renamed the Grand Treasurer, was established principally to supervise the safe distribution of those central funds belonging to the Committee of Charity [K2] and could award up to 5 guineas to any Freemason deemed worthy. Similar, smaller charities were also established locally throughout the country. In Liverpool in 1806, a number of Antient lodges united to form their own particular charity known as The Charity Committee of Ancient Freemasons. It could award up to £5 at any one time during a year to any distressed member. The Secretary, Bro Joseph Gillmer, was presented with a fine silver gilt jewel in 1811 for his dedication and hard work [K3].

The Committee of Charity became the Fund of Benevolence with the Act of Union; eventually evolving into the Board of Benevolence, comprising of both the Board of General Purposes and Fund of Benevolence. The first Grand Master, the Duke of Sussex, founded a Lodge of Benevolence with all Grand Officers, Masters and Past Masters eligible for membership. Three Grand Officers, to act as the Master and Wardens, were appointed annually by him and were empowered to award up to £10 to a Freemason and £5 to a widow. The size and the irregularity of the attendance of this Lodge made it cumbersome, but it still continued until 1884, when it became a Board. It continued as such, with minor modifications, until the creation of the Grand Charity in 1981. The President of the Board of Benevolence was permitted to wear a specific apron to identify his position [K4].

The Royal Masonic Institute for Girls was founded in 1788 by Bartholomew Ruspini, an Italian dentist and Freemason. Its purpose was to establish a charitable foundation for the daughters of Freemasons who had died or fallen on hard times. A house in Somers Town, Euston was first chosen in 1789 and named The Royal Cumberland Freemason School for Little Children, after the wife of the Duke of Cumberland, the then Grand Master. Funds were raised by benefactors such as Anthony Ten Broeke [K5]; and by holding an annual dinner and sermon, the first being held on the anniversary of the foundation. These events were great social occasions and tickets had to be purchased: one such ticket for the event on the 11 and 12 April 1791 was signed by the then Deputy Grand Master Sir Peter Parker, Admiral of the Fleet and a great patron and friend of Horatio Nelson [K6]. The school proved so successful it became necessary to move to a larger establishment in nearby St George's Field. Since then it has moved several times. The School, now at Rickmansworth in Hertfordshire, proudly declares that it is the oldest girls' school in the country. In 1976 it became an open, fee-paying school, accepting girls from all backgrounds and faiths. The daughters of Freemasons can still attend but may select elsewhere if more convenient to their circumstances. In 1790, the artist Thomas Stothard painted the Chevalier Bartholomew Ruspini, leading the girls into Grand Lodge to be presented to the Prince of Wales, later King George IV [K7]. This painting proved so popular that it was later reproduced as an engraving by Francesco Bartolozzi [K8]. Bartolozzi was born in Florence in 1727. He travelled throughout Europe before settling in London, where he became a great friend of Stothard and other established artists [K9]. He joined the Lodge of the Nine Muses in London and produced a number of Masonic engravings, such as the aforementioned ticket, which again was based on a painting by Stothard.

A corresponding charity was founded by the Antient Grand Lodge in 1798 under the patronage of its Grand Master, John, 4th Duke of Atholl. Its aims were similar, but with the difference that these unfortunate children were educated at the nearest school to their home, and it was not until 1857 that a school was opened in Wood Green in north London. A new school was latterly built in Bushey, Herts., but eventually closed in 1979. In 1986 the two Charities merged to form the Masonic Trust for Girls and Boys. The Charity now funds the education of any child up until the completion of their education. The Trust received Royal patronage in 2003 and is now known as the Royal Masonic Trust for Girls and Boys and still aims: 'To continue to relieve poverty and provide an education and preparation for life for the children of the family of a Freemason and, where funds permit, for any children, as their fathers would have done, had they been able so to do.'

In 1829 an energetic and charismatic individual, Dr Robert Thomas Crucefix, was initiated into the Burlington Lodge in London. His progress in the Craft was meteoric, for in 1836 he was appointed a Grand Junior Deacon. Crucefix was also instrumental in popularising many of the other Orders within Freemasonry.

The Industrial Revolution had, by now, dynamically altered the social structure of the country. Many thought the cities were paved with gold, and to a few they were, but in reality many were reduced to penury. How to handle the poor became a national crisis. The publication of the Poor Law Amendment Act in 1834 attempted to resolve the problem by creating the controversial Union Workhouses. Crucefix was one of many who recognised that a large percentage of the inmates were just elderly, reduced by poverty to spend their last days in a Workhouse. What if they were Freemasons? What followed was a controversial and bitter period within the Masonic community. The Crucefix faction thought that the construction of an alms house was the solution; however the Grand Master, the Duke of Sussex, opposed the idea. He suggested that the introduction of an annuity fund would be sufficient to prevent any unfortunate member having to enter such an establishment. This controversy further deteriorated with Crucefix's introduction of *The Freemason's Quarterly Review* **[K10]**, a magazine designed to inform Freemasons on the history and philosophy of the Craft. It also became the platform to advertise his alms house project. Crucefix was conscious that the average Freemason often wanted more knowledge about the Craft, whilst to the Grand Master it was a threat to his control over both the management as well as his interpretation of the Order. The argument, at times, became extremely acrimonious and led to Crucefix's temporary expulsion. A truce was declared with the formation of two separate Charities: Crucefix's Building Fund for an Asylum and the Duke's Royal Masonic Benevolent Annuities Fund. When the Duke of Sussex died in 1843 attempts were successfully made to unite the Charities, thereby forming the Royal Masonic Benevolent Institution. Sadly Crucefix died just before the opening of the Asylum in 1850.

A portrait of Crucefix was commissioned by the Burlington Lodge in 1837. It was hoped the painting, by Bro Moseley, would hang in the Main Hall of the Asylum but until completion it would remain within their Lodge. It eventually was displayed in the Hall at the Home in Croydon, where it remained until the building's eventual closure in 1956. Recently this painting has been rediscovered and now hangs within Freemasons' Hall. In the nineteenth century a copy was made, which is in the Library and Museum of Freemasonry **[K11]**.

Dr Crucefix was so admired within the Craft that in 1841 he was presented with a testimonial in the form of a silver candelabrum **[K12]**. The presentation dinner was held at the New London Hotel (formerly known as Radley's), Bridge Street, Blackfriars, the venue of the innumerable meetings held to formulate the plans for a Home for elderly Freemasons. The candelabrum was made by William Evans, a silversmith working at New Street, Covent Garden and consists of a central column surmounted by a figure depicting Charity. The figures of an elderly man leaning on a stick, a boy reading and a girl with her workbag are at the base and represent the then three Masonic Charities. Dr Crucefix was associated with them all, but it is with the Royal Masonic Benevolent Institution that he is best remembered.

Charitable fundraising events have been held since the early eighteenth century and by the nineteenth century individuals who donated an agreed sum were designated Stewards and permitted to wear a Stewards' jewel. These were originally designed with a fabric tassel, such as the jewel worn at the 1869 festival for the Royal Masonic Institution for Boys, which raised £12,000 **[K13]**, whilst that for the Royal Masonic Benevolent Institution of 1878 raised £10,000 **[K14]**.

Dinners were held annually for each of the three Masonic Charities, usually at the Freemasons' Tavern, and comprised of an official ceremony, followed by a dinner, and finished with a musical presentation. An eminent Freemason was invited to act as President. In the 1850s these events became the final act in the fundraising period of a Masonic Province. The Provincial Grand Master for that particular Province would preside and during the celebrations the final sum raised was announced. The Stewards' Jewels can be distinguished by the colour of the ribbon – each charity having its own colour – whilst the actual metallic jewel is usually a representation of the emblem of each Province, as illustrated by the 1874 Stewards' Jewel issued by the Province of Suffolk. The jewel may be worn for up to a year after the termination of the Festival, although in some cases, such as Royal Patronages, it may be designated as a permanent jewel. During the Second World War these jewels were, of necessity, made of cardboard.

Freemasonry has always had individuals who have dedicated time and money for the betterment of others: Charles Edward Keyser was such a person. Born in 1847, he was educated at Eton and Trinity College, Cambridge and there initiated into the Isaac Newton Lodge. He amassed a considerable fortune on the Stock Exchange, which enabled him to purchase the estate at Aldermaston Court in 1893, along with the title of Lord of the Manor of Aldermaston. He donated much of his fortune to Masonic and non-Masonic charities and had personally funded a field hospital during the Boer War. A Patron, Trustee and Chairman of both the Board of Management of the Royal Masonic Institution for Boys as well as the RMBI, he was appointed Provincial Grand Master for Hertfordshire. He donated a Charity Collar which included bars recording his many charitable donations **[K15]**.

Another philanthropic Freemason was Benjamin Bond Cabell, who had presided at the 1851 Festival for the RMBI. In his public life he was a lawyer, the Tory Member of Parliament for St Albans, and in later life the High Sheriff of Norfolk. Conscious of the great loss at sea around the British coast, he decided in 1868 to fund a lifeboat at Cromer. Shortly afterwards in 1871 members of Lodge of Faith No. 141, London, raised £260 and petitioned Grand Lodge to provide the additional funds to purchase a lifeboat. Grand Lodge agreed and provided the funds for a 30ft vessel, together with a lifeboat carriage to get it to the water. HRH Albert Edward, Prince of Wales, had not long been installed as Grand Master when in 1875 he was sent on a diplomatic tour of India. Grand Lodge decided to celebrate his homecoming by contributing £4,000 towards two lifeboat stations and their lifeboats. One was set up at Clacton-on-Sea and its boat named *Albert Edward*, whilst the other was situated at Hope Cove, Devon and named *Alexandra* after the Princess of Wales **[K16]**. These events were extensively reported in both the local newspapers as well as the national press.

The New Masonic Samaritan Fund was formed in 1990, largely to replace the role previously carried out by the Royal Masonic Hospital. There had been for some time a compelling desire to have a hospital specifically for Freemasons and their families, and by 1916 enough money had been raised to purchase the former Chelsea Women's Hospital in the Fulham Road, London. This hospital, of necessity, was being used for wounded soldiers but with peace it was renovated and became known as the Freemasons' Hospital and Nursing Home. Demand however created a need for a larger hospital and in 1933 the Royal Masonic Hospital, funded by private subscriptions (largely from Freemasons), was opened in Ravenscourt Park, west London. In 1948 a School of Nursing was opened to train nurses to provide first-rate treatment for Freemasons. In most hospitals it was customary, on completion of a nurse's training, to present her with the nursing school's medal to be worn on her uniform. The Royal Masonic Hospital not only presented each qualified nurse with a badge but also a distinctive silver belt buckle displaying the Set Square and Compasses [K17]. It was inevitable that, as medicine became more specialised and expensive, especially in the field of surgery, the hospital could not sustain the demands required. It also was recognised that for many Freemasons outside the London area it was inconvenient. In 1990 it was decided to create a new fund, which would continue to give relief to members who could not afford private health care or were unable to obtain speedy and convenient treatment from their local NHS hospital. Finally, Grand Lodge recommended the closure of the Royal Masonic Hospital in 1992.

Freemasonry, by its very nature, has always tried to support individuals within the lodge who perhaps have fallen on hard times; or the members have maybe donated Christmas presents to widows to show they are not forgotten, and for this purpose a charity collection is made during each meeting. The collecting receptacle is usually a box, plate or bag but over the years a range of designs have been used. One of the more rare types is a broken column, symbolising life cut down in its prime, which was commonly seen as a headstone in Victorian cemeteries. Some lodges associated with flying have the central part of an old propeller. The Library and Museum of Freemasonry possesses a porcelain collecting box, made between the wars, in the shape of a bowler hat. It was probably used in the Holy Royal Arch Degree, the crown of the hat representing the vault [K18].

The values of Freemasonry are based on integrity, kindness, honesty and fairness, and charity has always been an important part of Freemasonry. The members have been, and still are, encouraged to practice charity not only for other members of the Craft but also for the community as a whole. This is not only achieved by financial donations but perhaps more importantly by the giving of their own time.

K1: Jewel from the Sea Captains' Lodge, 1757.

An enamel and silver gilt jewel presented to Thomas Marriott Perkins by members of the Sea Captains' Lodge in 1757. There were five lodges called Sea Captains' Lodge in the eighteenth century, meeting in ports around the country and it is most probable that Thomas Perkins belonged to the one based in London. Thomas Perkins first appears in Masonic records as a Grand Steward at the feast of 1756, although not associated with a particular lodge. He joined the Grand Stewards' Lodge and was Master in 1759-60. He visited the Lodge of Antiquity (now No. 2) on 10 July 1759 and joined the Lodge two weeks later on 24 July, his occupation listed as a West Indian merchant (the Lodge of Antiquity was known as the West Indian and American Lodge from 1761-70). He remained a member until 1768, although the Lodge records note that in 1762-3 he had gone abroad to the West Indies. He was appointed Provincial Grand Master of the Mosquito Shore in 1761, with Jamaica being added in 1762, and he held that position until 1770.

K2: *Laws Relating to the Committee of Charity, 1730.*

The *Laws Relating to the Committee of Charity* were first published in 1730.

The Moderns Grand Lodge established a Committee of Charity as early as 1727, only ten years after its formation. The Committee considered petitions from Brethren for financial assistance for members and their dependants. Charity, sometimes referred to as 'Relief' in the early years, has always been a central tenet of Freemasonry. The Antients Grand Lodge established a similar system when it was formed in 1751, and which was managed through the Stewards' Lodge. In 1814 the grant-making elements of the Committee of Charity and the Stewards' Lodge merged to form a Fund of Benevolence, managed in due course by a Board of Benevolence and ultimately in 1981 by the Grand Charity.

K3: Early Charity Jewel, 1811.

One of the earliest known Masonic charity jewels, it is of silver gilt and engraved plate, and was presented to Joseph Gillmer.

Prior to formal Charities being established by the two respective Grand Lodges, individual lodges often collaborated for charitable purposes. Joseph Gillmer, an accountant, was Secretary of the Charity Committee formed by five Antient lodges in Liverpool.

THE
LAWS
RELATING TO THE
GENERAL CHARITY,
And DISPOSAL thereof.

Printed in Pursuance of an Order made the
Seventh Day of *March*, 1747.

Richmond, G. M.

1724, *Nov.* 21. THAT for promoting the charitable Disposition of Free-Masons, and rendering it more extensively beneficial to the Society, a Collection be made in each Lodge, and paid into the Hands of a Treasurer, towards raising a Fund for the Relief of such distressed Brethren as shall be recommended by some Lodge contributing to the same.

Paisly, G. M.

1725, *Feb.* 28. THAT the Contributions of the several Lodges towards raising the above Fund be voluntary, and paid quarterly.

THAT no Brother shall partake of the said Charity until he shall have been Five Years a Member of some regular Lodge contributing to the same.

Kingston, G. M.

1729, *Dec.* 27. Ordered, THAT, for the future, every Lodge of Masons that shall be constituted by the G. M. or by his Authority, shall pay Two Guineas towards the Charity.

Norfolk, G. M.

1730, *Dec.* 15. THAT all Complaints, Informations, and Petitions, to the Grand Lodge, shall for the future be referred to the Committee of Charity; who are to examine the same, and report their Opinion thereon to the next quarterly Communication.

THAT

THE COMMITTEE, to whom it was refered to consider of Proper Methods to regulate the Generall Charity, after, severall Meetings for that Purpose, came to the following resolutions, which they Submit to the Judgment of the Grand Lodge as conducive to the End proposed by the Reference.

I THAT it is the Opinion of the Committee, that the Contributions from the Severall Lodges be paid Quarterly and Voluntary.

II THAT No Brother be recommended by any Lodge, as an Object of this Charity, but who was a Member of Some regular Lodge, which shall Contribute to the same Charity on or before the 21st Day of November 1724, when the Generall Charity was first proposed in the Grand Lodge.

III THAT No Brother, who has been Admitted a Member of any such Lodge since that time, or shall hereafter be so Admitted, be recommended till three Years after such Admission: And as to the Methods or rules to be Obseved by the Grand Lodge in relieving such Brethren who shall be Qualified as aforesaid, whom they shall think fitt, upon Application to themselves, to relieve; Viz. Those concerning the Circumstances of the Persons to be relieved; the sums to be paid; the times or terms of payment; the Continuance, Suspending or taking off such Allowance, with the reasons thereof, whether arising from the Circumstances of the Assisted Brother being better'd, or from his behaviour in any respect rendring him unfitt to have it Continued; and in Generall all other circumstances Attending the regular and Ordinary distribution of the Charity, where the Grand Lodge think fitt to put any One upon it, the Committee are of Opinion They are most decently and securely lest to the Wisdom care and Discretion of the Grand Lodge, to do therein from time to time as cases shall happen, in a Manner most Agreeable to the Exigencies of them; Which as the Committee cannot foresee with any Certainty, so they are unable to Lay down any fixed proposalls concerning them; But as it may fall out that a Brother who is in all respects qualified for relief and in need of it, may by the pressure of his Circumstances be forced to Apply perhaps a Good while before a Quarterly Communication may be had, or the Grand Lodge Assembled, for a present relief or subsistance till he can make his Case known to the Grand Lodge for their further favour: the Committee took that Case into their particular Consideration and as to that are humbly of Opinion.

IV THAT three pounds, and no more, may be given to any particular distressed Brother who shall be recommended by any Lodge as an Object of this Charity, without the Consent of the Grand Lodge.

K4: Apron of the President of the Board of Benevolence, 1870.

In 1814 the grant-making elements of the Committee of Charity of the Moderns and the Stewards' Lodge of the Antients merged to form, under the United Grand Lodge of England, a Fund of Benevolence, managed in due course by a Board of Benevolence and ultimately in 1981 by the Grand Charity. The President of the Board of Benevolence was a Grand Office in its own right, reflecting the importance of charity within the structure of Freemasonry. In 2016 the Grand Charity and the other Masonic Charities have merged to form a new, all-encompassing Masonic Charity to be known as the Masonic Charitable Foundation.

K5: Anthony Ten Broeke, c.1766.

A portrait in oils, attributed to Samuel Drummond (1766-1844), of the merchant, Freemason and benefactor, Anthony Ten Broeke.

Anthony Ten Broeke (1735-1812) obtained British citizenship in 1777. He was Master of Caledonian Lodge No. 325 – later New Caledonian Lodge No. 134 – in 1766. In 1771 he was expelled from the Craft with ten other members of the Lodge for writing a letter to the Provincial Grand Master of the Austrian Netherlands, which the Moderns Grand Lodge considered defamatory. After apologising, he was reinstated in 1777. In 1788 he was a Founder member of the committee of the Royal Cumberland Freemasons' School, later re-named the Royal Masonic Institution for Girls.

The collar Anthony Ten Broeke is seen wearing in the painting is one of a number of similar collars made for the officers of Caledonian Lodge No. 134 and still in use today.

K6: Ticket for a Church Service, Sermon and Dinner in support of the Royal Cumberland Freemasons' Charity School for Girls, 1791.

The attendance at a church service followed by dinner was an accepted way of raising funds in support of the school, either by means of a generous donation, or – as in this instance where no collection was made – by the price of the entrance ticket, which was 7s. 6d. (some £40 itm).

K7: Ruspini leading a Procession of Girls from the Masonic School into Freemasons' Hall, 1802.

A painting by Thomas Stothard (1755-1834), an English painter, illustrator and engraver. The Chevalier Bartholomew Ruspini (1730-1813) was an eminent and successful dentist as well as a prominent Freemason. In 1788, with the Duchess of Cumberland as Patron, he founded the Royal Cumberland Free Mason School for Girls. The painting shows Ruspini leading a procession of girls from the School into Freemasons' Hall. In the foreground are (left to right) Anthony Ten Broeke, Lord Moira (wearing uniform), the Prince of Wales (Grand Master), James Heseltine (Grand Secretary), William Forssteen, James Galloway (an interpreter), the Persian Ambassador, the Ambassador's Secretary, and Ruspini.

K8: Ruspini leading a Procession of Girls from the Masonic School into Freemasons' Hall, 1802.

An engraving by Francesco Bartolozzi, after the original painting by Thomas Stothard. Engraving was the only means available at the time to make images in a printed format. It is interesting to compare the engraving with the original painting by Stothard [K7].

K9: Business card for Chevalier Bartholomew Ruspini, engraved by Bartolozzi, c.1775.

Bartolozzi, a leading engraver of the day, was a fellow Freemason and friend of Ruspini. From the very earliest days of organised Freemasonry occasional one-off financial grants were made to individuals and to the children of deceased Brethren. In the case of the Moderns, these came from the Committee of Charity; and with the Antients from the Stewards' Lodge. There was however no continuous provision until Ruspini established the Royal Cumberland School. The original school was on the site of what is now the British Library. At the end of their school life, the girls would, in most cases, either return to their families or go into domestic service. School life was well-disciplined and caring but very basic – by way of example, the usual fare for meals consisted mainly of gruel, bread and beer, with boiled mutton as the highlight of the week. Some ten years later William Burwood and the United Mariner's Lodge established a similar Charity for boys. The two Charities grew, becoming in due course the Royal Masonic Institution for Girls and Royal Masonic Institution for Boys respectively. They eventually merged to form the Royal Masonic Institution for Girls and Boys in 1982.

K10: *Freemason's Quarterly Review*, 1834.
Published by Robert Crucefix.

The magazine, established in 1834, was very much a mouthpiece for Crucefix. He was at odds with the Grand Master, who (it would be an understatement to say) did not share the same enthusiasm as Crucefix for the need for a facility for aged and sick Freemasons. Although there was much more to it, the essential difference between the two was that the Duke of Sussex favoured relieving the needs of those requiring assistance by means of granting annuities, whilst Crucefix felt that a more hands-on approach was required by providing a supportive environment in the form of a home or asylum. In the end both methods were utilised but ironically the Asylum in Croydon was opened shortly after the death of Crucefix, who did not live to see the fruits of his labour.

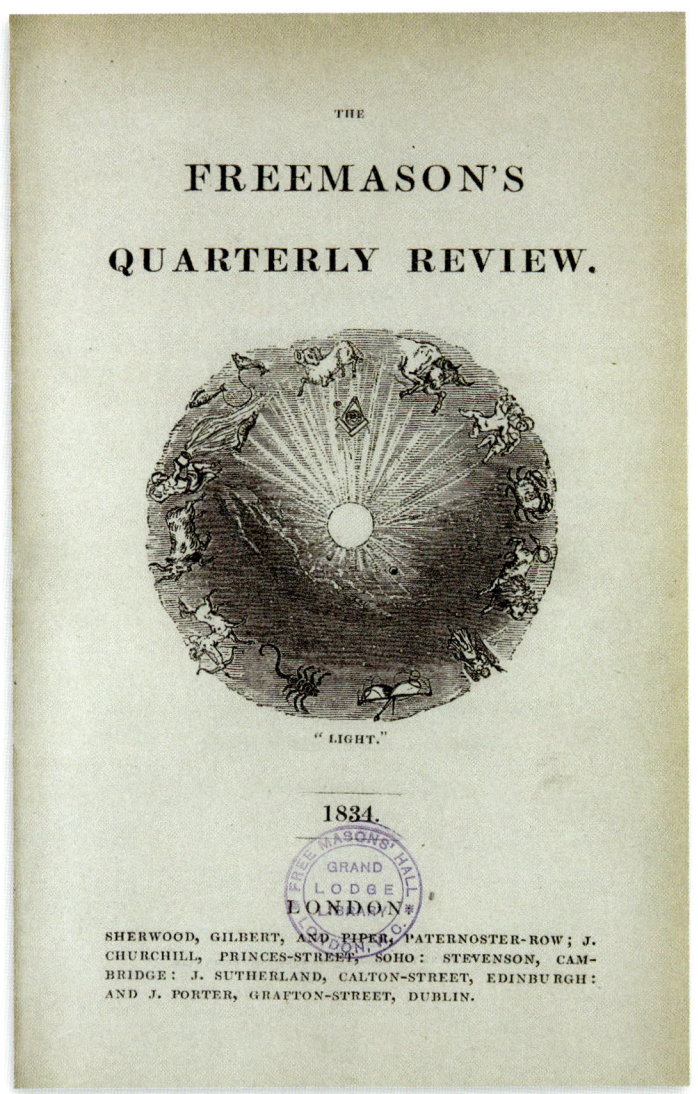

K11: Dr Robert Crucefix, *c.*1837.

Dr Robert Crucefix (1797–1850) was born in Holborn, London and educated at Merchant Tailors' School. He became a Freemason in 1829, was appointed Junior Grand Deacon in Grand Lodge in 1836, and developed a considerable interest in the Christian Orders of Freemasonry, becoming the first Sovereign Grand Commander of the Ancient and Accepted Rite (Rose Croix) in England.

K12: Silver Candelabrum presented to Dr Robert Crucefix, 1841.

The candelabrum was presented to Dr Robert Thomas Crucefix (1797-1850), who was the founder of the Asylum for Aged and Decayed Freemasons – now the Royal Masonic Benevolent Institution – and was a governor of the Masonic Charities for both the boys and the girls. The two Charities are represented by the figures at the base, with the figure of Charity herself surmounting the column.

The presentation was made at a meeting held at the New London Hotel, Bridge Street, Blackfriars on 24 November 1841, to mark his contribution towards Freemasonry and primarily the development of what is now the Royal Masonic Benevolent Institution. The piece was designed and manufactured by William Evans at his workshop in New Street, Covent Garden. The figure at the top of the column is Charity. Around the foot of the column are three figures: an elderly man leaning on a stick, with a dog to one side as the symbol of fidelity; a boy standing reading and a girl with her workbag. Together they represent the three Masonic Charities then in existence – the Asylum for Aged Masons, the Girls' School and the Boys' School.

K13: Charity Steward's Rosette: Royal Masonic Institution for Boys, 1869.

The financing of the three original Masonic charities had always been a major issue. Having founded the Girls' School, within a year Ruspini realised that long-term funding was required. A church service was organised to celebrate the first anniversary of the School, followed by a charity dinner. The event had a large Masonic presence and the very generous donations made amounted to £82. 10s. 6d., a little over £9,000 itm. The event was styled a Festival and the monies raised called the Appeal: thus started the Festival System which endures to the present day and is by far the major source of income for all the Masonic Charities.

Donations received from Freemasons are recorded by the various Charities in the name of the individual donor and accrue on a cumulative basis towards certain honorifics, which also entitle the holder to particular voting rights. The Masonic Charities each have an Annual Festival, hosted by one of the forty-four out of the forty-seven different Masonic Provinces (Guernsey and Alderney, Jersey and London are not included). It means that each Masonic Province can expect to host a Charity Festival every eleven years. Most Provinces limit the money-raising activities to a five-year period, and the normal expectation is that a member should try to achieve the minimum status of what is known as a 'Steward' by donating a sum of £500 during the five-year period. Other levels such as Vice-Patron, Patron and Grand Patron can be achieved by donating larger amounts.

The higher levels of donation are recognised by the respective Charities with an appropriate jewel appended to a collar or collarette.

K14: Steward's Jewel: Royal Masonic Benevolent Institution (RMBI), 1878.

Ever since the inception of the Festival system badges or jewels, issued by the individual Provinces hosting a Festival, are worn by members to show that they have made the appropriate donation required to qualify as a 'Festival Steward'.

K15: Charles Edward Keyser's Grand Lodge Charity Jewel, with Collar adorned with bars, *c.*1900.

It became quite fashionable in Victorian times to append multiple 'Festival Steward' bars – awarded for additional Stewardships – and other qualifying Charity jewels to collars, in order to demonstrate to the Masonic world at large the level of generosity exhibited by the wearer. This collar and jewel belonged to wealthy stockbroker Charles Edward Keyser (1847-1929). Each jewel represents one Festival Stewardship, the cost of which was 10 guineas or some £900 itm – a very expensive collar!

K16: Launch of the Lifeboat *Albert Edward*, funded by Freemasons, at Clacton-on-Sea, 1875. ➤

Tangible projects are very popular amongst Freemasons, as those donating to a good cause can literally see how their money has been utilised. Freemasonry is probably unique in that all charitable donations come from members of the Craft, rather than collecting contributions from members of the public or other similar sources. Freemasonry has been funding lifeboats since 1871. At Clacton the first three lifeboats, all named *Albert Edward*, were gifts to the Royal National Lifeboat Institution from the Freemasons of England. The first was presented in 1878, in commemoration of the safe return from his tour in India of their Grand Master King Edward VII, then the Prince of Wales.

K17: Royal Masonic Hospital Nurse's Silver Belt Buckle, *c.*1960. ➤

The Royal Masonic Hospital and Nurses' Home opened at Ravenscourt Park, West London in 1933 and closed in 1992. A School of Nursing was established in 1948, which quickly gained a worldwide reputation for training skilled nurses of the highest calibre. The distinctive and highly-coveted Royal Masonic Hospital nurse's silver belt buckle, awarded on qualifying as a nurse at the Hospital, has achieved iconic status amongst the medical profession.

As early as 1911, members of Malmesbury Lodge No. 3156 became interested in the possibility of starting a Masonic hospital or nursing home. Approval for the idea by Grand Lodge came in 1913 and fundraising began in 1916. The impact of the First World War was such that the Freemasons' War Hospital was opened on the site of the former Chelsea Hospital for Women in Fulham Road, London in the same year. Over 4,000 servicemen were treated at the Hospital by the end of the War. After the First World War the Freemason's Hospital and Nursing Home opened in the Fulham Road premises and accepted its first patient in 1920. The site proved to be too small and a new site was sought at Ravenscourt Park, West London. Money for the new Hospital was raised through donations, with donors being awarded what became known as the Permanent Steward's Jewel. The Royal Masonic Hospital was opened in 1933.

Although the Hospital was highly successful and very well respected, in later years fewer and fewer Masons, and indeed their families, wanted to travel to London for treatment. At the same time running costs were escalating and the situation rapidly became untenable. In 1992, after considerable debate and heart-searching, Grand Lodge recommended the closure of the Hospital. The decision, and indeed the way it was arrived at, was far from popular with many members of the Fraternity, particularly those who had supported the Hospital over the years – a case of the heart ruling the head if ever there was one, but in retrospect even the harshest of critics would now accept that it was the only viable decision.

K18: Porcelain Charity Box in the shape of a Vault, c.1935.

There are many types of container used for collecting coins for charitable funds in the course of a lodge meeting. This is a rare example of Masonic imagery, which would be a very familiar piece of symbolism to a member of the Royal Arch degree; manufactured during the Sampson Hancock period of Crown Derby Porcelain. It was used by the Chapter of Unity No. 4841 in Derbyshire at their Festive Board.

Charity is a central tenet of Freemasonry, but is entirely a matter for every individual Mason. The amounts donated should not be to the detriment of himself or his family. A collection is usually taken during every lodge meeting, though sometimes this is deferred to the dinner afterwards. The amount donated on each occasion is a matter for the individual concerned but is unlikely to be less than £1.

Royal Freemasons and the Rulers of the Craft

Dr Paul Calderwood

Over the past 300 years one of the most striking – and enduring – features of Freemasonry has been the powerful appeal and enjoyment that it has extended to so many of the nation's rulers.

Within that group of rulers, the most conspicuous have been those members of the British Royal Family who became Freemasons or provided the organisation with valuable patronage. They numbered well over two dozen people and included five Kings and four Queens.

As members of the Craft, this royal group included King George IV, King William IV, King Edward VII, King Edward VIII and King George VI; as well as their Royal Highnesses the Duke of Connaught, Prince Arthur of Connaught, three Dukes of Kent, Prince Michael of Kent and Prince Philip.

As patrons or supporters, it also included Queen Victoria, Queen Mary, Queen Elizabeth the Queen Mother, Queen Elizabeth II; as well as Princess Louise (Duchess of Argyll), Princess Mary (the Princess Royal), Princess Margaret of Connaught and Princess Patricia, among others.

This long-running association has generated an abundance of treasured items that illustrate the history of the Fraternity and the strong appeal that the organisation has had for many of the nation's most distinguished figures.

In Britain, the close association between royalty and Freemasonry can be traced back to the 1730s and the very earliest days of organised Freemasonry. It was just twenty years after the formation of the Premier Grand Lodge that the first member of the British Royal Family entered the Order – when Frederick Lewis, Prince of Wales, was initiated in an Occasional Lodge that was convened at Kew Palace. His example was followed six years later in 1743 by his brother, the Duke of Cumberland, who – characteristically – was initiated in a military lodge in Belgium. Frederick Lewis never became King, for he died in 1751 at the age of 44 (pre-deceasing his father King George II by nine years).

However, after the death of Frederick Lewis, three of his sons also became Freemasons: namely, Edward Augustus, Duke of York in 1765; William Henry, Duke of Gloucester in 1766; and Henry Frederick, Duke of Cumberland in 1767. These three sons were appointed Past Grand Masters in 1767 and one of them (the Duke of Cumberland) subsequently held active office as Grand Master of the Moderns Grand Lodge from 1782 until his death in 1790.

Although their older brother, the Prince of Wales (later King George III) did not become a Mason, six of his sons did. They were:

- William, Duke of Clarence (later King William IV) in 1786
- George, Prince of Wales (later King George IV) in 1787
- Frederick, Duke of York, also in 1787
- Augustus Frederick, Duke of Sussex, in 1788
- Edward Augustus, Duke of Kent, in 1789
- Ernest, Duke of Cumberland (later King of Hanover) in 1796

Whilst Prince of Wales, George succeeded his uncle, the Duke of Cumberland, as Grand Master of the Moderns Grand Lodge in 1790 **[L1] [L2]** and he held that office until 1813, when he was succeeded by his brother, the Duke of Sussex. In that year, the Duke of Sussex and their brother the Duke of Kent (the Grand Master of the Antients Grand Lodge) **[D10]** signed the Act of Union that created the United Grand Lodge of England (UGLE) and, in consequence, the Duke of Sussex became the first Grand Master – an office that he held for thirty years, until 1843 **[L3]**.

North of the English border, a similar pattern of close royal involvement with Freemasonry was established from an early date. Since the creation of the Grand Lodge of Scotland in 1736, the following members of the Royal Family have been Grand Patrons: George, Prince of Wales (King George IV) in 1804; King William IV in 1830; Albert Edward, Prince of Wales (King Edward VII) in 1871; King Edward VIII in 1936; and King George VI.

The prestige with which these British Royals endowed the organisation, both north and south of the border, was augmented by a host of foreign monarchs. Overseas royal Freemasons with whom the British Royals had family or imperial connections included, in Denmark, King Christian IX, Frederick VIII, and Christian X; in Greece, King George II; in Sweden, King Oscar II, King Gustav V, and King Gustav VI; as well as – further afield – the Maharajah of Cooch Behar, the Maharajah of Gwalior, the Amir of Afghanistan and the Sultan of Zanzibar. Several of these royal Brethren were in fact 'English' Freemasons. King Christian IX, for example, joined a lodge under the jurisdiction of the UGLE, and the King of Greece and the Sultan of Zanzibar were both initiated into English lodges; while King Christian X and King Gustav V were appointed as Past Grand Masters.

In England and Wales, an important part of the history of royal endorsement of Freemasonry has been played by the ladies. Arguably the most notable of these was Queen Victoria, who was not only the daughter of a Grand Master (the Duke of Kent) but also became the mother of two later Grand Masters. She smiled on Freemasonry in a variety of ways – particularly in support of Masonic charities. In 1852 she became Patron (and, from 1883 onwards, Grand Patron) of the Royal Masonic Institution for Boys; although she probably would not have been 'amused' in 1900, when Richard Eve, Trustee of the RMIB, was reported in *The Times* as saying that she 'was now the oldest annual subscriber'. In 1882 Queen Victoria **[L4]** also became Chief Patroness of the Royal Masonic Institution for Girls **[L5]**. She continued to hold these offices, endorsing both the Boys and the Girls Institutions, until her death in 1901 **[L6]**.

Two of her sons, the Prince of Wales **[L7] [L8] [L9] [L10]** and the Duke of Connaught, were to become successive Grand Masters of the UGLE – an office that might also have been held by another son, Leopold, Duke of Albany. Leopold was appointed Provincial Grand Master of Oxfordshire in 1876, but his Masonic career and his life were both cut short by his unexpected death in 1884.

Leopold's older brother, the Prince of Wales **[L11]**, was without doubt the most high-profile Freemason within the British Empire – from the date of his Initiation in 1868 until his death in 1910. He was a keen and very active Mason who deserves much of the credit for the great expansion that the UGLE experienced during his Grand Mastership. His brother, the Duke of Connaught **[L12]**, was another keen and active Freemason and – until 2005 – held the record as the longest-serving Grand Master of the UGLE, having served for thirty-eight years.

In addition to these three sons, several of Queen Victoria's grandsons also became senior members of the Fraternity, including Prince Albert Victor Christian Edward, Duke of Clarence and Avondale (the elder son of the Prince of Wales), who was appointed Provincial Grand Master for Berkshire in 1890; and Prince Arthur of Connaught, who became Provincial Grand Master for the same province in 1924.

This enthusiasm was also echoed by the grandsons of King Edward VII: the Prince of Wales (later King Edward VIII) **[L13] [L14]** and the Duke of York (later King George VI) **[L15] [L16]**. Highlighting the importance that Freemasonry played in their lives, George VI wrote, in recording the moment of his brother's Abdication in 1936: 'When David and I said goodbye we kissed, parted as Freemasons and he bowed to me as his King'.

Further underlining his own very strong attachment to Freemasonry, George VI in the following year took the unprecedented step of becoming the only Royal ever to preside over a meeting of Grand Lodge *after* becoming King. It was an act that he proudly repeated in 1939, when he installed his younger brother, Prince George, Duke of Kent as Grand Master – and on two other occasions after that.

Following in Prince George's footsteps two of his sons, Edward, Duke of Kent **[L17]** and Prince Michael of Kent, have continued this proud family tradition as rulers within Freemasonry. Indeed the present Duke of Kent has been the Grand Master for the past fifty years – a unique achievement. Meanwhile, his brother, Prince Michael **[L18]**, is close to equalling the record (thirty-eight years) set by HRH the Duke of Connaught as the longest-serving Grand Master of the Grand Lodge of Mark Master Masons.

Throughout the past three centuries members of the Royal Family have given Freemasonry valuable endorsement and so raised the public profile of the Masonic Orders. For Freemasonry, the benefits of this association have been seen – in rising membership figures and soaring morale.

However, within the British ruling classes, it was not only members of the Royal Family who enthusiastically embraced Freemasonry. Among the leaders and rulers of British society in a wider sense, a similar fascination was felt, for example by many of the Lords Temporal and Spiritual. Almost a thousand members of both became active Freemasons. Their ranks ranged from the Duke of Devonshire and the Marquis of Zetland to the Archbishop of Canterbury, a number of Presidents of the Wesley Conference and several Chief Rabbis.

Equally, large numbers of British politicians drawn from all parties have been proud to affirm their membership of the Craft. Their numbers have included, for example, Prime Minister Winston Churchill **[L19]** and the Leader of the House of Commons, Viscount Crookshank. The many Government posts in which British Freemasons have served have included those of Lord Privy Seal (Arthur Greenwood), Lord High Chancellor (F.E. Smith), Solicitor General (Sir Ian Percival), Home Secretary (Edward Shortt), Health Minister (Sir Gerard Vaughan), Environment Minister (Sir David Trippier), Secretary of State for India (Leo Amery), Secretary of State for Air (Sir Kingsley Wood), Postmaster General (Lord Stanley) and Fisheries Minister (Tony Baldry), as well as many others.

Similarly in local government, countless elected and appointed members have enjoyed the friendship and fulfilment of Freemasonry. In London almost one hundred Lord Mayors of the City have been Masons, and in towns and cities throughout England and Wales (including

Liverpool, Manchester, Bradford, York, Hull, Leeds and Cardiff) many hundreds more Mayors were enthusiastic, proud and well-known Freemasons.

Beyond Britain's shores, within its vast Empire and the Commonwealth that succeeded it, similarly long lines of ruling figures have also delighted in their membership of Freemasonry. They have included the Governor Generals of Australia, of India, of New Zealand, of Canada, and of South Africa; as well as the Governors of Victoria, South Australia, Madras and Bombay; and a Lieutenant Governor of Guernsey [L20]. Their substantial ranks have been swollen by Dominion Prime Ministers in Australia and New Zealand, plus Maharajahs, Khans and a wide range of native rulers.

Looking back over the past 300 years, one is bound to ask why did so many of Britain's leaders – and most especially members of the Royal Family (who, after all, enjoyed all the privileges of social pre-eminence) – choose to associate themselves so strongly with Freemasonry? No general answer could possibly fit all instances. Many of those who are unsympathetic to the organisation would be only too quick to claim that its attractions (in their view) may have included financial gain and the opportunity to exercise undue influence; but, since wealth and influence are an intrinsic part of royalty, these are unlikely to have tempted many Princes and Dukes to enter the Brotherhood. Freemasons themselves generally describe the attractions as a combination of some, or all, of the following: friendship, networking, family ties, peer pressure, love of tradition, a desire to perpetuate a cultural heritage, philosophical reflection, moral improvement, benevolence and social care. Most of these motives appear to have played a part in attracting the interest of royalty. Additional motives – for royalty – might also include a sense of public duty: acknowledging the need to be identified with the major institutions of the country in order to cement loyalty to the throne. The lack or inaccessibility of relevant records, which would identify more closely the specific motives that attracted each of these members of the Royal Family to Freemasonry, makes it difficult to state precisely which factors played the dominant part in each case. A varying mixture of the motives listed above was probably at work in most instances.

Arguably, this set of individuals might be divided into four groups. Firstly, those for whom the convivial aspects of Freemasonry were uppermost – probably embracing the fun-loving, sociable Kings Edward VII and VIII and Prince George, Duke of Kent. Secondly, those for whom the moral aspects and sense of public duty had an especially strong pull – probably including the Duke of Connaught, Prince Arthur of Connaught, King George VI, the present Duke of Kent and Prince Michael of Kent. Thirdly, the group for whom a sense of public duty and an interest in benevolence represented the main link to Freemasonry probably encompassed non-Masons such as King George V and the female members of the Royal Family mentioned above. Lastly, there were those with a connection, but for whom the appeal of Freemasonry was not so strong. Clearly, the level of royal involvement in Freemasonry in the United Kingdom declined substantially after 1952. Nonetheless, the present Queen has steadfastly supported the RMBI, RMIG and RMIB since her accession and her husband – more than sixty years after his Initiation – is still a subscribing member.

Over the past three centuries as a whole, members of the Royal Family and other rulers undoubtedly gave Freemasonry celebrity endorsement, raised its public profile, swelled its ranks and generated great pride.

L1: Throne commissioned for George Augustus, Prince of Wales, later King George IV, 1791.

Grand Master's throne with a carved framework of gilt lime wood, flanked by a pair of Doric columns. The throne's arms and supports are formed from a double scroll of acanthus leaves with a lion's mask and paw at the tip of each arm and the base of each support. The seat rails are carved with rosettes and incorporate on the front a rectangular plaque, carved with a Volume of the Sacred Law between the points of a pair of Compasses. The throne is surmounted by a carved wood ducal coronet, partially gilded and partially painted red, with a painted ermine trim; this is flanked below by two gilt cradles, on which are mounted a terrestrial globe and a celestial globe.

Soon after George Augustus, Prince of Wales (later George IV) became the first Royal Grand Master of the Moderns Grand Lodge in 1790, a ceremonial throne and two Warden's chairs, replete with Masonic symbolism, were commissioned for use in the new Freemasons' Hall in London. The London cabinet maker Robert Kennett, based at 67 New Bond Street, charged £157. 10s. (£17,000 itm) and took three months to complete the set in gilded lime wood.

George Augustus (1762-1830) was the eldest son of George III, whom he succeeded in 1820 following a period from 1789 when he acted, during the illness of the King, as Prince Regent. He was initiated on 6 February 1787 by his uncle the Duke of Cumberland at the Star and Garter in Pall Mall. In the same year he founded the Prince of Wales's Lodge (now) No. 259 and was its Permanent Master from 1787 to 1820. The Lodge has the privilege of annually nominating a Grand Steward and its members are permitted to wear aprons with garter-blue edging. Whilst Prince of Wales he became Grand Master, in succession to his uncle, in 1790 and held that office until the Union of the two Grand Lodges in 1813, when he accepted the title of Grand Patron of the Order.

L2: King George IV, *c.*1825. ▶

The oil painting on canvas from the studio of Thomas Lawrence (1769–1830) shows George IV wearing the robes of the Order of the Garter, the highest chivalric order in the United Kingdom.

George Augustus (1762-1830) was the eldest son of George III, whom he succeeded in 1820 following a period from 1789 when he acted, during the illness of the King, as Prince Regent. He was initiated by his uncle, the Duke of Cumberland, on 6 February 1787 at the Star and Garter in Pall Mall. In the same year he founded the Prince of Wales's Lodge (now) No. 259 and was its Permanent Master from 1787 to 1820. The Lodge has the privilege of annually nominating a Grand Steward and its members are permitted to wear aprons with garter-blue edging. Whilst Prince of Wales he became Grand Master, in succession to his uncle, in 1790 and held that office until the Union of the two Grand Lodges in 1813, when he accepted the title of Grand Patron of the Order.

L3: Augustus Frederick, Duke of Sussex, 1885. ▼

Portrait in oils by Barnett Samuel Marks (1827-1916), painted in 1885 to replace the original which was destroyed in a fire at Freemasons' Hall, London in 1883.

The appearance of the Duke wearing traditional highland dress may in part be explained by the fact that Augustus Frederick had been created Duke of Inverness in 1801. His second wife, Lady Cecilia Gore, whom he had married in 1831 without the consent or knowledge of the King and hence contrary to the Royal Marriage Act, was made the Duchess of Inverness, in her own right, in 1840.

L4: Loyal Address: To Queen Victoria, 1896. ➤

From the District Grand Lodge of Wellington, North Island, New Zealand to Queen Victoria, offering congratulations on celebrating her Diamond Jubilee.

L5: Centenary Jewel: Royal Masonic Institution for Girls, worn by Albert Edward, Prince of Wales, later King Edward VII, 1888. ▽

The Prince of Wales was very supportive of the three Masonic Charities at the time – the Royal Masonic Benevolent Institution, the Royal Masonic Institute for Girls and Royal Masonic Institute for Boys. He presided at the Festivals of all three of them: twice at the RMIB (1870 and 1898) and the RMIG (1871 and 1888), and once at the RMBI (1873).

The Festival system, developed during the Victorian era, has continued to the present day and all the Masonic Charities each now have an Annual Festival, hosted by one of the forty-four out of the forty-seven different Masonic Provinces (Guernsey and Alderney, Jersey and London are not included). It means that each Masonic Province can expect to host a Charity Festival every eleven years. Most Provinces limit the money-raising activities to a five-year period and the normal expectation is that a member should try to achieve the minimum status of what is known as a 'Steward' by donating a sum of £500 during the five-year period. Other levels such as Vice-Patron, Patron and Grand Patron can be achieved by donating larger amounts.

L6: Loyal Address: To Albert Edward, Prince of Wales, later King Edward VII, 1901.

From the members of the Craft, who after holding an impromptu meeting on the Union Castle Royal Mail Steamship *S.S. Norman*, sent congratulations to the Prince of Wales on his having avoided injury when on 20 May 1901 the mast collapsed on board the yacht *Shamrock II*. The Prince was a competitor in the 11th America's Cup, in the yacht designed by the Scottish naval architect George Lennox Watson and built by William Denny and Brothers.

A Loyal Address is a very public means for any organisation to show its allegiance and loyalty to the Monarch or a member of the Royal Family, and in that regard Freemasonry is no exception. Included here are a number of diverse examples on very different occasions that amply illustrate the art of the calligrapher and the devotion of Freemasons to the Royal Family over many years.

L7: King Edward VII as Grand Master, 1885.

A portrait by Louis William Desanges (1822–87), himself a Freemason. He was an English artist of French heritage, and is known today for his paintings of winners of the Victoria Cross and military themes.

Edward VII (1841-1910), the eldest son of Queen Victoria, was initiated in 1868 in Sweden by King Oscar II of Sweden and Norway (1829-1907). He was a most enthusiastic Mason and very supportive of Freemasonry. He became a member of Royal Alpha Lodge No. 16 in 1870, serving as Master from 1871 to 1872, in 1877 and again from 1882 to 1886. He went on to join Union Lodge No. 52, Prince of Wales's Lodge No. 259 and Grand Master's Lodge No. 1. He was the Founding Master of Navy Lodge No. 2612, Household Brigade Lodge No. 2614 and Sancta Maria Lodge No. 2682. He was Grand Master from 1874 until his accession in 1901, when he became Protector of the Craft. He also found time to be First Grand Principal of the Royal Arch, Grand Master of the Mark, Grand Master of the Knights Templar and Grand Patron of the Ancient and Accepted Rite. Reigning monarchs are precluded from serving as Grand Master but as he wished to continue his connection with Freemasonry he took on the role of Protector of the Craft.

L8: Jewel: Commemorating the Installation of Albert Edward, Prince of Wales, later King Edward VII, as Grand Master, 1875. ➤

Following the death of the Duke of Sussex there was a gap in royal participation in the Craft, simply because there were no Princes of the Blood Royal eligible to join. This lapse was remedied when Edward VII was initiated in Sweden in 1868. The involvement of the Prince of Wales in Freemasonry was a major factor in the growth of membership and the increase in the number of lodges in the late nineteenth century.

L9: Golden Jubilee Jewel: Commemorating the 50th anniversary of the reign of Queen Victoria, 1837-87.
This particular jewel belonged to Albert Edward, Prince of Wales, later King Edward VII, 1887. ◂

The Golden Jubilee of Queen Victoria in 1887 and the Diamond Jubilee of 1897 were both the subject of major national and Masonic celebrations. On 21 June 1887 an Especial meeting of Grand Lodge was held in the Royal Albert Hall to commemorate the Golden Jubilee, attended by some 7,000 Freemasons including two of the Queen's sons – the Grand Master, Albert Edward, Prince of Wales, and the Duke of Connaught; together with Lord Lathom, the Pro Grand Master.

Admission fees were charged and raised £6,000 (almost £600,000 itm), which was divided between the three Masonic Charities of the time – the Royal Masonic Benevolent Institution, the Royal Masonic Institute for Girls and Royal Masonic Institute for Boys.

All subscribing Masons were entitled to wear a commemorative jewel, and those who attended the meeting at the Royal Albert Hall were permitted to have an additional bar, and a further device if they acted as a Steward at the meeting.

L10: Diamond Jubilee Jewel: Commemorating the 60th anniversary of the reign of Queen Victoria, 1837-97.
This particular jewel belonged to Albert Edward, Prince of Wales, later King Edward VII, 1897.

The Golden Jubilee of Queen Victoria in 1887 and the Diamond Jubilee of 1897 were both the subject of major national and Masonic celebrations.

As in 1887, an Especial meeting of Grand Lodge was held in the Royal Albert Hall on 14 June 1897 to commemorate the Diamond Jubilee, attended by some 7,000 Freemasons including two of the Queen's sons – the Grand Master, Albert Edward, Prince of Wales, and the Duke of Connaught; together with the Pro Grand Master, the Earl of Carnarvon.

Admission fees were again charged and raised £7,000 (over £700,000 itm), which was divided between the Prince of Wales Hospital Fund and the three Masonic Charities of the time – the Royal Masonic Benevolent Institution, the Royal Masonic Institute for Girls and Royal Masonic Institute for Boys.

Also as in 1887 all subscribing Masons were entitled to wear a commemorative jewel, and those who attended the meeting at the Royal Albert Hall were permitted to have an additional bar, and a further device if they acted as a Steward at the meeting.

L11: Loyal Address: To King Edward VII, 1901.

From the Grand Lodge of Manitoba, Winnipeg, Canada to King Edward VII on the death of Queen Victoria, expressing sympathy over her death and congratulating him on his accession to the Throne.

To the King's Most Excellent Majesty,

May it please Your Majesty,

We your Majesty's loyal subjects, members of the Fraternity known as the Grand Lodge of Manitoba, Ancient Free and Accepted Masons, now in annual assembly, desire to humbly express the profound sorrow with which we learned of the death of Her Majesty Queen Victoria, and to convey to you our sincere and fraternal sympathy. As Masons we ever rejoiced that her late Majesty was a most gracious and generous patroness and supporter of our Order, and encouraged the observance of its teachings and principles by allowing her children to become members of it, and to take upon themselves high offices, which greatly tended to the benefit and advantage of the fraternity. We long realized in her the symbol of unity of our Empire and that her labour was continually spent in studying the best interests and wellfare of her subjects. Thus she evidenced her belief in the reciprocal rights and duties of Soverign and subject and that true happiness came to her from "Her Throne, broad based upon her people's will".

We further beg to tender to you our loyal congratulations on your succession to the Throne. We pray that the Great Architect of the Universe may extend to you the happiness of a prolonged life, the blessings of peace, and that you may further witness the continued happiness and prosperity of your subjects, feeling confident that their well-being will be as dear to your heart as to that of your illustrious Mother, and be enhanced by your gracious and beneficent rule.

As members of our Ancient Fraternity we have learned with much thankfulness that you will be pleased to accept the position of Protector of English Free Masons. We can join with our English brethren in paying tribute to the great services which you have rendered the craft, and we feel that the manifold agencies for good associated with Freemasonry all over the British Empire are very much indebted to your fostering care and Patronage.

Dated at the Masonic Temple in the City of Winnipeg, in the Province of Manitoba, Canada, this 2 day of June A.D. 1901. A.L. 5901, in the First Year of His Majesty's Reign.

R. S. Thornton
Grand Master.

Attest:

James A. Ovas
Grand Secretary.

W. R. LEWIS.

L12: Loyal Address: To Arthur, Duke of Connaught and Strathearn, 1906.

From the District Grand Lodge of Transvaal to Arthur, Duke of Connaught and Strathearn, on his visit to South Africa in 1906 in his capacity as Grand Master.

Arthur, Duke of Connaught and Strathearn (1850-1942) was the third son of Queen Victoria. His record as a Freemason is second to none, as is the service he rendered to English Freemasonry over a period of more than fifty years.

Initiated in the Prince of Wales's Lodge No. 259 on 24 March 1874, he was the Permanent Master from 1903 until his death in 1942; he was also a member of Royal Alpha Lodge No. 16, serving as Master in 1880. He subsequently joined and in due course became Permanent Master of: London Irish Rifles Lodge No. 2312, Aldershot Army and Navy Lodge No. 1971, Household Brigade Lodge No. 2614, Jubilee Masters Lodge No. 2712, Old Wellingtonian Lodge No. 3404, Royal Colonial Institute Lodge No. 3556, and Nil Sine Labore Lodge No. 2736.

Appointed as Senior Grand Warden in 1877, he was Provincial Grand Master for Sussex in 1886-1901 and District Grand Master for Bombay in 1887-1901. Appointed Past Grand Master in 1891, he served with great distinction as Grand Master from 1901 to 1939, whilst at the same time undertaking the duties of First Grand Principal, Grand Master of the Grand Lodge of Mark Master Masons, Grand Master of the Knights Templar, and Grand Patron from 1911 to 1942 of the Ancient and Accepted Rite.

L13: Apron presented to Edward, Prince of Wales, later King Edward VIII, on his Initiation, 1919.

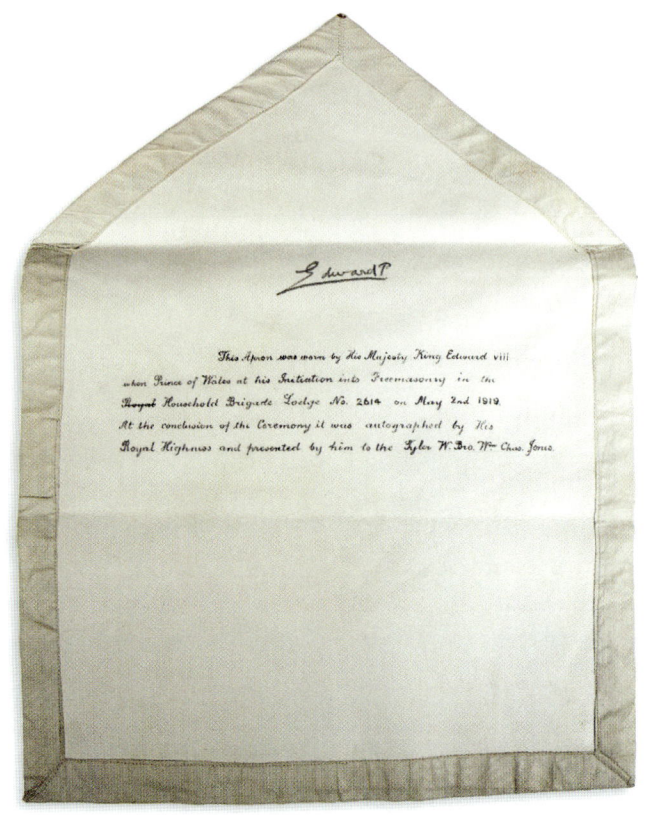

The apron was worn by Edward, Prince of Wales at his Initiation in the Household Brigade Lodge No. 2614 on 2 May 1919. At the conclusion of the ceremony it was autographed by him and presented to the Tyler of the Lodge. In England every Initiate is presented during the course of the ceremony with a plain white, lambskin apron.

Edward Albert, Prince of Wales (1894-1972) was the eldest son of George V and Queen Mary. He was initiated into Household Brigade Lodge No. 2614 in 1919 and went on to join St Mary Magdalene Lodge No. 1523, Lodge of Friendship and Harmony No. 1616 and Royal Alpha Lodge No. 16. He was a very active Freemason: a member of the Royal Arch, the Mark Degree, the Ancient and Accepted Rite and the Royal Order of Scotland. He was appointed as Provincial Grand Master for Surrey in 1924, and as Past Grand Master on his Abdication as King Edward VIII in 1936, when he took the title of the Duke of Windsor.

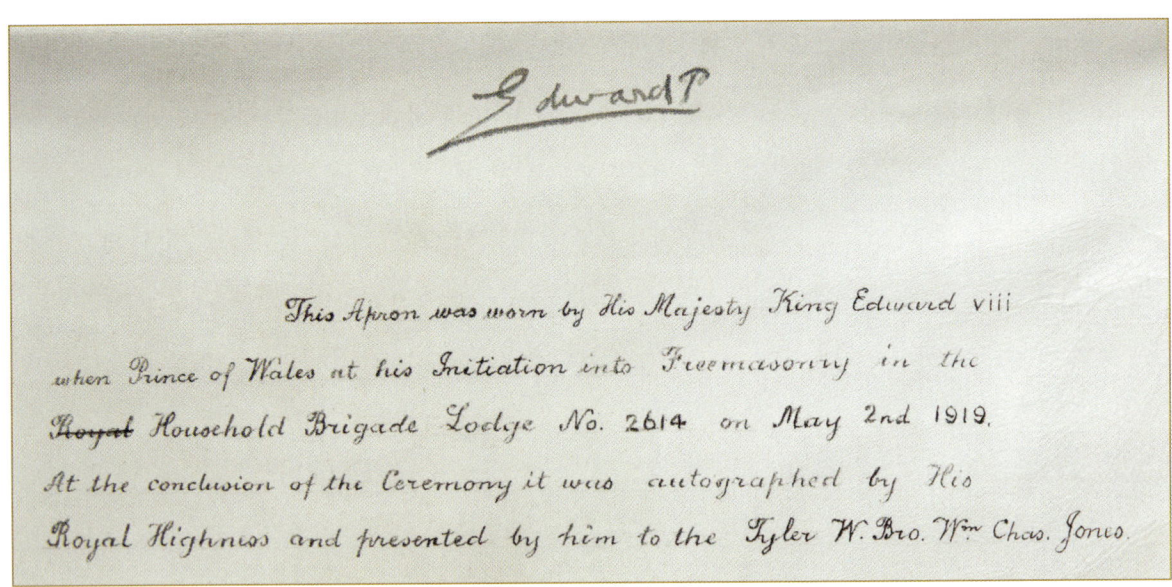

L14: Past Grand Master's apron, worn by the Prince of Wales, later King Edward VIII, 1936.

L15: Invitation to the Initiation of Albert, Duke of York, later King George VI, 1919.

Although George V was not a Freemason, but his two sons - who respectively became King Edward VIII (1894-1972) and King George VI (1895-1952) – were both active Freemasons.

In recent times the most enthusiastic of Royal Freemasons has undoubtedly been Albert, Duke of York, who succeeded his brother Edward VIII on his Abdication in 1936 as King George VI.

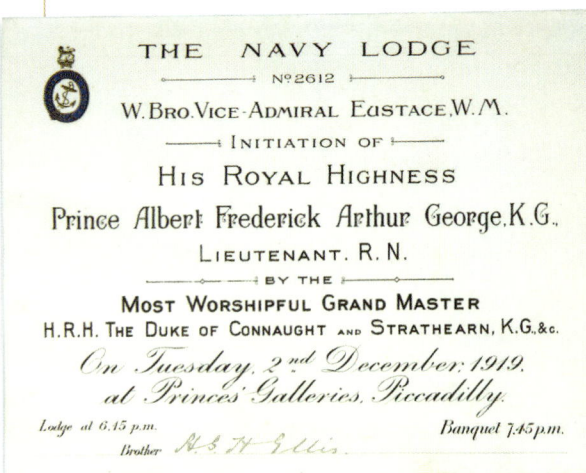

He was initiated in Navy Lodge No. 2612 in London on 2 December 1919, and in response to his toast at the dinner following his Initiation, the Duke of York is reported as saying:

I have always wished to become a Freemason, but owing to the war I have had no opportunity before this of joining the Craft. All my life I have heard of Freemasonry, and though there has always been a certain mystery attached to it, I have learned that Freemasons in this country have been a great help to the poor and friendless, and have been notable for their efforts on behalf of children.

L16: RMBI 1931 Festival Souvenir: Chairman, Albert, Duke of York.

In 1924 the Duke of York was installed as Provincial Grand Master of Middlesex. The Duke relished the role and took an active part in the work of the Province. In 1931 he also became the Provincial Grand Master for Middlesex in the Mark. The same year he presided in over the Royal Masonic Festival. The Festival raised £116,329. 19s. 5d. – over £7 million itm. A magnificent total, given that all the monies donated would have been from the pockets of individual Masons, the majority of whom would have been members of lodges in Middlesex.

He later acknowledged that his tenure as Provincial Grand Master helped him overcome his stammer and he attributed the improvement '… to the ritual and ceremonies I was obliged to conduct as a Freemason and Provincial Grand Master.'

In 1936 following the death of George V and the accession of Edward VIII, the Duke was approached, to take on the role of Grand Master Mason of Scotland, during its bicentenary year - but there was a problem: to be Grand Master Mason of Scotland one had to be a member of a Scottish lodge. It says everything about the man that, rather than choose an 'upmarket' lodge in Edinburgh, he joined instead Glamis Lodge No. 99, a small village Lodge, the Master of which was a postman.

In the ordinary course of events, on acceding to the throne the previous protocol was for the King not to take any further active part in Freemasonry but to become Patron of the Craft, as in the case of George IV, and Protector of the Craft with Edward VII. However, George VI wished to continue his active association with Freemasonry and at an Especial meeting of Grand Lodge, held to celebrate the Coronation at the Albert Hall on 30 June 1937, he was installed as Past Grand Master.

As far as his Royal duties allowed, the King continued to be actively involved as a Freemason until shortly before his untimely death, and this included the Installation of three successive Grand Masters.

The first Installation was that of his younger brother, George, Duke of Kent (1902-42), the fourth son of George V and the father of the present Duke of Kent. The Duke of Kent succeeded his great-uncle, the Duke of Connaught, as Grand Master and was installed by the King in his capacity as Past Grand Master at a ceremony at Olympia on 19 July 1939, witnessed by some 12,000 Freemasons.

Albert

Royal Masonic Benevolent Institution.
89th Annual Festival, 12th March 1931.
R.W. Bro. H.R.H. The Duke of York, K.G. Patron,
Past Grand Warden,
Provincial Grand Master for Middlesex,
Chairman.
Presented by the Committee of Management to
W. Bro. Major Sir Francis Burdett, Bart. P.P.G.W. Middlesex.
Steward on the occasion when the sum of £116,328-19-5 was raised by 6,674 Stewards.

L17: Edward, Duke of Kent, 1975.

The portrait by Arthur Derek Hill, CBE (1916–2000), an English portrait and landscape painter, was commissioned by the United Grand Lodge of England. The Duke is wearing the robes of the Order of the Garter, the highest chivalric order in the United Kingdom. The stained glass window in the background has a border made up of Set Squares and Compasses, which surround an Ionic capital.

The present Grand Master, Edward, Duke of Kent (1935-), the elder son of George, Duke of Kent (q.v.) is the third Duke of Kent to be a Mason and the third to be elected a Grand Master. He is also the eighth Royal Grand Master in English Freemasonry. His father George, Duke of Kent, was Grand Master from 1939-42. The present Duke was initiated on 16 December 1963 in Royal Alpha Lodge No. 16 and became Master in 1965. He was appointed as Senior Grand Warden in 1966, and installed as Grand Master on 27 June 1967 at an Especial Grand Lodge held at the Royal Albert Hall at the celebration of the 250th Anniversary of the United Grand Lodge of England. The Duke was exalted in Westminster and Keystone Chapter No. 10, of which he became First Principal in 1966 and was installed as First Grand Principal in 1967.

L18: HRH Prince Michael of Kent, 1987. ▷

A portrait painted in 1987 by Howard Morgan (1949-) shows the Prince wearing his regalia as Grand Master of the Grand Lodge of Mark Master Masons (GLMMM), who commissioned the portrait. In the foreground is a representation of Noah's Ark, a reference to the fact that the GLMMM has authority over the Degree of the Royal Ark Mariner in England and Wales.

HRH Prince Michael of Kent (1942-) is the younger son of George, Duke of Kent (q.v.). He was initiated on 13 June 1974 in Royal Alpha Lodge No. 16 and was the Master in 1977. He joined the Prince of Wales's Lodge No. 259 on 21 October 1975 and served as a Grand Steward in 1982. Appointed as Senior Grand Warden in 1979, he was installed as the Provincial Grand Master for Middlesex in 1982, an office he still holds. Exalted on 5 June 1979 in the Prince of Wales's Chapter No. 259; he was advanced as a Mark Master Mason in Milestone Lodge of MMM No. 1000 on 28 June 1979 and elevated as a Royal Ark Mariner in Milestone Lodge of RAM No. 1000 on 25 October 1979. He has served as the Grand Master of the Grand Lodge of Mark Master Masons since 1982.

L19: Master Mason's Apron belonging to Sir Winston Churchill, 1902. ▽

Sir Winston Churchill (1874-1965) was a British statesman and Prime Minister from 1940 to 1945 and again from 1951 to 1955. Churchill was also a British Army officer, a historian, a writer and an artist. He won the Nobel Prize in Literature, and was the first person to be made an honorary citizen of the United States. He was also a Freemason, being initiated into Studholme Lodge No. 1591 (now United Studholme Alliance) in London on 24 May 1901 and became a Master Mason on 5 March 1902. He was not however very active in the Craft and never progressed beyond the rank of a Master Mason.

L20: Silver Gilt Ceremonial Flagon, 1806.

The Doyle Cup is one of two silver gilt ceremonial flagons presented to Lieutenant General Sir John Doyle by the Freemasons of Guernsey. He had a distinguished military career, but nearly ruined himself financially due to his generosity while Lieutenant Governor of Guernsey.

The cup combines aspects of Doyle's Freemasonry and military career. The lid bears the arms of the Masonic Antients Grand Lodge and a Royal Crown. The handle is a crocodile – the unofficial badge of all officers who had served in the Egyptian campaign; the spout bears the Prince of Wales feathers. All would have been meaningful to Doyle, who was Colonel of the Prince of Wales Royal Irish Regiment, had been initiated in Prince of Wales's Lodge, and been the Prince's Private Secretary. Also illustrated on one side is a depiction of the battle for Chew's House in Philadelphia during the American War of Independence, where Doyle was wounded in action; and on the other side are a number of ornate Masonic symbols.

John Doyle (1756-1834) was an officer in the British Army and served with distinction in the American War of Independence and the French Revolutionary Wars. After acting as Private Secretary to the Prince of Wales, he was appointed Lieutenant Governor of Guernsey from 1803 until 1813, when he was knighted. Promoted to General in 1819, he was created a baronet in 1825.

John Doyle was initiated in London in 1792 in the Prince of Wales's Lodge under the Moderns Grand Lodge. In 1807 he was a Founder of Doyle's Lodge of Fellowship, Guernsey under the Antients Grand Lodge, where he had to be 'remade' a Mason before being installed as Worshipful Master. In 1810 he became a Founder and Master of Doyle's Military Lodge, Guernsey, under the Moderns Grand Lodge. In 1820, soon after the 1813 merger of the Moderns and Antients Grand Lodges, the two Lodges amalgamated and became Doyle's Lodge of Friendship No. 84, Guernsey. In 1822 Doyle was appointed Deputy Grand Master of the United Grand Lodge of England.

Location and Contact Details
of Featured Museums and Libraries

London
London
[1] Library and Museum of Freemasonry
Freemasons' Hall, 60 Great Queen St,
London WC2B 5AZ
Monday to Friday 10.00 to 17.00
Tel: 020 7395 9257
Email: libmus@ugle.org.uk

Bristol
Bristol
[2] Bristol Freemasons' Hall Library and Museum
Freemasons' Hall, Park Street, Bristol BS1 5NH
Monday and Thursday: 09.00 to 12:30;
or by arrangement
Tel: 0117 954 9840
Email: prov.sec@provinceofbristol.org.uk

Derbyshire
Littleover
[3] Library & Museum of the Provincial Grand Lodge of Derbyshire Freemasons
Masonic Hall, 457 Burton Road, Littleover,
Derby DE23 6XX
Wednesday and Thursday: 10.30 to 12.30:
September to June; or by arrangement
Tel: 01332 272202
Email: library@derbyshiremason.org

Essex
Wickford
[4] Essex Provincial Masonic Library and Museum
2 Station Court, Station Approach, Wickford,
Essex SS1 7AT
Tuesday: 10.00 to 13.00: or by arrangement
Tel: 01268 571610
Email: enquiries@essexpgl.org.uk

Hertfordshire
St Albans
[5] Hertfordshire Provincial Museum and Library
Fleet House, 10 Parkway, Porters Wood,
St Albans, Herts. AL3 6PA
Monday to Friday 09.00 to 15.00
Tel: 0116 254 5325 **Email:** archivist@pglherts.org

Leicestershire
Leicester
[6] Provincial Masonic Library and Museum
Freemasons' Hall, 80 London Road,
Leicester LE2 0RA
Monday to Friday 09.30 to 12.00
Tel: 0116 254 5325 **Email:** library@pglleics.co.uk

Northumberland
Gosforth
[7] The John Sherwood Stephenson Library and Museum
Provincial Office, 17 Lansdowne Terrace,
Gosforth, Newcastle upon Tyne NE3 1HP
Tuesday and Thursday afternoons: 13:30 to 15.30:
or by arrangement
Tel: 0191 213 6990 **Email:** provsec@pgln.org

Nottinghamshire
Nottingham
[8] Masonic Museum & Library
Masonic Hall, 25 Goldsmith Street,
Nottingham NG1 5LB
Monday to Friday: 10.00 to 16.00
Tel: 0115 947 3829
Email: masonslibandmus@hotmail.com

West Lancashire
Warrington
[9] Warrington Museum of Freemasonry
Winmarleigh House, Winmarleigh Street,
Warrington WA1 1NB
Wednesdays: 09.30 to 13.00: or by arrangement
Tel: 01925 651468
Email: curator@themasonicmuseum.co.uk

Worcester
Worcester
[10] Worcestershire Masonic Library and Museum
Masonic Hall, Rainbow Hill,
Worcester WR3 8LX
Tuesday and Thursday: 10.00 to 12.00;
second Saturday of the month from March to
September: 10.00 to 16.00
Tel: 01905 24971
Email: info@worcestermasonicmuseum.co.uk

Jewels of the Craft
Web: www.jotc.org.uk

The Treasures of English Freemasonry 1717 – 2017

Catalogue and Index of Images

Artefacts	Date	Page
A16: Ancient Egyptian Mason's Maul	c.1400 BC	34
A1: Wren Maul	1675	16
H1: Sword of State of the United Grand Lodge of England	1735	201
A20: Lodge Meeting in a Bottle, made by a French Prisoner of War during the Napoleonic Wars	c.1795	38
F9: Scrimshaw carved by a French Prisoner of War during the Napoleonic Wars	c.1795	149
G4: Master's Tablet	c.1800	187
J15: Wooden Workbox made by a French Prisoner of War during the Napoleonic Wars	c.1800	236
A18: Snuffbox made from a silver-mounted cowrie shell	1810	37
G10: Craft First Degree Tracing Board by Josiah Bowring	1819	193
G11: Craft Second Degree Tracing Board by Josiah Bowring	1819	194
G12: Craft Third Degree Tracing Board by Josiah Bowring	1819	195
A17: Powder Horn	1820	37
F10: Master's Hat: St Paul's Lodge No. 6400	c.1830	148
F11: Master's Storage Box, St Paul's Lodge No. 6400	c.1830	148
F35: First Degree Tracing Board	1864	175
A22: Masonic Toast Rack	c.1872	43

Artefacts	Date	Page
E11: Gavel used by Ad Astra Lodge No. 3808	1918	131
A23: Masonic Jelly Mould	c.1921	42
K18: Porcelain Charity Box in the shape of a Vault	c.1935	267
Books		
G7: *Orbis Miraculum or The Temple of Solomon portrayed by scripture-light…* by Samuel Lee	1659	188
B1: *To all godly people, in the Citie of London*	1698	49
B4: *Book of Constitutions*: Frontispiece	1723	51
B3: *Constitutions of the Free-Masons*	1723	50
B6: *Engraved List of Lodges*	1725	53
J1: *Book of Constitutions*	1734	222
C4: *Ahiman Rezon* with the bookplate of Laurence Dermott	1756	70
G9: William Preston: *Illustrations of Masonry*	1772	190
G6: *An Accurate Description of the Grand and Glorious Temple of Solomon by Jacob Juda Lyon*: Frontispiece - a reprint of the 1675 publication	1778	188
C1: *Book of Constitutions*: Frontispiece showing the interior of Freemasons' Hall	1784	69
J11: Bible presented to the Lodge of the 18th Regiment of Foot No. 351 [Irish Constitution]	1787	233
D19: *Book of Constitutions*: Frontispiece showing Soane's Ark of the Masonic Covenant	1815	117
Ceramics		
J4: Meissen Ceramic Group of two Freemasons	c.1744	225
J5: Meissen Ceramic Figure of a Freemason	c.1745	226

Catalogue and Index of Images

	Ceramics	Date	Page
	J3: Ch'ien Lung punch bowl, decorated with Masonic symbols and the arms of the Moderns Grand Lodge	1760	224
	F30: Two Ceramic Figures after the Meissen original modelled by Johann Joachim Kändler	c.1774	170
	C15: Teapot in Liverpool creamware	c.1780	85
	F29: Three Graduated Jugs	c.1790	168
	J9: Cup and saucer in Sèvres porcelain	1794	230
	C16: Teapot in Wedgwood creamware	c.1794	85
	C17: Jug in Sunderland lustreware	c.1810	84
	H5: Earthenware Dish showing the Freemasons' Tavern	1820	204
	F22: Shaving Bowl	c.1820	161
	F15: Lodge of Repose Loving Cup	1933	155
	B14: Wedgwood Vase	1992	63

	Documents		
	B5: Earliest Grand Lodge Minute Book	1723	52
	B2: *Haddon Manuscript*	1723	49
	C2: Swan and Rummer Lodge Minute Book	c.1725	69
	K2: Laws Relating to the Committee of Charity	1730	251
	C20: Warrant for Lodge No. 203, meeting at King's Arms Punch Bowl, Shad Thames, London	1766	88
	C18: Early Antients Grand Lodge Certificate	1767	86
	C19: Early Patent of Appointment of a Provincial Grand Master	1769	87
	J19: Loyal Address: To the Duke of Manchester, Grand Master	1778	241
	A9: By-laws of Royal Denbigh Lodge No. 505: Frontispiece	1787	29

	Documents	Date	Page
	J13: Lodge Certificate of Frederick Abell	1799	235
	D3: Royal Arch Register of the Antients Grand Lodge	1800	96
	D10: Articles of Union	1813	107
	F16: Grand Lodge Certificate belonging to Samuel Lancaster	1813	157
	D13: International Compact	1814	111
	L4: Loyal Address: To Queen Victoria	1896	277
	L6: Loyal Address: To Albert Edward, Prince of Wales, later King Edward VII	1901	278
	L11: Loyal Address: To King Edward VII	1901	283
	L12: Loyal Address: To Arthur, Duke of Connaught and Strathearn	1906	284
	D20: Arms of the United Grand Lodge of England	1919	119
	H12: Freemasons' Hall - Clerk of Works' Diary	1928-1929	214

	Engravings		
	G8: *The Builder's Dictionary*: Frontispiece	1734	191
	B7: *Cérémonies et coutumes religieuses de tous les peuples du monde*	1737	54
	B8: *Night* by William Hogarth	1738	55
	B9: *Grand Procession of Scald Miserable Masons*	1742	56
	G5: *King Solomon's Temple*: Robert Sayer	c.1760	187
	D12: Engraving on the 'Sussex Plate': a silver candelabrum presented to the Duke of Sussex to mark his twenty-five years as Grand Master	1838	108
	D2: Lodge of Perfect Union: Frontispiece of the Charter	1800	97
	K8: Ruspini leading a Procession of Girls from the Masonic School into Freemasons' Hall	1802	257

298

The Treasures of English Freemasonry 1717 – 2017

	Engravings	Date	Page
	H8: Cockerell's Freemasons' Hall	1869	210
	K16: Launch of the Lifeboat *Albert Edward*, funded by Freemasons, at Clacton-on-Sea	1875	265
	Ephemera		
	E1: Lodge Summons – Turk's Head	1766	123
	J2: Letter from Henry Price, Provincial Grand Master of New England, to Thomas French, Grand Secretary, Moderns Grand Lodge	1769	223
	K9: Business card for Chevalier Bartholomew Ruspini, engraved by Bartolozzi	*c.*1775	256
	J7: Letter from Prince Hall, Master of African Lodge No. 459	1785	229
	K6: Ticket for a Church Service, Sermon and Dinner in support of the Royal Cumberland Freemasons' Charity School for Girls	1791	254
	E2: Lodge Summons – King's Head Tavern - Friendly Lodge No. 466	1796	125
	E3: Lodge Summons - Bedford Lodge No. 205	1813	124
	E4: Lodge Summons - St George's Lodge No. 164	1815	127
	E5: Lodge Summons - Royal York Lodge of Perfect Friendship No. 243	1821	126
	E6: Lodge Summons – Lodge of Honor and Generosity No. 274	1822	126
	E7: Lodge Summons - Grand Master's Lodge No. 1	1824	129
	E8: Lodge Summons - St John the Baptist Lodge No. 53	1825	128
	E9: Lodge Summons - Lodge of Peace and Harmony No. 82	1826	130
	L15: Invitation to the Initiation of Albert, Duke of York, later King George VI	1919	288
	L16: RMBI 1931 Festival Souvenir: Chairman, Albert, Duke of York, later King George VI	1931	289
	F7: Six Commemorative Masonic Postage Stamps	1938-1978	147
	F6: Anti-Masonic Serbian Postage Stamps	1942	146

	Ephemera	Date	Page
	F8: Victory 3d. Postage Stamp	1946	147
	E10: Lodge Summons - Globe Lodge No. XXIII	2003	131
	Furniture		
	F26: Master's Chair	*c.*1760	167
	F32: Georgian Masonic Chairs	*c.*1790	172
	L1: Throne commissioned for George Augustus, Prince of Wales, later King George IV	1791	272
	F25: 'Wooler' Master's Chair	*c.*1806	165
	F24: Leicester Masonic Table	*c.*1825	163
	F27: Warden's Chair	*c.*1840	166
	Glassware		
	C12: Glass Rummer	1700	80
	C14: Beilby Firing Glass	*c.*1760	83
	C13: Bristol Blue Decanter	1770	82
	Jewels		
	B13: Sisson Jewel	*c.*1727	60
	A3: Sackville Medal	1733	18
	C3: Enamel jewel with Antients Grand Lodge Coat of Arms	*c.*1755	71
	K1: Jewel from the Sea Captains' Lodge	1757	249
	J8: Jewel of *Loge L'Immortalité de L'Ordre*	1767	228
	C10: Pierced Jewel inscribed to John Gale	*c.*1770	78
	H3: Freemasons' Hall Medal	1780	203

Catalogue and Index of Images

	Jewels	Date	Page
	F28: Limoges Enamels	c.1780	169
	C21: Country Steward's Jewel	1789	89
	A4: Grand Steward's Hogarth Jewel	c.1789	19
	F5: Silver Pierced Jewel	c.1790	145
	F37: Provincial Grand Master's Collar Jewel belonging to John Dent	1792	176
	F2: Pierced Jewel St Georges East York Militia Lodge No. 356	1796	143
	J14: Jewel made by a French Prisoner of War during the Napoleonic Wars	c.1800	234
	D5: Moira Jewel	1800	100
	D4: Nine Worthies Collar Jewel designed by Thomas Harper	1801	98
	F21: Past Master's Jewel	1803	159
	D14: Royal Arch Breast Jewel designed by Thomas Harper	1807	113
	K3: Early Charity Jewel	1811	250
	F3: Pierced Silver Jewel belonging to Christopher Fenton	c.1814	142
	C11: Past Master's Gallows-Pattern Collar Jewel	1815	81
	A13: Jewel commemorating the dedication of the Freemasons' Hall in Bath	1819	33
	D17: Collar jewel worn by Augustus Frederick, Duke of Sussex	c.1820	114
	G3: Wellington Lodge Jewel	1820	184
	F1: Chapter Jewel belonging to Francis Lambert	1821	141
	F34: Commemorative Jewel	1827	174
	F4: Member's Jewel	c.1830	144

	Jewels	Date	Page
	J20: Burnes Medal	1843	241
	E14: Member's Jewel - Polish National Lodge No. 534	1846	133
	F36: Past Master's Collar Jewel	1866	177
	K13: Charity Steward's Rosette: Royal Masonic Institution for Boys	1869	260
	H9: Freemasons' Hall Steward's Jewel	1869	211
	L8: Jewel commemorating the Installation of Albert Edward, Prince of Wales, later King Edward VII, as Grand Master	1875	281
	K14: Steward's Jewel: Royal Masonic Benevolent Institution (RMBI)	1878	262
	L9: Golden Jubilee Jewel: Commemorating the 50th anniversary of the reign of Queen Victoria, 1837-87.	1887	281
	L5: Centenary Jewel: Royal Masonic Institution for Girls, worn by Albert Edward, Prince of Wales, later King Edward VII	1888	276
	A2: Collar Jewel for the Past President of the Board of General Purposes	1894	16
	L10: Diamond Jubilee Jewel: Commemorating the 60th anniversary of the reign of Queen Victoria 1837-97.	1897	282
	K15: Charles Edward Keyser's Grand Lodge Charity Jewel, with collar adorned with bars	c.1900	263
	D15: Modern Royal Arch Jewel	1900	112
	F18: Selection from the John Gandy collection of nearly 600 Founder's Jewels	1900-1930	159
	F19: Founder's Jewel - Cassiobury Lodge No. 3234	1907	158
	F20: Founder's Jewel - Caldwell Lodge No. 3201	1907	158
	E12: Founder's Jewel - Atbara Lodge No. 3407	1909	132
	E13: Founder's Jewel - United Dooars Lodge No. 3351	1909	132
	E15: Past Master's Jewel - Rose of Denmark Lodge No. 975	1910	135
	E16: Bladon Miniatures	c.1910	135

The Treasures of English Freemasonry 1717 – 2017

	Jewels	Date	Page
	F23: RMIB Steward's Jewel presented to Sir Thomas F. Halsey	1912	161
	A5: Jewel designed by Alphonse Mucha for Dilo Lodge, Czechoslovakia	*c.*1920	21
	H10: Silver Hallstone Jewel	*c.*1920	213
	J22: Order of King Carl XIII of Sweden	1930	243
	E20: Founder's Jewel - Serenity Lodge No. 5917	1943	137
	E19: Founder's Jewel - Tranquillus Lodge No. 5912	1943	137
	J16: Jewels made by English Prisoners of War during the Second World War	1943	236
	E17: Founder's Jewel - New Era Lodge No. 5991	1944	135
	E18: Founder's Jewel - Ringway Lodge No. 6024	1945	137
	J17: Jersey Provincial Grand Lodge, jewels made from calico	1945	239
	E21: Past Master's Jewel - Riddlesdown Lodge No. 6107	1945	136

	Jewellery		
	A21: Pocket watch and case mounted with Grand Steward's Hogarth Jewel	*c.*1770	40
	J21: Casket in silver with gold and diamond chip decoration	1875	242
	F14: Devonshire Casket	*c.*1947	154
	K17: Royal Masonic Hospital Nurse's Silver Belt Buckle	*c.*1960	265

	Music		
	H2: Ode and Anthem composed for the Dedication of the Temple at Freemasons' Hall	1776	202
	A8: 'Act on the Square Boys' - a Music Hall song	*c.*1875	26

	Newspapers and Magazines		
	D1: *Freemasons' Magazine*: frontispiece from the first issue	1793	95

	Newspapers and Magazines	Date	Page
	K10: *The Freemasons' Quarterly Review*	1834	258
	A6: *The Freemason* newspaper: title page of the first issue	1869	23

	Paintings		
	B11: Senior Warden of an Early Lodge	*c.*1735	59
	B10: Colonel John Pitt	*c.*1750	58
	K5: Anthony Ten Broeke	*c.*1766	253
	H4: Freemasons' Tavern	1783	205
	C5: William Preston – Portrait	1800	73
	K7: Ruspini leading a Procession of Girls from the Masonic School into Freemasons' Hall	1802	255
	D9: Edward Augustus, Duke of Kent and Strathearn	1813	106
	G2: John James Howell Coe	*c.*1819	185
	A10: Silhouette of a Freemason	*c.*1820	28
	A14: Lodge Room at Kaira, India	1821	32
	L2: King George IV	*c.*1825	275
	D6: Augustus Frederick, Duke of Sussex	1827	103
	H6: Watercolour of Sir John Soane's Hall, showing the Ark of the Masonic Covenant	1828	207
	K11: Dr Robert Crucefix	*c.*1837	259
	J12: Masonic ship: the *William & Ann* of London	1855	235
	H7: Reception of HRH the Prince of Wales as Past Grand Master	1869	209
	L3: Augustus Frederick, Duke of Sussex	1885	274

301

Catalogue and Index of Images

	Paintings	Date	Page
	L7: King Edward VII as Grand Master	1885	279
	A12: Goose and Gridiron Tavern	1892	30
	J6: George Washington	1899	227
	D8: Duke of Atholl	1901	105
	H11: Freemasons' Hall: the winning competition scheme by Ashley and Newman	1927	212
	L17: Edward, Duke of Kent	1975	291
	L18: HRH Prince Michael of Kent	1987	293

	Photographs		
	H13: Freemasons' Hall during construction (i)	1928-1929	215
	H14: Freemasons' Hall during construction (ii)	1928-1929	216
	H15: Freemasons' Hall: The Grand Temple	1928-1929	217
	H16: Freemasons' Hall: The Dais in the Grand Temple	1928-1929	217

	Poetry		
	A7: 'The Mother Lodge'	1896	25

	Regalia		
	C7: Moderns Apron	c.1760	76
	C9: Antients Apron	c.1790	78
	C6: Moderns Apron	c.1790	76
	J10: French Napoleonic Apron	c.1805	231
	C8: Antients Apron	c.1806	77
	B12: Early Masonic Apron	c.1810	61
	F17: Hand-Decorated Apron belonging to Samuel Lancaster	c.1813	156

	Regalia	Date	Page
	F33: Early Lambskin Apron	c.1815	173
	D18: Apron worn by Augustus Frederick, Duke of Sussex	c.1817	116
	F31: Thomas Wildman's Chain	1822	171
	D16: Grand Registrar's Purse	c.1830	115
	K4: Apron of the President of the Board of Benevolence	1870	252
	J18: Apron worn at a Meeting during the Siege of Ladysmith	1899	238
	L19: Master Mason's Apron belonging to Sir Winston Churchill	1902	292
	L13: Apron presented to Edward, Prince of Wales, later King Edward VIII, on his Initiation	1919	286
	L14: Past Grand Master's apron worn by the Prince of Wales, later King Edward VIII	1936	287
	F13: Apron of the Provincial Grand Master for Derbyshire	c.1938	153

	Sculpture		
	A19: William Preston - Death Mask	1818	39
	D7: Bust of the Marquess of Zetland	c.1845	104
	A11: Statue of Augustus Frederick, Duke of Sussex	1847	31

	Silverware		
	L20: Silver Gilt Ceremonial Flagon	1806	295
	D11: 'Sussex Plate': a Silver Candelabrum presented to the Duke of Sussex to mark his twenty-five years as Grand Master	1838	109
	K12: Silver Candelabrum presented to Dr Robert Crucefix	1841	261
	G1: Silver Gilt Cornucopia and Ewers	1852	183
	A15: Epergne in silver and glass	1887	35
	F12: Silver Coffee Pot presented to F.J. Sawby	1892	151

The Contributors

John Belton
Initiated in 1980 and currently a full member of Quatuor Coronati Lodge No. 2076 (QC), John is also a member of other orders in other places. His early research interests majored on the post-1947 decline of Masonic membership across the English-speaking world. More recent themes have included Revolutionary Fraternalism linking London to the Italian Risorgimento, and *The English Masonic Union of 1813: A Tale Antient & Modern*. Educated as a microbiologist, he is by profession a marketer and exporter working for a major multinational pharmaceutical company. In retirement, John is, by inclination, a Masonic searcher-out of curiosities, and of mislaid history.

Dr Paul Calderwood
Paul Calderwood graduated in history from the University of Leicester. Subsequently, he was awarded a PhD by Goldsmiths College, University of London. His thesis has been published as a book, *Freemasonry and the Press: A National Newspaper Study of England and Wales,* which was the basis of the 2013 Prestonian Lecture. Articles by him have appeared in various publications including the *Journal for Research into Freemasonry and Fraternalism*. He was awarded the Norman B. Spencer Prize for his essay on 'Freemasonry and Architecture in twentieth century Britain' by QC in 2010 and he became a full member of the Lodge in 2014.

Dr James Campbell
Dr James Campbell is Director of Studies in Architecture and the Seear Fellow in Architecture and Art History at Queens' College, Cambridge. He trained as an architect, practising in the US, Hong Kong and London before returning to do a PhD at Cambridge in architectural history. A Fellow of the Society of Antiquaries, he has published widely. As well as an interest in Freemasonry, his specialist fields are seventeenth century architecture, the history of building construction, and the development of library design. A successful writer, his books have been translated into eleven languages. He is a full member of QC and was Prestonian Lecturer in 2011.

Diane Clements
Diane Clements is a graduate in Modern History from the University of Oxford. Subsequently she worked as an investment banker – most of her banking career was spent at Barings, the oldest merchant bank in London until its spectacular and appropriately historic collapse in 1995.

Diane has been Director of the Library and Museum of Freemasonry at Freemasons' Hall in Great Queen Street since 1999. Working with a team of dedicated professional curators, librarians and archivists, she has supervised its recent development with particular focus on making the collections more accessible on site and online.

Dr James Daniel
'Jim' Daniel, a Freemason since 1961, was once a cultural diplomat (1964-89), a Grand Secretary General of the Ancient and Accepted ('Scottish') Rite (1989-98) and a Grand Secretary of the UGLE (1998-2002). After retiring in 2002 and with several publications on Masonic history already to his name, he was awarded a doctorate by the University of Sheffield in 2010 with a thesis on 'The 4th Earl of Carnarvon (1831-1890) and Freemasonry in the British Empire'. A Past Master of QC (and many others) he is the Prestonian Lecturer for 2017.

Dr David Harrison
David Harrison gained his PhD from the University of Liverpool in 2008, with a thesis that focused on the development of English Freemasonry. The thesis was subsequently published in 2009 as a book, *The Genesis of Freemasonry*. A follow-up work entitled *The Transformation of Freemasonry* was published the following year, with both works receiving critical acclaim. David has subsequently continued to publish work on the history of English Freemasonry, most notably *The Liverpool Masonic Rebellion and the Wigan Grand Lodge* in 2012 and *The York Grand Lodge*, which was published in 2015. Harrison regularly appears on TV and radio discussing his work, and frequently contributes to Masonic magazines such as *The Square*, *Freemasonry Today* and *Philalethes*.

Professor Aubrey Newman
Educated at Glasgow and Oxford Universities, Aubrey taught history at the University of Leicester, where he is Professor Emeritus of History. His interests have been mainly in eighteenth century history, in particular with the links between London and the Provinces. He was initiated into Masonry in 1967 and was Master of his Lodge before joining the Leicester Lodge of Research No. 2049 and QC, also becoming Master of both. The Prestonian Lecturer in 2003, he is also Past President of the Jewish Historical Society of England.

Hugh O'Neill
Born on the Wirrral in 1937, Hugh was educated at Wimbledon High School for Girls – it was war-time – and St John's, Leatherhead. He trained in electronic engineering and communications, leading to electronic process control, wind turbines, and nascent business computer technology. From the mid-1980s John had his own IT consultancy business, providing services for small and medium-sized enterprises. Having retired in 2002, he has immersed himself in Masonic research and became a full member of QC in 2012.

Dr John Reuther
John Reuther was raised and educated in Islington, North London, before qualifying as a Biomedical Scientist at the Royal London Hospital. Subsequently he gained a Master's degree in Medical Microbiology at the University of Surrey and a Doctorate in the Faculty of Medicine at St Thomas' Hospital. Most of his working career has been in medical microbiology within the Public Health Laboratory Service. Initiated into Freemasonry in 1973 in the Province of Essex, John became a Trustee of the Royal Masonic Benevolent Institution in 2006 and was appointed Deputy President in 2013. He was elected a full member of QC in 2016.

Image Acknowledgements

Images are reproduced by kind permission of the following:

© Howard Morgan	L18
© Royal Masonic Trust for Girls and Boys	K7
© Sir John Soane's Museum, London	H6
© Trustees of the Derek Hill Estate	L17
© AdobeStock/LiliGraphie/Beth Van Trees	Page 9, A7
Angel Lodge No. 51	F16, F17
Geoffrey Bond OBE, DL, FSA, Hon. Curator, Masonic Museum, Nottingham	F28, F29, F30
Globe Lodge No. XXIII	E10
Kings Arm's Lodge No. 28	G4
Lodge of Antiquity No. 2	A1
Lodge of Lights No. 148	F32, F35
Marquis of Lorne Lodge No. 1354	F33
Private Collection	A12
Royal Sussex Lodge No. 402	F26, F27, F31
Scots Lodge No. 2319	Page 9
The Diadem, Magazine of the Jewels of the Craft	F1, F2, F3, F4, F5

All other objects appearing in the book, unless otherwise stated, are from the Library and Museum of Freemasonry

Image Credits:

Peter Beck	F32, F33, F34, F35, F36
Ian Brown	F25
Editor	Page 9, A7, A12, E10, F6, F7, F8
Grand Lodge of Mark Master Masons	L18
Gary Hope	F26, F27, F28, F29, F30, F31
Paul Hurst	Page 7
Library and Museum of Freemasonry	A1, B7, B8, B9, B10, B11, D1, D6, D8, D9, D11, D12, D19, G2, G5, G10, G11, G12, H4, H7, H8, H11, H13, H14, H15, H16, J6, J7, J12, J19, K5, K8, K11, L1, L2, L3, L7, L17
Provincial Grand Lodge of Bristol	F9, F10, F11, F12
Provincial Grand Lodge of Derbyshire	F13, F14, F15, K18
Provincial Grand Lodge of Essex	F16, F17
Provincial Grand Lodge of Hertfordshire	F18, F19, F20, F21, F22, F23
Provincial Grand Lodge of Worcestershire	A4, D4, F37
John Reilly	F24
Robert J.G. Smith, Editor and Past President of Jewels of the Craft	F1, F2, F3, F4, F5

All other images by Tom Lee of Rocket Visual